mental
health and
going
to school

mental health and going to school

the woodlawn program of assessment, early intervention, and evaluation

Sheppard G. Kellam
Jeannette D. Branch
Khazan C. Agrawal
Margaret E. Ensminger

The University of Chicago Press
Chicago and London

Sheppard G. Kellam, M.D., is Director of the Community Mental Health Assessment and Evaluation Unit, Chief Consultant Psychiatrist at the Woodlawn Mental Health Center, and Associate Professor of Psychiatry, the University of Chicago.

Jeannette D. Branch, M. A., is Director of the Woodlawn Mental Health Center and Field Work Associate Professor of Psychiatry, the University of Chicago.

Khazan C. Agrawal, M.S., is Chief of Data Processing in the Community Mental Health Assessment and Evaluation Unit, Woodlawn Mental Health Center, and Research Associate in the Department of Psychiatry, the University of Chicago.

Margaret E. Ensminger, M.A., is Sociologist in the Community Mental Health Assessment and Evaluation Unit, Woodlawn Mental Health Center, and Research Associate in the Department of Psychiatry, the University of Chicago.

The University of Chicago Press, Chicago 60637
The University of Chicago Press, Ltd., London

International Standard Book Number: 0-226-42968-7
Library of Congress Catalog Card Number: 74-10341

Contents

v

Contents

Figures

Tables

Preface

Woodlawn is a black, urban neighborhood community on the south side of Chicago. This book is about the mental health of Woodlawn children as they enter first grade and progress through their early school years. Our investigation of this major social and psychological transition in the lives of young children spanned the years 1964–70 and was deeply rooted in the development of a concept of community mental health—what it is and how it relates to a total mental health system. The theoretical framework that emerged provides a basis for designing programs of service and research in communities.

Mental Health and Going to School describes a community-wide program of assessment, early intervention, and evaluation for first-grade children. Throughout this book one of the issues with which we are concerned is the development and maintenance of a working relationship between the agency and the community—a relationship which we contend is crucial to successful neighborhood-based programs of research and service.

The conceptual development concerning community mental health and the total mental health system led us to define two dimensions of mental health: first, a societal dimension that involves the adequacy of one's social performance as viewed by society; and second, an individual dimension that involves psychological well-being. Major research goals were to study these two dimensions of mental health and to determine how they may be interrelated over the course of the child's early school years. The results are based on repeated community-wide studies, both concurrent and longitudinal, of the children in all twelve Woodlawn elementary schools from first grade through third grade.

The twelve schools were divided into two matched groups. By the flip of a coin, one group was designated "intervention schools" and the other "control schools." The six intervention schools participated in an intervention program that was carried out in the classroom and employed a design derived from the conceptual framework and base line data collected prior to intervention. Children in intervention schools were systematically compared to those in control schools on measures of both dimensions of mental health.

Finally, *Mental Health and Going to School* is concerned with the theoretical, clinical, and policy implications of the conceptual framework, the result of the studies of the two dimensions of mental health, and the evaluation of the intervention program.

One of the central ideas which we will attempt to elaborate in this report is that, in order to succeed, community programs—service or research or both—require close, complex relationships to many parts of the social-political structure of the local community as well as of the broader society. The Community Mental Health Assessment and Evaluation Unit derives its role in Woodlawn through the Woodlawn Mental Health Center and its community board. The research money which supports the unit comes from a variety of sources, mainly the National Institute of Mental Health, and is administered through the University of Chicago. The Woodlawn Mental Health Center is a service facility of the Chicago Board of Health and also receives support from the State of Illinois Department of Mental Health. In the development of the center and in the development of this program of assessment, early intervention, and evaluation, a variety of public and private institutions played crucial roles.

In the months immediately preceding the formation of the center in Woodlawn, Faye Price, M.S.W., working out of the Mental Health Division of the Chicago Board of Health, had negotiated with a number of community service agencies and had supported their directors in meeting the Honorable Richard J. Daley, mayor of Chicago, and requesting a mental health clinic for the neighborhood. Many community leaders accompanied this group of agency leaders, and the occasion was indeed one of the early joint activities of professional agencies with citizen leadership. This activity was a forerunner of our own beginning negotiations, which were focused somewhat more toward the leadership of the citizen social and political organizations but also included important relationships with service agencies.

As a result of months of negotiation with the leaders of the community's social and political organizations, an advisory board was formed of community citizens. This board provided the basic sanction to do this program and has continued to function in this capacity. Its current members are: Mr. Lawrence Carroll, attorney at law (chairman), Mrs. Emily Banks, Mrs. Rose B. Bates, Mrs. Josephine J. Berryhill, Dr. Paul Boswell, the Reverend Arthur Brazier, Mrs. Henry G. Clark, Mrs. Viola Cotton, the Reverend Thomas H. Ellis, Mr. Orville Fitzgerald, Mr. Elzena Hart, the Reverend E. J. Morris, Jr., the Reverend Tom Nairn, Mr. John W. Oldham, Mrs. Zonita Owens, Mr. Joseph Pitts, Mrs. Rosa Pitts, the Reverend A. L. Reynolds, Mr. A. L. Smith, Mrs. Bertha Tisdell, Mr. Wheeler Warr, Mr. Ferman B. Watson, and Mrs. Dorothy West. The late Mr. William C. Ward was also a member.

The Board of Health of the city of Chicago played a basic role at the time of the development of the center. Dr. Samuel Andelman, who was then commissioner, and Dr. Murray C. Brown, the current commissioner provided the necessary Board of Health support. At the time of the center's beginning, the Honorable Neil Hartigan, lieutanant governor of Illinois, was at the Chicago Board of Health and was important in facilitating the formation of the center and the program reported here. The Mental Health Division of the Board of Health was more directly involved in the development of administrative and professional support from the Board of Health. Dr. Thomas McGee, former director of the division, and Dr. Vladimir Urse, current director, have been very important to us.

From the beginning, the Woodlawn Mental Health Center was to provide a program of research and service directed at important clinical problems in the then newly evolving area called community mental health. Dr. Harold Visotsky, former director of the Department of Mental Health of the state of Illinois, and Dr. Melvin Sabshin, head of the Department of Psychiatry at the University of Illinois Abraham Lincoln College of Medicine, helped make this arrangement. Dr. Sabshin also took part in the discussions of the early ideas which went into the research reported here.

With the gradual development of a clearer understanding of the relationship of public and private institutions to local community areas, the transition from the University of Illinois Department of Psychiatry to the University of Chicago was brought about. Dr. Daniel X. Freedman, chairman of the Department of Psychiatry at the University of Chicago, was instrumental in helping us make this transition, since the Woodlawn community and the resources of the university are immediately adjacent to each other. Dr. Freedman and many members of the Department of Psychiatry have continued to support service, training, and research aspects of the center.

The project required active collaboration with the twelve elementary schools of Woodlawn. Nine of these are Chicago Board of Education public schools, and we are indebted to Dr. James Redmond, general superintendent, for his support at the city-wide level. It is hard to describe adequately the critical participation and support given at all stages of this program by Dr. Curtis C. Melnick, Area A associate superintendent. Dr. Donald Blyth, superintendent of District 14, Mr. Michael R. Fortino, former superintendent of District 21, and Mr. Jack Mitchell, current superintendent of District 21, were all important in supporting the acceptance of the program and its continuation over the many years of our collaboration with the schools. The Right Reverend William E. McManus, formerly superintendent of the Roman Catholic Archdiocese School Board, was important in getting the program accepted in the three Catholic schools of Woodlawn.

We shall comment from time to time throughout this report on the participation of the faculties of the twelve Woodlawn elementary schools in the assessment as well as the intervention aspects of the program. This report is itself one of the products of the collaboration. The authors have all developed many personal relationships with many members of the faculties during these years and recognize that without such a collaborative, mutually respectful partnership this study would not have been possible.

The direction of the first-grade intervention program and the training of school and mental health staff associated with the intervention were the primary responsibility of Sheldon K. Schiff, M.D., until June 1970. Dr. Schiff and Dr. Kellam shared responsibility as codirectors of the center until April 1970. Jeannette Branch, formerly chief of Children's Mental Health Services at the center, assumed the position as director of the Woodlawn Mental Health Center on 1 July 1970. The third member of the original team of codirectors and cofounders, Edward H. Futterman, M.D., left the center in 1965. Dr. Futterman shared with us the trials and problems of the center's formative period and made an important contribution to its development.

A major idea in this report concerns the relationship between research and service in community programs. There are important scientific reasons for combining these two operations in certain kinds of human service programs. In addition, it is essential in the development of a relationship between professional staff and community that adequate quid pro quo be provided to each for the effort of the other. For the community, the provision of service was a vitally important part of the agreement, even though community leaders recognized clearly that in the long run adequate systematic research was required into mental health need and its alleviation. Clinical service to the community remains the central function of the center, and this has been crucial in the development and evolution of the research. The research problems with which the Community Mental Health Assessment and Evaluation Unit are primarily concerned are closely related to the development of clinical care systems. Even so, without the service provided by the clinical staff, this research would not be acceptable to the community.

There is a less formal and less structured side to the politics of community program development which is equally essential. Occasionally, there has been need for informal explanation and discussion among various members of the staff, community leaders, and political leaders in the broader society. At such times "knowing somebody" becomes essential, and we have been indebted over these ten years to Mr. Earl Ross, a lawyer and businessman, whose expertise lies in the area of solving problems in the legal, business, political, and professional worlds. Any professional developing community-based programs will probably have experienced the need for facilitators who are wise from both a rational and a political standpoint.

The administration of this unit has depended heavily over the years on Cecilia Bethe, who has been superb in maintaining its business aspects. Her relations with the city, university, and, most important, the Woodlawn Mental Health Center staff and board have been a mainstay of this work. Parin Vergee has been, over the last year, increasingly important in supporting the data processing and analyses and the development of this manuscript.

About a year and a half before the completion of this manuscript Anne Petersen, Ph.D., joined the staff of the Community Mental Health Assessment and Evaluation Unit as staff psychologist and as research associate (assistant professor) of the Department of Psychiatry. Her training has been in psychological measurement and statistics and her experience very much related to the kind of work which we report in this book. Her participation in the dissection and careful scrutiny of analyses, concepts, and inferences made an important contribution to this report. Many aspects of the work were tightened, particularly such areas as the description of the methods for developing the social maladaptive modes (which will be elaborated in this report), the relationships between social adaptational status and psychiatric symptoms, and the overall conceptual development of the study. All of the authors look on Anne Petersen's contribution as very large and her work is very much reflected in the report's final appearance.

Loretta Hardiman has been our editor for over five years. We have all learned important aspects of the anatomy and physiology of this book from her. The interplay over ideas between her and the rest of the staff has been vitally important in the development of concepts, their description, and the analyses and summary conclusions drawn from the work. She has been responsible for most editorial aspects of manuscript preparation. Phillip Hallen and the Maurice Falk Medical Fund suggested the usefulness of an editorial unit and then made it possible by providing financial support.

Past staff members of the Community Mental Health Assessment and Evaluation Unit have been important in the earlier stages of the data collection and analyses. We are grateful to Sally Lipshutz, Lena Polite, Jane Ryder, Serpil Seren, S. S. Swaminathan, and Doris Van Pelt.

In the last few years several social, behavioral, and medical scientists have read the manuscript and offered important critical comments on almost all its aspects. We would like to acknowledge the advice and criticisms of these colleagues: Professors Ilene Bernstein, George Bohrnstedt, Keith Conners, Bruce Dohrenwend, Dr. Jarl Dyrud, Professor Donald Fiske, Dr. Daniel X. Freedman, Professors Richard Hill, Barbara Lerner, and Lee Robins.

Neither these reviewers nor the public and private institutions which supported this work have any responsibility for the problematic aspects of the concepts, methods, results, or conclusions presented here.

The research reported in this monograph was supported financially by: State of Illinois Department of Mental Health Grant Number 17-224, Psychiatric Training and Research Fund (three-year grant, 1965-68); State of Illinois Department of Mental Health Grant Number 17-322, Psychiatric Training and Research Fund (two-year grant, 1968-70); Public Health Service Research Grant Number 5 RO1-MH-15760, National Institute of Mental Health (five-year grant, 1968-73); Research Scientist Development Award Grant Number 1 KO1-MH-47596, National Insitute of Mental Health (awarded to Dr. Kellam in 1970 for a five-year period); Preparation of publications reporting this research was supported by a three-year grant from the Maurice Falk Medical Fund (1968-71).

mental
health and
going
to school

1   Introduction

It is now common knowledge that for a great many people there is no access to mental health services, nor is there even indirect benefit through programs of intervention in schools or other community settings. The problem is not only one of access to service but also of determining the kinds of services which would best enhance the mental health of those people whose needs are not being met.

It is also common knowledge among consumers that human service agencies are not coordinated with one another or with the institutions of the community generally. This fragmented service to only certain segments of the population represents what may be called a nonsystem, and there is overwhelming evidence that the public is deeply concerned about the disarray of services in education, health, welfare, and almost every other area in which society has attempted to provide support for meeting human need.

"Community mental health" is the currently popular phrase referring to efforts to broaden mental health services and make them more readily available to more people in more effective forms. Every direct encounter with mental disorder persuades those involved—patients, families, friends, physicians, social agencies—that there is a need for more services; but it is equally important to consider how such services should be designed and, particularly, how service agencies should go about developing a viable relationship with the communities they seek to serve.

The effect of increasing public awareness of the disarray in human services has not been lost on human service professionals. For many such professionals, the specter of being pressed to closer involvement with the community raises fantasies of hordes of people descending on outpatient clinics or hospitals. Anyone who teaches young professionals in community mental health sees this anxiety, an anxiety born of a lack of understanding about how neighborhood-based services, once in action, could provide more systematic functioning of backup facilities such as university outpatient clinics, privately practicing psychiatrists, and hospitals. Conceptual frameworks must be evolved to address the question of how to design neighborhood services and relate them to the other components of the total mental health system.

Many mental health professionals fear that neighborhood-based services could diminish their authority. Where the neighborhood is urban and poor, the human service agencies have traditionally not involved the residents in policy-setting processes. This situation is coupled with the almost complete absence of any services which are closely integrated into the social and political structure of such neighborhoods. When mental health professionals have attempted to move closer to the community, they have often found that the community's first priority is power-sharing. In the eyes of many communities, power-sharing means having a role in policy-making; it means being in on the setting of priorities and having a voice in recruiting staff, determining sites, and developing programs.

Even though a variety of models for relating to the community have evolved over the years, the results still need to be integrated and examined analytically. First, we need to examine systematically the various aspects of community mental health—to determine what we know and do not know about what community mental health should be and how it should function. We need to determine what kinds of research will be most helpful in moving us toward the immediate goal of coordinated mental health services and the long-range goal of a coordinated human service system. Second, the concomitant of this analytic approach is the issue of how to develop ways of relating to the community which recognize the community's roles as well as the professional-technical roles in policy-making and other aspects of programming. We have already seen how serious difficulties can arise when mental health projects do not first gain and then retain the community's sanction to operate (Aberle 1950; Kellam and Schiff 1966; Roman 1969).

In this study we attempt to analyze some of the basic aspects of community mental health and to describe the development of a longitudinal, community-wide project in assessment, prevention, early treatment, and evaluation based in the Woodlawn community on Chicago's south side. At every step, including the writing of this book, the ongoing sanction of the community has been a primary issue. In particular, the evolution and function of the Woodlawn Mental Health Center Board is described as an essential ingredient of the project.

What Is Community Mental Health?

Many attempts have been made to define community mental health. In view of the work of others who have designed and implemented such programs and of our own years of work in Woodlawn, it appears to us that the term denotes neither an established body of theory nor a set of proven practices. In fact, for some mental health professionals, the term seems to suggest a new subspecialty. Rather than a subspecialty of any one of the mental health professions, we suggest that community mental health be seen as a broadened purview of all the mental health professions—to include a concern for all people in need rather than just those who come to clinics or hospitals, as well as a more intense concern with enhancing mental health and preventing mental illness community-wide. Basic to this view of community mental health is the inclusion of the local community and its social institutions and functions—both those which are inside the community and those which extend beyond it. It should be clear that including the local community means including all the population, healthy and ill; this allows us to study the preconditions of health and of illness and provides for the eventual development of programs for preventing illness.

Such a view makes it necessary for us to consider those processes—biological, psychological, and social—which may have important relationships to the causes of mental illness and/or the development of mental health. Not the least of our problems is how to study processes which are so far-ranging and different from each other in their conceptualization, in the ways in which they are measured, and in the rules for making inferences. It is important to stress that this view of community mental health does not replace theory from biology, psychiatry, and psychology. Rather it implies a need for increased integration across these disciplines and for the addition of perspective and disciplines from the social sciences, some of which have established traditions for the study of mental illness and related concepts.

While this view of community mental health and what it entails is logical in the abstract, we recognize the enormity of the task of actually developing concepts in this broader purview, integrating data from vastly different disciplines, drawing inferences, and ultimately applying them to the development of training and service programs. On the other hand, as mental health professionals we cannot turn away from the problem because of its size and complexity; we must, however, be cautious and systematic in our approach to the task.

The diversity of factors which may be expected to impinge on the individual to bring about a condition of mental health or illness suggests that, in the interest of both research and treatment, we need a total mental health assessment and service system, the first level of which is highly integrated into the community. It is in the community, after all, that we can reach both the healthy and ill populations—and it is here (though not exclusively so) that biological, psychological, and social processes interact with each other and act on the individual to enhance mental health or induce mental illness. In later sections we shall discuss in more detail the design of a potential total mental health system involving three levels of care and the importance of the first level of care in the community.

The Broadened Purview and
Concepts of Mental Health

Let us now turn to the question of how the broadened purview of community mental health may influence our concepts of mental health. Historically the focus of investigators' research interests have influenced their definitions of mental illness or health. Once supernatural causes had been discarded as explanations of mental illness, concepts of mental illness became somewhat more systematic, but they have always been developed in relation to a particular purview.

In this century, for example, a number of concepts of mental health and illness were developed by psychoanalysts, and each concept grew out of the main focus of the particular stage of development of psychoanalytic theory. The concept of neurosis based on intrapsychic conflict around drive satisfaction developed early, when psychoanalytic interest was focused mainly on instinctual drives and their inhibition. Later, as the focus shifted to ego function, concepts of mental illness shifted to the nature of psychological defenses and their adequacy in dealing with or warding off intrapsychic conflict. More recently, ego psychologists have defined mental health and illness by putting a greater emphasis on the interaction between the external environment and intrapsychic structures and the effects of this interaction on the growth of personality and the formation of symptoms. Hartmann describes the growing interest in these effects: "the more we begin to understand the ego and its maneuvers and achievements in dealing with the external world, the more do we tend to make these functions of

adaptation, achievement, etc., the touchstone of the concept of health"
(1964, p. 4).

Other concepts of mental health and mental illness, each derived
from a particular purview, have emphasized different aspects of
psychological well-being. John Hughling Jackson's concern with neurological structure and function led him to formulate a particular view of
mental illness, just as the importance of reinforcement to B. F.
Skinner, Albert Bandura, and many others strongly influenced the
development of their concepts of mental health and mental illness.
Ludwig Binswanger, Victor Frankl, and Rollo May were clearly
influenced by their existential focus in the development of their
concepts. Each investigator tends to define mental illness in terms of
the processes which are within his focus of interest. The broadened
purview implied by "community mental health" is also influencing
concepts of mental health and illness.

A Two-Dimensional View
of Mental Health

If one accepts the idea that community mental health is a broadening
of the purview of the mental health professions to include the social
institutions and processes within and beyond the community, we can
ask: What is the nature of the interface between the individual and the
community and, indeed, the broader society? Probably a very basic
aspect of the interface is *the way one is seen by significant others*; this
may have critical importance to the way one feels about oneself and
consequently to one's mental health.

What is meant by "significant others"? Here a simple conceptual
framework that we have called the Life Course–Social Field concept
may help, and we shall enlarge upon this framework throughout this
book. Every individual in society passes through stages of life, each of
which involves the individual in specific social fields in which there are
persons who judge the adequacy of the individual's performance in that
field. The process involved is a highly interactional one, and the result
is what we call the *social adaptational status* of the individual. We
conceive of this interactional process and the resultant social adaptational status as the basic interface between the individual and society.
Social adaptational status is a societal judgment of the individual's
performance and is therefore external to the individual. In contradis-
tinction to social adaptational status, there is the question of how the
individual himself is feeling inside, that is, his psychological well-being.

Conceptually these two ideas are quite distinct; however, they may have great impact on each other.

From our point of view, these two components—social adaptational status and psychological well-being—represent two major dimensions of mental health. One represents mental health from the viewpoint of society; the other represents mental health from the viewpoint of the individual. This two-dimensional concept of mental health is a product of the expanded purview and builds on a variety of concepts from social and behavioral sciences. Charles Horton Cooley and George Herbert Mead were both concerned with the individual's perception of how others see him and its effect on the sense of self.

Adequacy of role performance as discussed by Parsons has very important similarities to social adaptational status:

> The primary criteria for mental illness must be defined with reference to the social *role-performance* of the individual. Since it is at the level of role-structure that the principal direct interpenetration of social systems and personalities come to focus, it is as an incapacity to meet the expectations of social roles, that mental illness becomes a problem in social relationships and that criteria of its presence or absence should be formulated. This is of course not at all to say that the state which we refer to as mental, as of somatic, illness is not a state of the individual; of course it is. But that state is manifest to and presents problems for both the sick person and others with whom he associates in the context of social relationships, and it is with reference to this problem that I am making the point about role-performance. [1964, p. 258]

It is possible to think of social adaptational status as an elaboration of Parsons's role theory, in that it further specifies the relationship between stages of life and specific social fields and the manner in which social tasks are presented to the individual by specific person(s) in each social field who have societal authority to define the tasks and rate the individual's performance.

The social adaptational process and the resultant social adaptational status for the individual occur in a social field which is part of the social structure and function of the broader society. The larger society has impact on the characteristics of each social field and therefore on the social tasks presented the individual and on the social adaptational status—an idea which reminds us of Merton's thoughts regarding the influence of the broad society on the individual.

> Our primary aim is to discover how some *social structures exert a definite pressure upon certain persons in the society to engage in nonconforming rather than conforming conduct.* If we can locate groups peculiarly subject to such pressures, we should expect to find fairly high rates of deviant behavior in these

groups, not because the human beings comprising them are compounded of distinctive biological tendencies but because they are responding normally to the social situation in which they find themselves. [1968, p. 186]

There is ample empirical evidence that there are important relationships among aspects of the larger society, the local community, and the mental health of the individual. For the most part, it is not yet clear what is cause and what is effect. There appears to be a strong inclination by many investigators to think that biological, experiential, and social factors converge—each with more or less impact—to induce mental health or mental illness.

Some of the classic work in the area includes Faris and Dunham's (1939) investigation of the relationship between the ecological characteristics of urban communities and psychiatric hospitalization; Hollingshead and Redlich's (1958) study of the relationship between an individual's social class and the kinds of psychiatric treatment offered; Clausen and Kohn's (1959) attempt to replicate Faris and Dunham's results in a rural community; the Stirling County studies of social disorganization and mental illness (A. H. Leighton 1959; Hughes et al. 1960; and D. C. Leighton et al. 1963); and the study by Srole et al. (1961) of mental illness and its correlates in an urban population. These are but a few of the studies which justify the serious concern of mental health professionals with a purview which includes a wide variety of data from many sources.

The research reported in this book is centrally concerned with the relationship of social adaptational status (hereafter cited as SAS), the societal view of mental health, to the psychological well-being of the individual. We have stated that both the research and service aspects of the broadened purview that we feel characterizes community mental health require an integrated mental health system, the first level of which is highly integrated into the community. Since our work was a first-level project carried out in a neighborhood-based community mental health center in Chicago's Woodlawn community, it may be helpful to discuss what we mean by community and by an integrated mental health system.

The Community and
the Mental Health System

The two-dimensional concept of mental health just described implies that mental health professionals necessarily have an interest in the com-

munity. The phrase "community," however, needs to be examined in relation to a mental health system which allows research and services to
develop at all stages of the individual's life and at all phases of the clinical
course of patients. Roland Warren (1963) defines community as "that
combination of social units and systems which perform the major social
functions having locality relevance. This is another way of saying that
by community we mean the organization of social activities to afford
people daily local access to those broad areas of activity which are
necessary in day-to-day living (p. 10)."

Warren defines five major functions which have "locality relevance": (1) production-distribution-consumption; (2) socialization; (3)
social control; (4) social participation; and (5) mutual support. While
all these functions may take place at the local level, they are not
exclusively community functions. As Warren states, "the organization
of society to perform these functions at the community level involves a
strong tie between locally based units such as businesses, schools,
governments, and voluntary associations and social systems extending
far beyond the confines of the community (p. 10)."

Health services, including mental health services, are part of the
community's mutual support function. Warren's concept of mutual
support refers to the help given individuals and families in times of
crisis when their needs are not satisfied by the usual pattern of
behavior. We would also include those preventive measures which are
available on a community-wide basis to avert such crises.

According to Warren's definition, many neighborhoods, urban as well
as rural, would more or less qualify as communities. Such areas are
often identified by a local name. In addition, they usually have
known boundaries, their own shopping facilities, various neighborhood
voluntary associations, and health and welfare services. Communities
may also have locally based political organizations which play a role in
city, state, and federal politics. Indeed, this kind of political organization has been known to result in the close scrutiny of mental health and
other human services by local citizen leaders.

Warren's concept of community is a general one, but it is sufficient
in considering how mental health research and service can be community-based. Concepts of community are important because they
guide us in the development of methods of observing and intervening in
such local social fields as the family, the classroom, or the voluntary
community association. Janowitz (1967) and, more recently, Suttles
(1972) have formulated more specific concepts of various kinds of
urban communities. The type of community to be served may have

implications for how mental health or other human service personnel in certain kinds of urban communities can best relate to the local social and political organization. We shall have more to say on this subject later in relation to Woodlawn, but let us now return to the idea of a well-functioning mental health system and examine how such a system may relate to the idea of community.

Three Levels of Research and Service

We have found it useful to envision a mental health system in which there are three levels of care. The first level should be highly integrated into the local community and include those aspects of study and service related to prevention and early treatment. Total populations of people, both healthy and ill, would be served—in other words, this first level would have a community-wide focus. Studies at this level would very often be epidemiologic and would require a great degree of involvement in the various social and political contexts of the community. It is at this first level of the mental health system that we would be most deeply immersed in the local community. The Woodlawn project that is the subject of this book is generally prototypical of a first-level program.

The second level would be more specialized and occur in more traditional outpatient settings, such as the private practitioner's office or the mental health clinic of the local hospital. The second level of care is conceived as serving fewer people but a wider geographic area than served by the first level. The essential characteristic of this level would be the concern with outpatient populations already in need. Here there would be more direct service by professionals, as contrasted with the first level, where community residents who know the community's institutions and values, who have been trained in basic mental health skills, and who would have professional supervision and backup, would play key roles.

The third level of the mental health system would consist of hospital and its variations. At this level the population requiring extensive, specialized professional care would be serviced and relevant research in such areas would be carried on. Typically, the third level would serve a much broader geographic area and a more disturbed population than the second level—just as the second level would serve a broader area than the first, which would be closely related to a single, local community or neighborhood.

This view of a mental health system implies a high order of integration across the three levels, with the first level doing the kinds of research and service which follow from the close relationship to populations of healthy as well as ill individuals. It is here that programs of prevention could be most easily developed. The second and third levels focus on populations already in need and therefore cannot function in areas of prevention except to alleviate morbidity as effectively as possible. Generally, such a system takes into account the viability and importance of the concept of local community while acknowledging the reality of the impact of the broader society on every individual.

Circumscribing the Community

I consider it of the greatest importance that the clinic make itself responsible for the mental health work of a fairly well circumscribed unit of population, so as to make possible studies of the social situation and of the dynamic factors which lead to the occurrence of mental derangements which must be attacked for purposes of prevention. [Meyer 1948, p. 361]

This was the opinion of Adolph Meyer in 1913. Circumscribing the community still seems to be an essential step in the development of mental health research and services at the first level. It involves demarcating a boundary around a finite population with whom the mental health professional is to work. While such demarcation defines a population, the mental health system we have described requires that a boundary also encompass the local manifestations of values, social relationships, and institutions which may impinge on the mental health of individuals in that population. It is not possible, of course, to circumscribe all of the social institutions and processes affecting individuals, since our concept of the local community is not one of an isolated entity walled off from the rest of society but, rather, a much more open concept accommodating those local manifestations of services, values, and social processes which affect people. There is no implication that it is not in the context of the broader society that such phenomena occur.

Circumscribing the community permits us to assess the kinds and prevalence of mental health need in the population and the conditions with which need is associated. We are then in a position to plan first-level intervention on the basis of both assessed need and associated conditions and to place programs within the community—near the individual or in that part of the social system where the problem can be addressed. The concern with prevention which is typical of the first level of our integrated mental health system is also well served by circumscribing the local community. Prevention, as we have said, requires that one pay attention to healthy individuals rather than wait for mental illness to occur. Circumscribing the population provides an opportunity to study the preconditions of mental illness (or even the preconditions of mental health) which may exist in the social system and to conduct research into the etiology of mental health need that otherwise would not be possible. Intervention can be viewed broadly, then, as changing a condition or conditions affecting a whole population; narrowly, as intervening in a specific social field in which the individual is having trouble; more narrowly, as intervening with the individual himself. It should be noted that intervention with the individual can be done as part and parcel of first-level research and service or may be accomplished by referring the individual to the second or third level of the system.

The degree to which mental health and other human service professionals understand that the community is an entity with local values, aspirations, and institutions is an important issue in setting boundaries. Mental health workers must be familiar with both the concept of community and the specific population they serve. The need for this quality would seem to be obvious—yet, more often than not, it has been lacking in traditional services. Frequently, the lack of a concept of community on the part of agency professionals has led each of the variety of agencies serving a community to set boundaries that have no relationship to those of other agencies or to those recognized by community residents. This is one of the primary reasons that it has been almost impossible to coordinate human services at the neighborhood level.

The mental health system described here is not totally dissimilar to traditional mental health services; there is, however, a significant difference in the degree to which first-level research and service are developed. Traditional research and services have not emphasized the development of first-level care in the community. There is also a difference in the degree to which various kinds of programs in traditional services have been integrated with each other in a functioning, efficient system. The lack of attention to first-level research and service explains in part why many professionals do not have a working knowledge of the local community.

The circumscribing process that represents the practical application of our concept of community must take into account the ideas of community residents regarding where their community begins and ends. There may be traditional boundaries which the residents respect but which are elusive to the nonresident. There is also a strong possibility that there may be far more political and social organizational structure in the local community than mental health professionals from outside recognize. For these reasons, negotiating boundaries with the people of Woodlawn was our first step in developing, together with community residents, a first-level mental health program of study and service for the community's young children.

The Role of the Community-wide Information System

The importance of community-wide measurement seems implicit in the concept of the mental health system described earlier, particularly at the first level. A community-wide system of periodic data collection can provide information on conditions potentially associated with both mental illness and health and indicate the strategic social fields for intervention. Periodic measures of other aspects of human need may include such diverse but socially relevant essentials as income, social opportunities, and affectional resources, the community's educational resources, and other factors which may be important to mental health. Finally, the measured evaluation of the impact of programs is essential if new programs with proved effectiveness are to be developed.

At the optimum, the two basic qualities of the community-wide information system should be its potential for including all members of the community, not just those who seek help at a clinic, and its use as a basis for planning and evaluating intervention. If the information system were closely related to planning, intervention, and evaluation of program impact, it could be the focusing agent for all human service agencies. It could be the basis on which current crisis response methods are augmented by first-level prevention and early intervention programs which link a variety of appropriate services together as part of a general response system.

Community-wide assessment of all first-grade children yielded early detection of a population of children who were having difficulties with their own feelings and/or were seen by their teachers as having difficulties with performance in school. If this information were used to initiate a home visit and an analysis of the problem by a person broadly skilled in assessing human need in collaboration with the parents, then the schools and other specific agencies could be involved at an early stage, thus broadening their role to include prevention and early intervention rather than merely crisis response.

This kind of information system provides a general response capabil-

2   Woodlawn

Prior to our arrival in Woodlawn in 1963, Saul Alinsky and the Industrial Areas Foundation had responded to a request by leaders of some community groups to help develop a basic political organization which would represent the aspirations of the community (Silberman 1964; Brazier 1969; Fish 1973). Woodlawn was undergoing a transition from middle-class white in the east and middle-class black in the west to an almost totally black community with a lower average income. As these changes occurred, many local groups felt the need for increased political organization at the neighborhood level. The problem of representing the local residents' self-interests around issues such as urban renewal, education, health, and other social programs was the major stimulus. Again, this process reflects the validity of the distinction between the local community and the city and even the broader society.

The Woodlawn Organization (TWO)—a confederation of more than one hundred block clubs, church groups, and other small organizations—was the most obvious outcome of the effort to organize this changing community, and this group was in full operation when we arrived. In addition, there were smaller, older, less militant organizations active in the community, like, for example, the West Woodlawn Council of Block Clubs, a confederation of groups based in a less transient area of the community.

Thus Woodlawn in this period was undergoing a political evolution against a background of rapid socioeconomic and racial change. Tables 1 through 3 present demographic data comparing the Woodlawn community to the entire city of Chicago in 1950 and 1966. The year 1950 was chosen because it indicates a good deal about Woodlawn before the period of the greatest change and because U.S. Census Bureau data were available. In 1966 we were two years into our studies

ity and is a basic function of the first level of the mental health system. However, the degree of intimacy of the kinds of information collected and the degree to which the system is integrated into the community depend on the active support (not just permission) of the community leadership. Therefore, early involvement of the community in decision-making processes affecting agency policy, priorities, and programming is probably the most fundamental issue in the development of an effective mental health system.

This issue is more than tactical. It goes back to the idea that every small community has political and social characteristics that should be understood and taken into account by all human service professionals. It means that there should be a formal mode of relating to the population to be served, and the potency of the community in this relationship should be clear. And it means that the first, second, and third levels of the mental health system, but particularly the first level, should be developed in keeping with the community's values and institutions. Services should not be imposed from the outside. The development and continued evaluation of the community sanctioning process are the only foundation on which effective services for large numbers of people can be built.

requires that one pay attention to healthy individuals rather than wait for mental illness to occur. Circumscribing the population provides an opportunity to study the preconditions of mental illness (or even the preconditions of mental health) which may exist in the social system and to conduct research into the etiology of mental health need that otherwise would not be possible. Intervention can be viewed broadly, then, as changing a condition or conditions affecting a whole population; narrowly, as intervening in a specific social field in which the individual is having trouble; more narrowly, as intervening with the individual himself. It should be noted that intervention with the individual can be done as part and parcel of first-level research and service or may be accomplished by referring the individual to the second or third level of the system.

The degree to which mental health and other human service professionals understand that the community is an entity with local values, aspirations, and institutions is an important issue in setting boundaries. Mental health workers must be familiar with both the concept of community and the specific population they serve. The need for this quality would seem to be obvious—yet, more often than not, it has been lacking in traditional services. Frequently, the lack of a concept of community on the part of agency professionals has led each of the variety of agencies serving a community to set boundaries that have no relationship to those of other agencies or to those recognized by community residents. This is one of the primary reasons that it has been almost impossible to coordinate human services at the neighborhood level.

The mental health system described here is not totally dissimilar to traditional mental health services; there is, however, a significant difference in the degree to which first-level research and service are developed. Traditional research and services have not emphasized the development of first-level care in the community. There is also a difference in the degree to which various kinds of programs in traditional services have been integrated with each other in a functioning, efficient system. The lack of attention to first-level research and service explains in part why many professionals do not have a working knowledge of the local community.

The circumscribing process that represents the practical application of our concept of community must take into account the ideas of community residents regarding where their community begins and ends. There may be traditional boundaries which the residents respect but which are elusive to the nonresident. There is also a strong possibility that there may be far more political and social organizational structure in the local community than mental health professionals from outside recognize. For these reasons, negotiating boundaries with the people of Woodlawn was our first step in developing, together with community residents, a first-level mental health program of study and service for the community's young children.

The Role of the Community-wide
Information System

The importance of community-wide measurement seems implicit in the concept of the mental health system described earlier, particularly at the first level. A community-wide system of periodic data collection can provide information on conditions potentially associated with both mental illness and health and indicate the strategic social fields for intervention. Periodic measures of other aspects of human need may include such diverse but socially relevant essentials as income, social opportunities, and affectional resources, the community's educational resources, and other factors which may be important to mental health. Finally, the measured evaluation of the impact of programs is essential if new programs with proved effectiveness are to be developed.

At the optimum, the two basic qualities of the community-wide information system should be its potential for including all members of the community, not just those who seek help at a clinic, and its use as a basis for planning and evaluating intervention. If the information system were closely related to planning, intervention, and evaluation of program impact, it could be the focusing agent for all human service agencies. It could be the basis on which current crisis response methods are augmented by first-level prevention and early intervention programs which link a variety of appropriate services together as part of a general response system.

Community-wide assessment of all first-grade children yielded early detection of a population of children who were having difficulties with their own feelings and/or were seen by their teachers as having difficulties with performance in school. If this information were used to initiate a home visit and an analysis of the problem by a person broadly skilled in assessing human need in collaboration with the parents, then the schools and other specific agencies could be involved at an early stage, thus broadening their role to include prevention and early intervention rather than merely crisis response.

This kind of information system provides a general response capabil-

TABLE 1. SELECTED POPULATION AND HOUSING CHARACTERISTICS, 1950 AND 1966

Characteristic	Woodlawn	Chicago
Total population		
1950	80,699	3,620,962
1966	78,182	3,465,782
Percent nonwhite		
1950	40.0	14.1
1966	98.0	28.0
Percentage of housing renter-occupied		
1950	87.7	68.5
1966	91.0	67.0
Percentage of housing units overcrowded (more than one person per room)		
1950	21.1	15.2
1966	23.0	12.0
Population (per sq. mi. in thousands)		
1950	37.5	17.2
1966	35.5	15.0
Area (in sq. mi.)		
1950	2.2	212.9
1966	2.2	224.0

Sources: The 1950 figures are from P. M. Hauser and E. M. Kitagawa, eds., *Local Community Fact Book for Chicago 1950* (Chicago: Community Inventory, 1953). The 1966 figures are from Pierre de Vise, *Chicago's Widening Color Gap*, Interuniversity Social Research Committee, Report No. 2 (Chicago Regional Hospital Study, 1967).

TABLE 2. SELECTED ECONOMIC CHARACTERISTICS, 1950 AND 1966

Characteristic	Woodlawn	Chicago
Median family income per year		
1950	$3,473	$3,956
1966	$5,508	$8,100
Percentage of persons on public assistance		
1950	4.5	3.1
1966	21.0	7.0
Percentage of labor force unemployed		
1950	4.5	2.8
1966	9.0	3.0

Sources: The 1950 figures are from P. M. Hauser and E. M. Kitagawa, eds., *Local Community Fact Book for Chicago 1950* (Chicago: Community Inventory, 1953). The 1966 figures are from Pierre de Vise, *Chicago's Widening Color Gap*, Interuniversity Social Research Committee, Report No. 2 (Chicago Regional Hospital Study, 1967).

TABLE 3. SELECTED FAMILY CHARACTERISTICS, 1966

	Percentage of Persons in Public Housing	Average Size of Household	Average Number of Children per Family	Percentage of One-Parent Families
Woodlawn	1.0	2.8	1.6	39.0
Chicago	4.0	3.0	1.2	18.0

Source: Pierre de Vise, *Chicago's Widening Color Gap*, Interuniversity Social Research Committee, Report No. 2 (Chicago Regional Hospital Study, 1967).

and, although there were no official census figures for that year, there were estimated data available in the de Vise report (1967).

In 1950, Woodlawn was crowded with 81,000 people in a community of 2.2 square miles, of which the eastern third is part of the city's Jackson Park. Forty percent of the population was black. Although the tables here do not show it, census data indicate that in 1950 Woodlawn's black population had a higher relative income and more education than the black population who would come later. By 1966, when 98 percent of the community's residents were black, Woodlawn was much poorer. Compared to Chicago generally, Woodlawn dropped sharply in median income while doubling its unemployment rate. It became what de Vise describes as a "new poor community" (1967).

Interestingly enough, the size of the total population changed very little from 1950 to 1966, although somewhere between 1960 and 1966 it began to decline. The percentage of renter-occupied housing and the degree of overcrowding remained stable, but both figures were higher than those for Chicago.

In 1950, Woodlawn was similar to Chicago in the proportion of employed men who were professionals or managers, but it had a larger proportion of men in service occupations and domestic occupations than the city as a whole. By 1966, the proportion of employed men who were in professional or managerial positions had declined considerably.[1] The deteriorating economic picture is illustrated also by public assistance figures. In 1966, there were three times as many Woodlawn residents on public assistance per one thousand population as there were city-wide, and more than twice the percentage of one-parent families.

While the description we have drawn reflects accurately some broad characteristics of Woodlawn, it does not indicate the degree of heterogeneity in the community, including the differences from one part of the community to another. For example, homeownership varied from more than 40 percent in some blocks to less than 1 percent in others. Education and income levels varied in the same way.

In 1963, psychiatrists E. H. Futterman, M.D., S. K. Schiff, M.D., and S. G. Kellam, M.D. (the first author), had obtained a commitment of support from the Chicago Board of Health, the State of Illinois Department of Mental Health, and the University of Illinois to set up a community mental health center in a Chicago neighborhood. Several community leaders in Woodlawn had requested a mental health facility from the city. This provided an opening for the Board of Health and the psychiatrists to inquire whether the residents of Woodlawn wanted the psychiatrists to come and collaborate in the development of community mental health programs in keeping with the community's needs.

The psychiatrists initially talked with the leaders of various community organizations as well as the professional directors of the service agencies in the area. They held a long series of discussions with many people in homes, offices, and other places throughout the community. For the residents, the main concern was whether the psychiatrists would take the community into account in planning and implementing programs.

The process of early engagement with the community has been recounted in more detail elsewhere (Kellam and Schiff 1966, 1968). It should be noted here, however, that negotiations around the issue of boundaries were very much a part of this early stage in gaining community sanction. Not only did many community residents have differing opinions as to where and what their community was, they also considered their ideas about boundaries to be just as important as more technical, professional criteria. Actually, the major contribution to be made by the psychiatrists in the discussion of what constituted the community's boundaries concerned the number of people that could be served with a reasonable degree of involvement. Professional studies—including the collection of census data—helped, but, in the final analysis, neither the professionals nor the studies could define the geographic area and institutions which constituted Woodlawn in the minds of the people who lived there.

By the time a decision had to be made, a community advisory board of citizen organization leaders had been formed. The membership included people with differing opinions about boundaries. After much debate over whether to include one area or another, a set of boundaries that were well grounded in tradition were agreed upon. These boundaries were identical to those described in Kitagawa and Taeuber

(1963) and are based on visible physical dividing lines—a cemetery on the south, railroad tracks on the west, the University of Chicago campus on the north, and Jackson Park on the east.

Formalizing the Relationship to the Community

Negotiations with the community leadership had shown that there was basic concern about the kind of relation the mental health center as an agency would have to them as a community. It was clear that negotiations had to continue until a formalized relationship had been developed in which the roles and responsibilities of the professionals were sanctioned by the residents.

There were several alternative methods of formalizing the relationship. Traditionally, Woodlawn's social service agencies had tended to band together as an interagency council which invited one or two community leaders to participate as representatives of the consumers. This had not been effective. It did not recognize community organizations and it provided no opportunity for citizens to develop a role in policy-setting.

Another possibility was the elected community board, but this method ignores minority opinion and places a great deal of power in the hands of any existing political machine. Advertising for interested residents to attend community meetings was still another alternative; however, lack of structure and lack of support for this method by existing community organization leadership led us to reject it too. Of course, we could have simply set up business in mental health programming so that consumers could use or not use the programs as they saw fit. This approach seemed especially dangerous, since the possibility of confrontation was enormous and there was no provision for community participation prior to design and implementation (Kellam and Branch 1971; Kellam et al. 1972).

Much more could be said about each of these models. They are summarized here only to establish why, in collaboration with the community, still another model—an advisory board comprising leaders from existing community organizations—was developed. Each member of the board thus represented a constituency of the community. The advisory board worked with the center's staff in establishing policy and setting priorities and collaborated in program design.

One of the board's most impressive contributions was to define community priorities as clearly being in the areas of children and

prevention. Board members voiced an intense interest in having Woodlawn children get off to the best possible start in school. They were
interested in a program of assessment and early intervention which
would occur within the elementary schools across the community. They
were also concerned that the capacity of the schools to respond to the
needs of the child, the family, and the community be enhanced.

This kind of mandate from the community suggested a first-level
program. Both the board and the mental health center staff saw the
goals of such a program as ones to be accomplished over time rather
than immediately. The process would entail continual assessment, the
development of intervention programs based on assessment, and evaluation and redesign of intervention over several years.

The community's mandate was in contrast to the position of the
social agencies in the community, both public and private, who were
practically unanimous in wanting a mental health disposition clinic to
help them handle schizophrenics and other severely disturbed segments
of the population more effectively.

The Life Course–Social Field
Concept

Since sanction to work in Woodlawn had come from the community
groups, the staff began to consider, in line with the board's expressed
interest, how to design and develop a community-wide, first-level
program for young children. The problem of selecting the population of
children was approached generally by relating mental health to the
social fields in the community.

What we have called the Life Course–Social Field concept is based on
the theoretical development of Erikson (1959, 1963), Havighurst
(1952), Neugarten (1968), and others over the last several decades. In
each case, there is a primary concern with the stages of life through
which all individuals pass. If the individual's life course is considered
from the community standpoint, specific social fields, such as the
school, the job, or the family, can be seen to have more or less importance at different stages. Everyone in a community is in one or another
stage of life and is functioning in several or all of the social fields relevant
to that stage. Each social field requires individuals within its sphere to
perform certain social tasks, and there are specific criteria of success
and failure.

Figure 1 shows our conceptualization of the stages of life along with a
series of major events which occur most often at times of transition

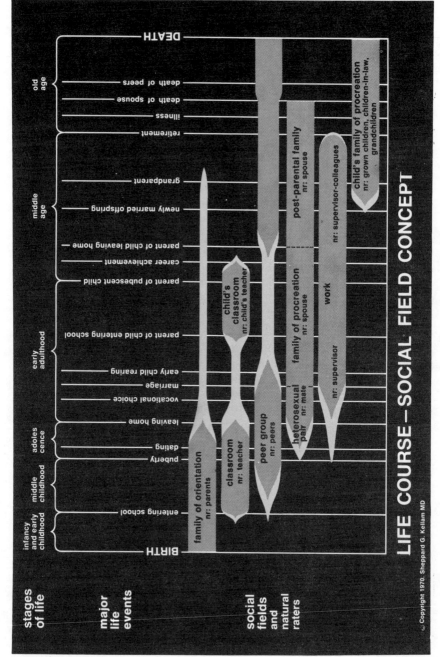

LIFE COURSE–SOCIAL FIELD CONCEPT

© Copyright 1970. Sheppard G. Kellam MD

Figure 1. Life Course–Social Field Concept

from one stage to the next. On this chart the stages of life and the major events intersect with specific social fields, such as the family, the classroom, or the job. The chart presents a generalized interpretation of the individual's life course. One must keep in mind that, for different individuals in Woodlawn and for those in different communities or societies, variations will be reflected in the way stages of life are delineated and in the array of major social fields.

Variations in the width of the horizontal bars representing social fields are meant to suggest the relative importance of each field at different stages, and this, too, will vary among individuals, communities, and societies. Differences in the shading of the bars indicate the beginning and end of the period during which these fields are likely to be most important to the individual. Again, this will vary from individual to individual and from community to community. Everyone is not involved in rearing young children in early adulthood, nor does every adult function in the work context. Still, the concept is useful in that it illustrates the relationships between an individual's stage of life and important aspects of societal structure and function. From a practical standpoint, the Life Course–Social Field concept indicates in which of the community's social fields a particular population at a given stage of life may be found.

The figure indicates also the presence of a so-called *natural* rater(s) —sometimes called the "socialization agent"—in each field (Lippitt 1968). The natural rater (indicated on the chart as *nr*) is the person (or persons) who defines the social adaptational tasks to be performed in the field and assesses, formally or informally, each individual's performance of these tasks. Parents function in this capacity in the family of orientation—as do the teacher in the classroom, certain members in the peer group, the spouse or mate in the heterosexual pair, the foreman in the work situation, and so on.

We found that the Life Course–Social Field concept was not only important in defining the societal dimension of mental health (in contrast to psychological well-being) but also helped deal with the practical problems of defining a specific community-wide population of children and then gaining access to them. According to this concept, the family and the classroom are the two major social fields in which young children can be found. It was our assumption that the peer group is not a major social field at this age. Young children do influence each other and show friendship preferences, but there do not appear to be distinct and stable patterns of peer relationships at this point. Such relationships do develop rapidly later on, however, as illustrated in figure 1. In terms of major life events, entering school is a time of transition for young children. It calls for adaptation to a new social field and the first real separation from home and parents. The child is faced with new tasks, new roles, and the need for a resynthesis of his identity.

Some kind of record of total population is essential for community-wide programming. When a youngster enters first grade, there is an official registration of his or her name and address. This is the first time, after their birth certification, that all children in the community are registered systematically; it gave us access to the total population of first-graders in Woodlawn.

In addition, the community's first-grade classrooms each collected in one place children from approximately thirty families. This arrangement made assessment easier and facilitated first-level intervention. The classroom also offered an opportunity to study the social adaptational tasks teachers set for children, and to study the teacher's ratings of each child's social adaptational status in the classroom in terms of these tasks. Essentially, such ratings are assessments of the child's performance by the social system of the school, an important societal aspect of assessing mental health need in young children. Finally, the classroom offered access to the school-family-community system. In a sense, it is the central social arena in which each of these fields come together to play out a major community function—effectively or ineffectively.

From the point of view of our board, Woodlawn classrooms had been too distant in their relationship to the home. Generally, the schools had not reached out to the community's families. School authorities felt similarly and indicated that there was a need to move closer to families in a more effective partnership. For these reasons, we suggested to the board that first-grade children should be the population for whom to program first. The board agreed and offered strong support for directing the resources of the Woodlawn Mental Health Center toward development of a first-grade program of community-wide assessment and early intervention.

3 Measuring Mental Health in First-Graders

Our examination of concepts of mental health led us to conclude that it would be useful to view mental health as consisting of two components. As discussed earlier, one involves an individual's psychological well-being, that is, that area of inner good feeling and self-esteem which has been the traditional concern of mental health clinicians and whose absence is noted by a set of feelings and/or behaviors traditionally termed "symptoms" of disordered psychological processes. The second involves social adaptational status, the judgment by society of the adequacy of the individual's social task performance.

It is crucial to understand the distinction between these two components of mental health in order to follow the analyses in this study. Social adaptational status is external to the individual. It is the judgment by a natural rater. Some such judgments, for example, school grades or a foreman's formal rating of the competence of a worker, are recorded. SAS is conceptually, therefore, distinct from the individual's *actual* performance. A grade of "excellent" is an example of a student's social adaptational status. The performance of the student may have been worthy of such a grade, but, nevertheless, this performance is conceptually distinct from the grade. Similarly, even though the judgment by a teacher that a child is shy may or may not be an accurate assessment of the child's actual behavior, it is possible to distinguish conceptually between the teacher's judgment and the child's behavior. Psychological well-being, in contrast to social adaptational status, is an internal state of the individual, although it is often possible to measure this state only by means of the observations by others.

A major portion of the remainder of this book is devoted to a series of studies which attempt to examine each of these two components of mental health and the ways in which they may be related. Our interest in these two components stems partly from the idea that the way a person is viewed by significant other people may have strong and important implications for the way that person feels about himself. Are the two components related over time and, if so, what is the relation? For example, is there an excessive cost in adapting to societal demands, a cost manifested by symptoms of anxiety or depression or other evidence of inner distress? Or does high social adaptational status bestow a psychological reward by generating psychological well-being? These are ways in which the two components of mental health may relate to each other.

**Measuring
Social Adaptational Status**

One of the major fields for first-grade children is the classroom, and the natural rater in this field—in the view of society—is the teacher. We had to determine the specific social adaptational tasks expected of children in the first-grade classrooms of Woodlawn as youngsters made the transition to the student role. The social context in which we were to make this determination was one of considerable tension and conflict between the community of Woodlawn and the larger city. In fact, whether the tasks expected of the children by the teachers were even appropriate was questioned by many Woodlawn parents.

The concept of social adaptational status and the social and political conditions surrounding the relationship between Woodlawn and the broader society dictated that the social adaptational status of Wood-lawn first-graders be based on the views of the teachers *in Woodlawn* of the tasks expected of Woodlawn's first-graders, rather than on the views of teachers in other neighborhoods. While a pilot study was conducted in nearby communities for the purpose of refining a teacher interview procedure, validity and reliability studies of the SAS instrument were carried out on ratings of Woodlawn children made by Woodlawn teachers. The rationale reflected the fact that the instrument was to measure a characteristic, SAS, which is field-specific; this meant that we had to be sure that it measured the SAS of Woodlawn children as judged by Woodlawn teachers.

The following pages describe the development of the instrument for measuring the SAS of Woodlawn children that was called TOCA, or "Teachers' Observations of Classroom Adaptation." The major validity and reliability discussion will center on the first Woodlawn community-wide ratings and their characteristics. Since we are concerned with exploring the concept of SAS as well as with validating the instrument for measuring it, we will discuss at greater length than usual some of the results of studies of the ratings in the section on validity.

Determining the Social Tasks
Expected of Woodlawn First-Graders

The first problem was how to ask the teachers what social task they expected of their first-grade students. When we asked several teachers what was expected, we found the answers tended to be vague phrases such as "developing citizenship" or "learning to think." More specific information was obtained, however, when the question was framed in terms of what the signs are that a child is not succeeding in school. The responses to this kind of question allowed us to infer the specific social tasks the teachers felt were important.

There were a total of fifty-seven first-grade classrooms in Woodlawn's nine public and three Roman Catholic schools. The fifty-seven teachers in charge of these classrooms were approached through the district superintendent in the case of the public schools and archdiocesan office in the case of the Catholic schools. Principals were asked to request their first-grade teachers to list the kinds of behaviors which caused them to think that a child was having difficulty assuming the student role, that is, maladaptive behaviors. This request was passed through the school hierarchy in the hope that it would elicit lists of behaviors which reflected the teachers' own viewpoints rather than their efforts to emulate mental health professionals.

The center's board were quite interested in the kind of response we would get from school administrators and faculty. They saw it as the first step in building a new alliance between the community and the schools around the issue of bettering the school situation for Woodlawn's young children. Board members made their concern very clear on both an individual and a collective basis and were very watchful as the project got under way.

Fifty-three of the fifty-seven teachers submitted lists. From the 435 maladaptive behaviors named, members of the center staff developed five categories of social tasks in which most of the teachers' descriptions could be placed. These categories were labeled "social contact," "authority acceptance," "maturation," "cognitive achievement," and "concentration," to reflect the general areas of behavior in which teachers set tasks in the classroom. (See table 4.)

The five social task categories inferred from the maladaptive cues

TABLE 4. DERIVATION OF SOCIAL TASK CATEGORIES

Maladaptive Behaviors	Categories of Social Tasks
Shy; timid; alone too much; friendless; aloof	Social contact
Fights too much; steals; lies; resists authority; is destructive to others or property; obstinate; disobedient; uncooperative	Authority acceptance
Acts too young physically and/or emotionally; cries too much; has tantrums; sucks thumb; is physically poorly coordinated; urinates in class; seeks too much attention	Maturation
Does not learn as well as he is able; lazy; does not come prepared for work; underachiever; lacks effort	Cognitive achievement
Fidgets; is unable to sit still in classroom; restless	Concentration

were meant to cover the range of social tasks presented to first-graders by their teachers. We could, of course, have inferred a variety of numbers of categories from the original 435 behaviors. More rigorous, systematic instrumentation would have entailed scaling the 435 behaviors, having a sample of teachers rate students on these scales, then factoring the ratings to arrive at a set of categories each of which would contain a group of scaled behavior items. However, it was clear that the teachers would not be willing to be involved in a lengthy, complicated procedure. Even in the developmental phase of instrument design, there was considerable pressure from the teachers to keep the procedures short. The five general categories enabled teachers to place a wide variety of behaviors under a task category such as cognitive achievement or social contact without having laboriously to rate larger numbers of more individual, more concrete behaviors.

The social contact category included behaviors such as "shy," "timid," and "alone too much," suggesting that first-graders were expected to develop an ability to relate to their classmates and the teacher. Behaviors such as "fights too much" and "resists authority" made up the authority acceptance category and suggested that first-graders faced the task of abiding by certain rules. The maturation category, which included such behaviors as "acts too young" and "cries too much," implied that teachers expected first-graders to behave with a certain degree of maturity and independence. The cognitive achievement category was based on behaviors that concerned working up to one's intellectual capacity as judged by the teacher. Paying attention and sitting still in the classroom were the types of behaviors that suggested the category we have called concentration.

Designing the Rating Instrument

Rating scales were devised for each of the five categories of social adaptational tasks to be assessed by TOCA, along with a sixth category, called "global adaptation," an overall scale of a child's behavior in his teacher's view. When a child was rated adapting on all five social task scales, he was rated adapting on the global adaptation scale. Teachers were instructed that a child who was rated maladapting on *any one* of the five social task scales was to be rated maladapting on the global adaptation scale; however, the degree of maladaptation was left to the teacher's judgment. For example, while a teacher could rate a child as severely maladapting on the social contact or concentration scales, she could feel that overall the child is only mildly maladapting. The global scale was meant to allow her to make such an overall assessment.

Each of the six scales was assigned four points so that teachers would have a range of possible ratings from *minimally adapting* through *severely maladapting*. The four possible ratings were:

0 = adaptive behavior at least within minimal limits
1 = mildly maladaptive behavior
2 = moderately maladaptive behavior
3 = severely maladaptive behavior

It is important to remember that these are not scales of symptomatic behavior as viewed by clinicians. They are scales of social adaptational behavior in the first-grade classroom as viewed by teachers and in relation to tasks defined by teachers.

Reasoning similar to that involved in the decision to use five single-item scales resulted in the decision to make four-point gradations on each TOCA scale rather than some higher number of gradations and to design the interview so that the interviewer did the writing—not the teacher. Other investigators have used more scales, each of which rated a more concrete behavior than do TOCA scales, and some such scales have finer gradations. Our solution represents a compromise between a desire for information concerning the degree of maladaptation and what we assessed to be the tolerance of Woodlawn teachers for the interview procedure.

After the TOCA instrument had been in use for several years, we became aware of the importance of TOCA's inability to measure the degree of adaptation as well as maladaptation. For example, when a child was rated adapting on one of the scales, we had no indication of the *degree* to which he was adapting in that area in his teacher's view. When a child was rated maladapting, however, the teacher was able to indicate also the degree to which he was maladapting. Clearly, the scales were biased toward a finer delineation of weakness than of strength. The original scales were retained, however, because year-to-year comparisons would have been difficult had they been changed.

TOCA was designed to be used in a standardized interview conducted by a member of the center staff. In a pilot test conducted in communities immediately adjacent to Woodlawn, TOCA was used with ten first-grade teachers who rated their students' social adaptational status in the classroom. The final design of the standardized teacher interview procedure was based on these preliminary experiences. (See Appendix A.) Pilot teachers reported that the categories were adequate representations of the social adaptational tasks facing first-grade children. The teachers had no difficulty using the categories to classify the kinds of behaviors they observed in their own classrooms.

The results of the pilot test indicated that the interview procedure was a feasible one; furthermore, reliability and validity studies of the pilot test data that are not presented here suggested that the instrument was appropriate for the intended purposes. Extensive validity and reliability studies conducted with the Woodlawn population itself are presented later in this report.

The Standardized Teacher
Interview: Rating the
Initial Population

The first community-wide ratings of Woodlawn first-graders were made in the fall of 1964 on a population of 2,010 children. (This total population is referred to hereafter as Cohort I.) Assessment was scheduled for the ninth week of school, to allow time for teachers to get to know their students well enough to rate them. The initial community-wide ratings took five weeks; subsequent ratings took about three weeks each. A schedule of TOCA assessments and assessments using other types of instruments is contained in Appendix B.

For the first and all succeeding assessments, ratings were obtained by a trained member of the center's staff in a standardized 45- to 50-minute interview with each first-grade teacher.[2] Interviews took place outside the classroom, so classes were covered by substitute teachers provided by either the center or the school.

The standardized interview began with a 5- to 10-minute period of engagement between the teacher and the interviewer. Often the discussion centered on the importance of the teacher's view of each student's progress in mastering first-grade tasks. Time was allowed for the teacher to question the purpose of the interview and to talk over anything else on her mind. She was given an interview form to read and refer to throughout the interview. Then, while the interviewer wrote, the teacher was asked to rate each of her students, separately, on each of the five scales of social adaptation and on the global scale. Termination consisted of about five to ten minutes of conversation, part of which usually concerned the responsibility a teacher feels when she must grade or rate a child without the benefit of collaboration with another person.

The interviewers were trained to avoid doing or saying anything that might bias the teachers' ratings. The scales had been developed using the teachers' language, and no attempt was made to get all teachers to rate with the same base line or level of expectation. The instrument designed to measure SAS was meant to assess how the child's performance was ordinarily viewed by his or her teacher, not how it might have been viewed after some sort of teacher training. From our standpoint, even though the teacher may have been permissive or demanding, or warm or cold, she had an official role in the social field of the classroom and in the school system. Thus we saw the teacher as having a central importance as the natural rater of the child's social adaptational status in the classroom, with each child in the class measured against the standards set by the teacher.

This does not imply that natural raters, including teachers, are totally objective. On the contrary, we have found that ratings are clearly related to certain characteristics of the individual rater, and these data are discussed later in this section when results of assessment are considered. Thus a program of intervention in first grade cannot ignore the teacher as a relevant aspect of the social system, just as it cannot ignore the family, the peer group, or the community.

Reliability of TOCA

As an instrument for measuring the social adaptational status of Woodlawn children, TOCA is based on a concept which puts both the definition of social adaptational tasks and the actual rating of children in the hands of one person—the classroom teacher. The instrument is intended to measure the teacher's view of the social adaptational status of the child in her classroom. We do not doubt that another rater, whether another teacher or a mental health professional, might have a totally different view of how well the child is performing his social tasks. However, in the conceptual framework we have outlined, such views are not relevant to the child's social adaptational status in the classroom. We are interested in the specific teacher's view, including her idiosyncrasies and whatever other factors influence this view. Therefore, interrater agreement is not relevant as a measure of the reliability of TOCA, any more than other views would be relevant to a child's school record.

The test-retest issue is another matter. Here we are very much interested in the question of whether the teacher's ratings of a child are whimsical or whether they represent a studied judgment persistent enough to be considered a useful expression of the child's adaptational status. In order to test this, we examined teachers' ratings for Cohort I made early in first grade, at approximately the end of the first quarter, in comparison to ratings from a sample of classes made six weeks later. We felt that this period of time was short enough to avoid the possibility of real change in the children but long enough to make it likely that teachers would have forgotten their original ratings. A longer interim would have increased the likelihood that real changes could have occurred in the child's behavior that would confound our study of test-retest reliability. Even so, we cannot be sure to what extent the degree of disagreement we found between the two sets of ratings was due to growth and development in the child or other confounding changes.

TABLE 5. TEST-RETEST RELIABILITY OF TOCA

TOCA Scales	Gamma	r†	t
Social contact	.76	.56	3.11**
Authority acceptance	.92	.79	0.43
Maturation	.82	.72	4.81**
Cognitive achievement	.85	.70	1.63
Concentration	.83	.70	6.04**
Global	.85	.70	3.94**

Note: These results were based on the reinterviews of 10 teachers who rated 282 Cohort I children 6 weeks after the initial ratings.
†r is the product-moment correlation.
** indicates that the test-retest means (early ratings minus retest ratings) were significantly different at the 0.01 level of probability.

Table 5 indicates that TOCA did demonstrate moderate reliability when the early and retest ratings were considered. Gamma values ranged from .76 to .92. The direction of the t statistics indicates a shift toward better adaptation. Either these children actually improved over the six-week period or the shift represents a placebo effect of the retesting procedures. From these studies of test-retest reliability, we concluded that TOCA was a sufficiently stable instrument to warrant further examination.

Validity of TOCA

The validity of the TOCA ratings was, of course, a primary concern in these studies. Validity has been described as the extent to which an instrument measures what it is purported to measure; this extent can be assessed only in relation to a given purpose. In the case of TOCA, the purpose was to measure the social adaptational status of first-grade children in Woodlawn. The discussion which follows is consistent with the American Psychological Association's published standards for psychological tests (1966).

Using the three types of validity—*content, criterion-related,* and *construct*—we tried to determine whether TOCA accomplished the appointed task. These three types of validity are only conceptually independent; in actual demonstrations they may overlap, depending on the intended use of the test.

Content validity is concerned with the inclusion in the measuring instrument of a proper sampling of the content or behaviors of interest. In regard to TOCA, the issue was whether the social tasks described in the instrument adequately represented those expected of first-grade children. The reader will recall that all of Woodlawn's first-grade teachers were asked to contribute, in their own language, lists of behaviors which to them indicated that a child was maladapting in the classroom. The request was routed through the school hierarchy in order to avoid the contamination which might have resulted had the request come directly from mental health professionals—that is, the teachers might have attempted to list "symptoms" rather than behaviors they considered maladaptive in the social field of the classroom. The large percentage of responding teachers and the number of behaviors submitted (435) gave us some assurance that the breadth of social tasks had been included. Further support for content validity was provided by the ease with which the 435 behaviors could be fitted into the five social task categories inferred from the maladaptive cues (see note 1).

Independently, two Woodlawn Mental Health Center staff members who had not been involved in making the categories attempted to place the 435 items into the five categories. They agreed on the category in which each item should be placed 76.3 percent of the time. Sixty items were judged unclassifiable by one staff member and seventy-five by the other. The unclassifiable items did not relate specifically to maladaptive behaviors but referred to conditions such as "poor nutrition," "bad family background," and so on. In practice, both during the pilot test and later during the actual assessments, teachers had no difficulty using these categories to rate all their students.

TOCA is intended to measure social adaptational status, a concept not generally measured in elementary schoolchildren by social scientists. We were not aware of other obvious traditional measures with which to compare TOCA for *criterion-related validity*. The nearest approximation to traditional alternative measures are intelligence test scores, achievement test scores, and grades, including conduct. There is, however, a basic conceptual difference between intelligence and achievement tests and TOCA in that test scores are not provided by a natural rater, as social adaptational status ratings are with TOCA. Still, these two kinds of tests are useful in terms of criterion-related validity, since performing well on them is a social task expected of schoolchildren. These comparisons would probably be just as appropriately considered under construct validity. Grades also differ from TOCA conceptually; however, TOCA's authority acceptance scale and the child's conduct grade may be somewhat similar. Even the cognitive achievement scale on TOCA is different from grades, since it specifically asks the teacher to consider whether the child is learning *up to his ability*.

We sought to determine whether there was any relation between TOCA and these measures, even though this was, at best, only an approximation of a test of TOCA's criterion-related validity. Some justification may be found by considering that intelligence tests, achievement tests, and grades are partly a series of obstacle courses for the children and as such can be considered measures of the child's adaptational status. For years, psychologists have interpreted IQ scores as measurements of a child's performance on a standardized test, not as direct reflections of innate intelligence. Binet himself indicated that children can learn to perform better on intelligence tests (Tuddenham 1962).

Figures 2 and 3 graphically illustrate the difference in the scores of adapting and maladapting children on both the Kuhlmann-Anderson Intelligence Test and the Metropolitan Readiness Test (MRT). The more maladapted children had lower IQ and MRT scores. Table 6 shows the strength of the relationships, indicated by gamma values, between TOCA and IQ and TOCA and the MRT scores. While most of the relationships we are about to consider are statistically significant,

Measuring Mental Health
in First-Graders

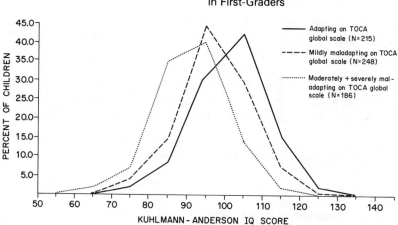

Figure 2. Distribution of IQ Scores of Adapting, Mildly Maladapting, and Moderately plus Severely Maladapting Children Early in First Grade. These data are derived from Global TOCA ratings and IQ scores of children in control public schools in Cohort I. The parochial schools are not included since they do not give IQ tests in first grade.

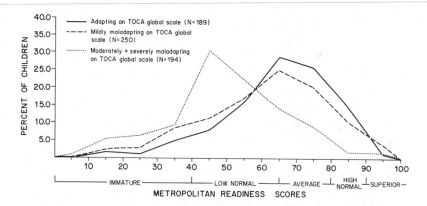

Figure 3. Distribution of Readiness Scores for Adapting, Mildly Maladapting, and Moderately plus Severely Maladapting Children Early in First Grade. These data are derived from Global TOCA ratings and readiness scores of children in control public schools in Cohort I. The parochial schools are not included since they do not give readiness tests in first grade.

particularly since the numbers are large, there is still the question of how strong the relationships are. We used gamma as the measure of strength of relationship. According to Goodman and Kruskal, "gamma tells us how much more probable it is to get like than unlike orders in the two classifications when two individuals are chosen at random from the population" (1954). The tables presenting the results of these tests (tables 6, 7, 8, and 9) show negative gamma values indicating that better (i.e., higher) scores or grades were generally associated with better (i.e., lower) ratings on TOCA scales.

Table 6 shows that the more maladapting a child was on any of the six TOCA scales early in first grade, the lower his score on the Kuhlmann-Anderson Intelligence Test was likely to be. The social

TABLE 6. GAMMA VALUES FOR TOCA RATINGS EARLY IN FIRST GRADE VERSUS IQ SCORES AND READINESS SCORES IN FIRST GRADE

TOCA Scales	First-Grade IQ† (N=649)	First-Grade Readiness† (N=632)
Social contact	-.26	-.40
Authority acceptance	-.53	-.27
Maturation	-.46	-.36
Cognitive achievement	-.40	-.20
Concentration	-.50	-.27
Global	-.51	-.37

Note: The results are based on 4 x 3 tables of the four TOCA levels (adapting, mildly maladapting, moderately maladapting, and severely maladapting) and three levels of IQ and three levels of readiness. The middle levels of both IQ and readiness included scores within one standard deviation of the mean. For Kuhlmann-Anderson Intelligence Test scores the levels were: below 87; 87-106; above 106. For the Metropolitan Readiness Test scores the levels were: below 41; 41-74; above 74. All chi square values were significant at the 0.01 level of probability.
This population consisted of Cohort I children in control schools.
† These results are for public schools only, since parochial schools do not give IQ and readiness tests in the first grade.

contact scale had the weakest relationship to IQ scores. The strongest relationship to IQ scores occurred with the authority acceptance scale. The cognitive achievement scale might have been expected to be more strongly associated with IQ than it was. However, this TOCA scale was intended to measure how well the child was *working up to his ability level*; the fact that teachers were instructed to take the child's ability into account may explain the lower gamma value for the relationship of this scale to IQ scores. In any case, it is clear that *performance on IQ tests is associated with performance on a variety of social adaptational tasks.*

Early first-grade ratings on all six TOCA scales were also associated with the Metropolitan Readiness Test scores obtained at about the same time in first grade. Again, the cognitive achievement scale was least strongly related to these scores. MRT was most strongly related to the ratings on the social contact scale. All of these results indicate the range of adaptational tasks that are related to *seemingly* narrow performance tests.

The relationships discussed here were all statistically significant at the 0.01 level. For each TOCA scale, chi square tests were performed on 4 X 3 tables—that is, the four levels of each TOCA scale versus the three levels of scores from first- and third-grade IQ tests and MRT test scores in first grade.

The grades (E, G, F, or U) the children received from their teachers in a variety of subjects were also compared to the four TOCA levels. Table 7 presents gamma values indicating the strength of relationships between early TOCA ratings and grades at the end of the first

TABLE 7. GAMMA VALUES FOR TOCA RATINGS EARLY IN FIRST GRADE
VERSUS FIRST-SEMESTER GRADES IN FIRST GRADE

Subject	TOCA SCALES						
	Social Contact	Authority Acceptance	Maturation	Cognitive Achievement	Concentration	Global	N
Reading	-.48	-.46	-.56	-.51	-.49	-.61	664
Oral language	-.47	-.40	-.53	-.34	-.34	-.49	694
Handwriting	-.30	-.42	-.47	-.37	-.40	-.49	681
Social studies	-.41	-.56	-.53	-.50	-.48	-.62	527
Arithmetic	-.43	-.45	-.52	-.48	-.44	-.59	681
Science	-.45	-.43	-.60	-.50	-.55	-.65	439
Conduct	-.02†	-.80	-.52	-.49	-.64	-.55	697

Note: The results are based on 4 x 4 tables of the four TOCA levels (adapting, mildly maladapting, moderately maladapting, and severely maladapting) and grade levels of excellent, good, fair, and unsatisfactory. Parochial schools were excluded, because their grades and subjects are not comparable to those of the public schools. This population consisted of Cohort I children in control schools.
† All chi square values based on these tables except this one were significant at the 0.01 level of probability.

semester in first grade. The table reveals that, generally, the better the adaptational ratings on six TOCA scales, the better the grades. The conduct grade was most strongly related to the authority acceptance scale (gamma = -.8) but had no relationship to the social contact scale. The remaining gamma values ranged from -.30 to -.65. TOCA's global adaptation scale showed a somewhat stronger relationship with grades generally than did the individual scales.

The results of these studies of TOCA in relation to other quasi-social adaptational measures suggest that TOCA yields data with sufficient criterion-related validity. The relationship between TOCA and IQ were moderately strong, although the gamma value for the relationship between the social contact scale and IQ was only −.26. Relationships between readiness scores and TOCA were less strong than those between IQ and TOCA. As mentioned above, the relationships between grades and TOCA were of moderate strength, with the strongest relationship occurring between the conduct grade and TOCA's authority acceptance scale. The latter result was particularly important, since both the conduct grade and the authority acceptance scale are measures of the teacher's view of the child's decorum in the classroom.

The criterion-related validity of TOCA was also examined over time by studying the relationships of TOCA ratings early in first grade to similar measures in third grade. The gammas (see table 8) for first-

TABLE 8. GAMMA VALUES FOR TOCA RATINGS EARLY IN FIRST GRADE VERSUS IQ SCORES AND READING ACHIEVEMENT SCORES IN THIRD GRADE

TOCA Scales	Third-Grade IQ† (N=355)	Third-Grade Reading† (N=365)
Social contact	−.39	−.31
Authority acceptance	−.44	−.43
Maturation	−.35	−.41
Cognitive achievement	−.40	−.37
Concentration	−.37	−.40
Global	−.50	−.47

Note: The results are based on 4 x 3 tables of the four TOCA levels (adapting, mildly maladapting, moderately maladapting, and severely maladapting) and three levels of IQ and three levels of reading achievement, the middle levels of which included scores within one standard deviation of the mean. Kuhlmann-Anderson IQ score levels were: below 83; 83-103; above 103. For the Metropolitan Reading Achievement Test scores, the levels were: below 20; 20-36; above 36. All chi square values based on these tables were significant at the 0.01 level of probability, except for two, which were significant at the 0.05 level of probability.
This population consisted of Cohort I children in control schools.
† These results are for public schools only, since parochial schools do not give IQ and reading achievement tests in third grade.

grade TOCA and third-grade IQ were slightly lower than those obtained in the first-grade concurrent study. All six TOCA scales were associated with IQ performance and reading achievement scores such that better early adaptation was associated with better scores on both third-grade tests.

The values of gamma for the relationships between TOCA ratings made early in first grade and the subject grades received in third grade are shown in table 9. Instead of the conventional .05 level of significance, the .10 level has been used throughout this book. It is hoped that sufficient data and discussion have been presented to guard against unwarranted inferences. For a discussion of this issue, the reader is referred to the footnote.*

Better adaptation in first grade was associated with better grades in third grade, although this relationship was less strong on the social contact scale than on the other TOCA scales. Apparently there was some drop in the strength of the relationship between first and third grade, although all except four were still statistically significant, most at the 0.01 level.

At the beginning of the discussion of criterion-related validity, grades, IQ, readiness, and achievement test performance were described as SAS measures only because children are expected to perform well on these tests. In fact, IQ and achievement tests are not judgments made by the natural rater, that is, the teacher; they are scores of the children's actual performance—therefore such scores are only quasi-social adaptational measures. Our results led us to conclude that

---

*We have used a level which to some extent guards against real differences being ignored. We quote from Blalock (1960, p. 125): "Significance levels commonly used in statistical research are the .05, .01, and .001 levels. It should be realized in view of the above discussion that there is nothing sacred or absolute about these levels. Although a person would usually be conservative in using such levels, if he actually did not want to reject the null hypothesis he would be on safer ground using perhaps the .10, .20, or even .30 level, thereby reducing his risk of a type II error."

In the same vein, McNemar (1963, pp. 63-64) says: "The null hypothesis is one which can be rejected but can never be proved; therefore to accept it too often because we insist on a high level of significance for rejection means that we are too apt to overlook real differences.... Those writers who advocate the .05 level for research workers in psychology cite R. A. Fisher, an eminent statistician, as their authority, *but* they fail to point out that Fisher's applications are to experimental situations in agriculture and biology where there is far better control of sampling than is ordinarily the case in psychology.

"If the findings of a study are to be used as the basis either for theory and further hypotheses or for social action, it does not seem unreasonable to require a higher level of significance than the .05 level. The answer as to what level, in terms of probability, should be adopted in order to call a finding statistically significant is not uninvolved. There is the balancing of risks: that of accepting the null hypothesis when to do so may mean the overlooking of a real difference against that of rejecting the null hypothesis which may lead to the acceptance of a chance difference as real. There is the question of the likelihood of independent verification, and, finally, there is the whim of personal preference: some individuals are more eager than others to announce a 'significant' finding; others are more cautious. It follows that no hard and fast rule can be given; a finding may be interpreted in terms of the probability of its occurence by chance and then it may be noted whether the P is near the significance level adopted *prior* to the experiment because it seemed appropriate when all factors were weighed."

Because of the small numbers involved in many categories of symptoms in epidemiologic research, including this study, there is a danger of missing important relationships if one is not careful in the use of significance levels.

TABLE 9. GAMMA VALUES FOR TOCA RATINGS EARLY IN FIRST
GRADE VERSUS FIRST-SEMESTER GRADES IN THIRD GRADE

Subject	TOCA SCALES						
	Social Contact	Authority Acceptance	Matura- tion	Cognitive Achievement	Concen- tration	Global	N
Reading	-.08 ns	-.36 **	-.28 *	-.22 **	-.30 **	-.30 **	363
Mathematics	-.20 ns	-.26 *	-.28 **	-.32 **	-.31 **	-.38 **	371
Speaking	-.23 *	-.32 *	-.36 **	-.25 *	-.34 **	-.32 **	370
Writing	-.17 ns	-.37 **	-.30 *	-.27 (*)	-.30 *	-.38 **	371
Spelling	-.32 **	-.46 **	-.38 **	-.35 **	-.43 **	-.44 **	369

Note: These results are based on 4 x 4 tables of the four TOCA levels (adapting, mildly
maladapting, moderately maladapting, and severely maladapting) and grade levels of
excellent, good, fair, and unsatisfactory. Parochial schools were excluded, because their
grades and subjects are not comparable to those of the public schools. This population
consisted of Cohort I children in control schools.
** indicates chi square values were significant at the 0.01 level of probability.
 * indicates chi square values were significant at the 0.05 level of probability.
(*) indicates chi square values were significant at the 0.10 level of probability
ns indicates chi square values were not significant at the 0.10 level of probability.

there is overlap between teachers' judgments and performance on
these tests; however, there is more to a teacher's judgments on TOCA
than is measured by any one of the quasi-social adaptational measures.
Multiple regressions indicate that IQ, readiness test scores, and grades
account for only 21 to 38 percent of the variance of each of the TOCA
scales, with grades being the strongest predictor of TOCA (see note 1).

Construct validity is perhaps the most important aspect of validity to
be addressed, particularly since social adaptational status is a relatively
unexplored concept. Compared to the criterion-related studies of
TOCA ratings, we are on more solid ground in establishing the validity
of the concept of social adaptational status and the instrument for
measuring it by attempting to predict events from what we know of the
concept. Thus in the following presentation of data and discussion, we
are concerned with the evidence for the construct validity of TOCA; but
we also explore the results in terms of what they reveal about the
concept of social adaptational status in Woodlawn first-graders. Are
TOCA ratings really measures of the social adaptational status of
Woodlawn first-graders?

Several characteristics of the children and their school experiences
were selected that should relate to TOCA if this instrument actually
yields valid measures of social adaptational status. The selection of
these characteristics was based on empirical evidence from other investigators, some of whom are cited in the discussion of our results. Tests
were conducted to see whether the TOCA ratings distinguished be-

tween children with hypothetically favorable characteristics and those
with less favorable characteristics. For example, the construct validity
of TOCA would be supported if the social adaptation ratings of first-
graders who had been to kindergarten were better than those of
first-graders who had not been to kindergarten. The same may be
said of older children in comparison to younger children, and generally, investigators have found girls in first grade to be better adapted
than boys of the same age. Therefore, girls would be expected to
have better TOCA ratings. It would be unreasonable to expect variables such as sex or age to explain all or even most of a child's
social adaptational status. However, there should be some predictable differences if TOCA has construct validity. The strength of the
relationship between TOCA and any of these characteristics would
depend, then, on the importance of the particular characteristic in
explaining social adaptational status and on the validity of TOCA as a
measure of that status.

Both analysis of variance and chi square tests were conducted comparing favorable and less favorable characteristics. The chi square tests
were done to obviate the problem of the questionable linearity of the
TOCA scales. There were very few differences between the results
obtained with chi square tests and the results obtained by analysis of
variance; therefore, only the results of analysis of variance are included
in table 10. Other cohorts produced results similar to those obtained
with Cohort I (see note 1).

The significant results from analysis of variance are indicated in
table 10 by a number. The numbers are the differences in the percent
adapting on each scale between the "favorable" and "less favorable"
populations. Both the results of analysis of variance and differences in
percent adapting are included, the latter for the reader interested in a
measure of the strength of the results. We tested combinations of
independent variables, two at a time, to see whether interactions
occurred—for example, whether older children who had been to kindergarten did better or worse than younger children who had been to
kindergarten. These results are cited in the following discussion (see
note 1).

In order to study the change in the relationship of the selected
characteristics to adaptation ratings over the school year, we concen-
trated on the population of children who were rated both early and at
the end of the school year. Thus, children who had been rated early in
the school year but had transferred to schools outside Woodlawn before
the year's end were excluded, as were children who came to Woodlawn

TABLE 10. DIFFERENCES IN PERCENTS ADAPTING BETWEEN CHILDREN WITH "FAVORABLE" CHARACTERISTICS AND CHILDREN WITH "LESS FAVORABLE" CHARACTERISTICS WHERE THESE DIFFER BY ANALYSIS OF VARIANCE

| | TOCA SCALES | | | | | | | | | | | |
| | Early in school year | | | | | | End of school year | | | | | |
"Favorable" vs. "Less Favorable" Characteristics	Social Contact	Authority Acceptance	Maturation	Cognitive Achievement	Concentration	Global	Social Contact	Authority Acceptance	Maturation	Cognitive Achievement	Concentration	Global
Girls (824) vs. boys (887)§	ns	12.7	7.2	7.7	12.0	9.2	ns	16.3	14.0	8.6	18.0	8.6
Older children (677) vs. younger children (692) (excluding repeaters)	3.8	ns	5.5	ns	ns	ns	ns	ns	6.0	3.6	ns	3.5
Kindergarten previous year (1203) vs. no previous schooling (166)	6.8	ns	4.9	ns	ns	6.8	ns	ns	ns	ns	ns	7.3
Kindergarten previous year (1203) vs. repeating first grade (289)	ns	13.2	ns	8.8	ns	10.0	ns	7.3	ns	ns	ns	9.6
Same school previous year (1005) vs. different school previous year (489) (kindergarten and repeaters only)	ns	11.0	13.5	8.9	17.5	12.8	8.2	8.5	13.2‡	10.7†	14.0	12.7
Same teacher all year (1225) vs. change of teacher during first grade (316)	12.8	ns	12.4	ns	11.1	ns	ns	11.3	ns	1.8†	7.1†	ns
Same school and teacher all year (1225) vs. change of school during first grade (60)	ns	ns	ns	ns	ns	ns	17.1	ns	13.4‡	17.8	ns	17.7

Note: This population included all the children who were in Woodlawn schools from early to end of first grade (N=1711), Cohort I.
* Opposite direction from prediction
† Interaction with intervention vs. control (where the favorable/less favorable were different on TOCA)
‡ The numbers in parentheses do not always add up to the total because of missing information in some cases and because some comparisons are not dichotomous.
§ The numbers in parentheses do not always add up to the total because of missing information in some cases and because some comparisons are not dichotomous.
ns=not significant at the 0.10 level of probability.

schools after the early ratings. These studies included both intervention schoolchildren and control schoolchildren. The division of the twelve Woodlawn elementary schools into intervention schools and control schools is described in detail in a later section; here, it is sufficient to say the results presented in table 10 were not different for intervention and control schools.

These results support the construct validity of TOCA. The following statements summarize the general inferences that were drawn from these studies, all of which were in keeping with the original hypotheses regarding the characteristics selected for study:

1. Girls were better adapted than boys.
2. Older children (excluding repeaters) had better adaptational status than younger children.
3. Children who had been to kindergarten had better adaptational status than those who had had no prior schooling.
4. Children who repeated first grade had worse adaptational status than nonrepeaters.
5. Children who came to first grade from another school had worse adaptational status than children who were in the same school the previous year.
6. Children whose teachers left in the middle of the first grade subsequently had worse adaptational status than children who kept the same teacher all year.
7. Children who changed schools during first grade had worse adaptational status than those who did not.

For those interested in more detail, the next several pages are devoted to an elaboration of these results.

Sex. Early in first grade and at the end of first grade, girls were better adapted than boys on all scales except social contact. Generally, about 9 percent more girls than boys were rated adapting on the TOCA global scale. A curious exception to this relationship occurred when the teacher left the class in the middle of first grade. In this instance, girls were rated less mature than boys by the teacher who was going on leave.

Ullmann has pointed out that in many studies, including his own, there is a noticeable disparity between frequency rates of maladaptation in boys as compared to girls (1952). In Ullmann's own assessment system, the only test in which he found girls to be more maladapted than boys was a self-rating instrument. Ratings by teachers and ratings by peers both indicated that boys have higher frequency rates of maladaptation in ways which are observable. Ullmann conjectured that girls internalize such difficulties. He also reviewed other hypotheses which attempt to explain why girls seem better adapted to school than boys—for example, girls develop the skills necessary for school earlier or girls have less role conflict than boys in sitting still, being submissive to the teacher, and so on.

Age. Even a small age difference was significant in a child's mastery of the social tasks of first grade. After repeaters had been excluded, the remaining first-graders were divided into two groups: those aged six to six-and-a-half, and those aged six-and-a-half to seven. Early in the year, older children were less shy and tended to be rated on TOCA as more mature than younger children. By the end of first grade, older children were rated better adapting than younger children on the cognitive achievement, maturation, and global scales. Younger children were no longer more shy than older children. Also, by the end of first grade, having gone to kindergarten seemed to make more difference to the older children. Older children who had not gone to kindergarten were less well adapted on the global scale than were the older children who had gone. Younger children, with or without kindergarten, were in between. This led us to conjecture that perhaps teachers expect older children to perform better, and the children can do so—but only if they are prepared by kindergarten.

In his survey, Rogers concluded that disparity in age (being more than one year older or more than one year younger than the median of the classroom group) had maladaptive consequences (1942). Hamalainen's findings were much the same (1952). Rogers's results showed that children who were underage or overage for the grade level were rated by principals as being less well adjusted emotionally. These children also fared worse in scholastic achievement.

Our results were not totally different, although one must remember the difference between our definition of "younger" and "older" and those used in the investigations of others. In our studies, older children (excluding repeaters) were better adapted than younger children except for those older children who had not been to kindergarten. Thus, being older was generally an advantage; but when it was associated with inadequate preparation, that is, not having gone to kindergarten, being older was associated with greater maladaptation.

Kindergarten. Repeaters were excluded from this analysis also so that we could examine the effect of kindergarten more clearly. Early in the year, children who had gone to kindergarten were better adapted on the social contact, maturation, and global scales than were children without prior schooling. On the other TOCA scales, having attended kindergarten made no significant difference. When confronted with an impending loss of teacher, children who had not been to kindergarten were rated more shy than children who had, and far more shy than children whose teacher was not about to leave. Thus kindergarten was associated with an advantage in social contact and may have provided some protection for the child who was confronted with the loss of the first-grade teacher. By the end of first grade, children who had been to kindergarten were still rated better adapted on the global scale, but they were no longer different from children who had not been to kindergarten in terms of social contact ratings.

Although the evidence from other studies is mainly from uncontrolled investigations, it suggests that kindergarten is associated with better achievement test performance and better physical, social, and emotional adjustment of children (Fuller 1960; Mindness and Keliher 1967; Hefferman 1971). Thus there is sound reason for testing construct validity by comparing children who had been to kindergarten with those who had not. If one wants to go further and find out whether ratings of better adaptation are *caused* by kindergarten or by other factors, such as better family support of the child who attends kindergarten, the research problem becomes more complicated.

In an article on early childhood education written in 1960, Fuller summarizes the results of research on kindergarten. She states that, for the most part, there has been a lack of careful research design and appropriate statistical tests. She also points out that the lack of control groups in the majority of studies is a critical shortcoming, especially since early childhood is a time of rapid growth. Without investigating comparable groups of children who have not been to kindergarten, it is impossible to tell whether any benefit is due to the effect of kindergarten, to the natural development of the child, or to the advantages of the family support received by children who are sent to kindergarten. This is true of our data too.

Since 1960, the plethora of new preschool programs has confounded the problem still further. It is now even more difficult to differentiate the impact of kindergarten from that of other preschool efforts. In terms of TOCA's construct validity, however, we found that the discrimination between children who had been to kindergarten and those who had not was sufficient, although the question of cause remains open.

Repeating first grade. Children who were repeating first grade were seen by their teachers as having more trouble accepting authority, more difficulty learning, and a higher rate of maladaptation on the global scale early in the year than children who had attended kindergarten the previous year. However, if the repeating child changed schools after failing, he did much better in cognitive achievement than the repeater who remained in the same school. The reason for this may be that remaining in the school where he or she has failed leaves a child with a label of failure which others reinforce and which he comes to believe also. There may also be a difference in the amount of family support; the family of the child who is transferred may be more actively involved in the child's educational achievement.

By the end of the year, children who were repeating first grade still had trouble accepting authority and still had a higher rate of maladaptation on the global scale, but they were no longer different in cognitive achievement from nonrepeaters who had been to kindergarten. In addition, if the repeater's teacher left during the year, the repeater seemed—in the view of the new teacher—to suffer more than the nonrepeater by being more shy and more immature and having more difficulty accepting authority. This suggests a continuing and increasing vulnerability on the part of the repeaters. The effect of prior failure on the student experiencing a loss of teacher is to increase the damaging impact of the current stress. We shall see later that earlier stress not experienced as personal failure, even if it is associated with a drop of SAS, tended to *decrease* vulnerability to the stress of loss of teacher.

Goodlad conducted an extensive survey of the effects of repeating a grade on a child's personal and social adjustment (1954). He found repeaters were more often rejected as friends by their classmates than were nonrepeaters, and that teachers more often rated repeaters for bullying. The frequency of bullying among repeaters relates to our findings that repeaters were rated significantly more maladapting on the authority acceptance scale.

Changing schools between years. Changing school between years is strongly associated with maladaptation. Early in first grade, on all scales except social contact, more children who had gone to a different school the previous year were rated maladapting than children who had continued in the same school. The only exception to this was the case of repeaters who changed schools. By the end of first grade, children who had gone to a different school the previous year were rated more maladapting on all six TOCA scales than children who had remained in the same school. These results were among the strongest on table 10; however, if one considers the Social Field–Life Course concept, such results are not surprising. Children who change schools must adjust to a new school, a new teacher, and new classmates. In addition, the characteristics of families and children who move may differ from the characteristics of families and children who do not move.

Change of teacher. The first-grade teachers who left in the middle of the year rated more of their children as shy, immature, and unable to concentrate than did teachers who remained with the class all year.

Girls were rated less mature than boys by teachers who were about to leave. This was one of the few cases in which boys were rated better adapted than girls, and we have no explanation for this. Children who were in a different school the previous year were rated less shy and less mature than children who were in the same school the previous year by the teacher who was about to leave. In fact, by the end of the year, children who had spent the previous year in a different school and had a first-grade teacher leave were rated slightly better at concentrating and just as social as children who had the same teacher for all of first grade and had been in the same school for kindergarten. *Therefore, even though it was a disadvantage for most children, changing schools prior to first grade seems to have been an advantage for children who faced change of teacher during first grade.*

These results cast light on a question that was raised early in our discussion of social adaptation concerning the impact on the individual of having to perform certain social tasks. Our findings suggest that exposure to a certain kind of prior stressful experience—that is, a fateful event, such as a change of school before first grade—reduced the adequacy of the children's performance in the view of the first-grade teacher. However, a later stressful event—the loss of the first-grade teacher—had less impact on the social adaptational status of these children than it did on children who had not experienced the prior stress of a change of school. There is, thus, the possibility that some kinds of prior stressful experiences—possibly those not associated with personal failure—may increase a child's later social adaptive capacity, while prior stress in the form of personal failure seems to lower future social adaptive capacity. Further research on this hypothesis would have far-reaching importance for understanding the relations between stressful experience, social adaptation, and mental health.

At the end of first grade, replacement teachers rated the children as having more difficulty accepting authority and concentrating. Paradoxically, they gave their students better ratings on the cognitive achievement scale than did teachers who remained with the same class all year. Yet by the end of the third grade, children whose first-grade teachers had left were rated by third-grade teachers as having *more* difficulty learning than children who had kept the same teacher throughout first grade (see note 1). This combination of results suggests that first-grade replacement teachers may have had a need to prove themselves that was reflected in their tendency to rate their students better in cognitive achievement. Generally, losing the first-grade teacher seems to have had a negative impact on the children's adaptation.

Changing schools midyear. Prior to the change, children who later changed schools during the course of first grade did not differ from students who remained in the same school and with the same teacher throughout the year. However, by the end of the year—after the change —there was a marked difference in these students. They were rated by their teachers as more shy and more immature and as having lower cognitive achievement than children who had stayed in the same school through first grade. There were 18 percent more children rated adapting on the global scale among those children who did not change schools.

'The literature is sparse on what happens to the adaptational process in children whose teachers leave in the middle of the school year or in children who transfer to another school. There are a few studies by other investigators which report that children who change schools during the year do much worse on various cognitive achievement measures than children who do not (Levine, Wesolowski, and Corbett 1966). Our own studies appear to be important additions in this area. We have noted that, in Woodlawn, a change of teacher during first grade was associated not only with maladaptation prior to the change but also with maladapting two years later. Children who were to change schools during first grade were not detectably different prior to the change; however, those children might have experienced sudden problems in the family or elsewhere which caused their change of school and their maladaptation.

If our conjectures are correct, changing teachers or changing schools carries severe consequences to many children's social adaptational status in first grade. It appears that the social adaptational process is dependent on a stable social field. Bloom illustrates this point extremely well when he demonstrates that a supportive, stable environment is vital for a child's growth and development and further states that on theoretical grounds, one can predict that such an environment is most important at times of maximal change or learning (1964). The results of our studies suggest that disturbances in the stability of a child's relationship to his classroom, his teacher, and/or his school are disruptive to the social adaptational process and may be considered as warnings of impending maladaptation. The impact of the disruption may be heightened or lessened, depending on the kinds of prior stressful experiences the child had.

In the spring of 1967, two years after first grade, follow-up studies were done on that portion of Cohort I still in any of the twelve Woodlawn schools. Although this was a smaller and more stable population (994), the third-grade results obtained by analysis of variance for this less mobile population (see note 1) showed that:

1. Boys were still more likely than girls to be maladapting on all scales except social contact.
2. Children who were younger than the average when they entered first grade were still more likely to be maladapting on the maturation scale.
3. Differences between children who had attended kindergarten and those who had not had disappeared.
4. Differences between children who had failed first grade and those who had not had increased since the end of first grade; repeaters were now more likely to be maladapting on all six scales.
5. Having attended a different school prior to first grade was no longer associated with being maladapted.
6. Children whose teacher left during first grade were more likely to be maladapting on the social contact, authority acceptance, cognitive achievement, and global adaptation scales.
7. Differences between children who had changed schools during first grade and those who had not were no longer present.

All of these studies of the validity of TOCA provide evidence that the instrument provides a valid measure of the child's social adaptational status in the first-grade classroom. Specifically, the studies of criterion-related validity indicate that TOCA is related to IQ, to achievement test performance, and to grades, but is clearly not identical to these other measures; the studies of construct validity confirm the capacity of TOCA to predict differences in social adaptational status between various populations of children. All these studies provide information concerning the concept of social adaptational status itself.

The results suggest that a child's social adaptational status in the first-grade classroom is partly determined by factors completely external to the child. Most of the seven favorable/less favorable comparisons did not derive from the *child's* capacities or performance but from events or conditions that happened to the child. This raises the question of *how* certain fateful events affect the child's performance. Does lack of kindergarten, for example, deprive the child of prior needed experience or training, thus lowering his performance in first grade so that the teacher rates him as maladapting? Or might such events affect a child's social adaptational status directly by leading the teacher to assume that lack of kindergarten invariably lowers the adequacy of a first-grader's performance, so that she rates him maladapting without actually observing his performance? The teacher's lowered expectation may affect not only the social adaptational status of the child but the child's performance itself. The work of Rosenthal and Jacobson (1966, 1968) tends to confirm such a possibility. They found that, when teachers were misinformed about the capacity of a student, the child's performance appeared to be influenced, with the change in performance being dependent on the kind of misinformation given the teacher.

Certainly, not all the determinants of social adaptational status are external to the child. One of the most intriguing results of the Woodlawn studies has to do with the relationship between prior stress and subsequent adaptive capacity. A change of school between kindergarten and first grade tended to lower social adaptational status just as prior failure in first grade did. While such events were strongly associated with greater maladaptation, they appear to alter the vulnerability of such children to the damage caused by a loss of teacher later during the course of first grade, but the changes in vulnerability are in opposite directions. This altered vulnerability seems to be clearly an internal process in the child; but it is also clear that the replacement teacher, in rating her children generally as higher achievers than those who kept the same teacher, was basing her assessment of the children's social adaptational status at least partly on factors outside the performance of the children.

We can summarize by saying that SAS, a judgment made by a natural rater in a specific social field, is partly determined by factors other than the performance of the individual being assessed. It is also apparent from these results, however, that social adaptational status is based partly on the person's performance. In other words, SAS is not purely a label attached to the child without regard to his performance. It appears very likely that SAS is developed out of an intense interplay between the teacher setting the tasks, the child's performance, and the teacher's judgment as to SAS; each stimulates the other and provides some of the determination for the other, while each appears to be determined by other factors as well. This interplay between the child and the teacher with its resultant SAS of the child was a major interest, both conceptually and in terms of research, throughout this project.

Results of the Initial Assessment:
Base Line Measures

The initial community-wide assessment, made at the time of the first report card in the fall of 1964, provided base line measures of social adaptation for all 2,010 Woodlawn first-graders. These first teacher ratings indicated that on the TOCA global scale, 36.3 percent of the children were rated mildly maladapting; 19.4 percent were rated moderately maladapting; and 13.6 percent were rated severely maladapting. Thus we found that, early in first grade, teachers viewed 69.3 percent of the children in this population as not performing adequately the stipulated social tasks of the first-grade classroom. Only 30.7 percent of Cohort I received teachers' ratings of adapting within minimal limits.

Even though these base line measures confirmed the board's feeling that the community needed an effective program of prevention and early treatment for its youngsters, there was deep concern over the large numbers of children being labeled as "not making it." When the results became known generally in the community, there was a great deal of discussion about what they did or did not mean. Members of the board, together with the center staff, discussed at length all the possible interpretations of the results. Board members were quick to reaffirm their position that the early school experience of Woodlawn children needed close examination and that the schools, the parents, and the community had to find a way to work together for change.

Further conference with the board and school faculties revealed that both were anxious for an intervention program to get under way. Accordingly, Woodlawn's twelve elementary schools were divided into two matched groups of six schools each in order to develop, implement, and systematically evaluate a community-wide intervention program. The following criteria were used in the matching: (1) number of first-grade classrooms and of first-grade students; (2) number of public schools and parochial schools; (3) frequency rates of maladapting children in first grade; (4) number of large and small schools as measured by the number of first-grade classrooms; and (5) percentage of impoverished families in the area served by the school.

Table 11 shows how the two groups of schools compared. The toss of

TABLE 11. CHARACTERISTICS OF INTERVENTION AND CONTROL SCHOOLS

Criteria	Intervention Schools	Control Schools
Number of schools, classes, pupils		
Total number of schools	6	6
Total number of classrooms	29	28
Total number of pupils	1066	944
Public vs. parochial schools		
Number of public schools	4	5
Number of parochial schools	2	1
Prevalence of global maladaptation		
Schools with less than 33% moderate or severe	3	3
Schools with 33% or more moderate or severe	3	3
Distribution of first-grade classrooms		
Schools with 3 or fewer first-grade classrooms	3	3
Schools with 4 or more first-grade classrooms	3	3
Economic level of school's enrollment area†		
1–25% of population with annual income of $3000 or less	1	2
26–29% of population with annual income of $3000 or less	2	1
30% or more of population with annual income of $3000 or less	1	2

Note: These data are based on characteristics present at the time of the initial assessment, fall 1964, except for "Economic Level of School's Enrollment Area," which is based on 1960 census data.

† Parochial schools were omitted, since their enrollment was scattered over wider areas which included many public school districts.

a coin determined which group of schools would receive a first-grade intervention program and which would be control schools. Those schools designated as either control or intervention remained so throughout these studies. From this point on, all analyses took into account this division of schools. Except for the analyses of the intervention program, almost all the results were derived from data on children who were in control schools. In a few cases, we report the results of analyses including all children from both control and intervention schools; where this occurs, we indicate it.

After the initial assessment, ratings of social adaptational status were repeated with Cohort I at the end of first grade in spring 1965. For Cohort II, ratings were made at the time of the first report card (roughly the ninth week), midyear, and the end of first grade. This was the standard schedule for the periodic assessment of each subsequent cohort of first-graders. In addition, two-year follow-ups were completed for the first four cohorts.

Table 12 shows percents of children rated adapting and percents rated maladapting on the six adaptation scales for all first-graders in

TABLE 12. TOCA RATINGS EARLY IN FIRST GRADE

Cohort	TOCA Scales (Ranked by percent adapting)	Percents of Children			Total N
		0	1	2 + 3	
I (1964–65)	Authority acceptance	71.4	10.7	17.9	
	Social contact	68.3	15.9	15.8	
	Concentration	57.6	16.7	25.7	944
	Maturation	56.8	18.3	24.9	
	Cognitive achievement	52.0	25.4	22.6	
	Global	31.1	36.5	32.4	
II (1965–66)	Authority acceptance	74.2	12.7	13.1	
	Social contact	69.9	14.6	15.5	
	Concentration	61.0	20.9	18.1	863
	Maturation	59.2	20.6	20.2	
	Cognitive achievement	58.1	20.9	21.0	
	Global	36.7	39.5	23.8	
III (1966–67)	Authority acceptance	75.3	14.1	10.6	
	Social contact	73.7	18.0	8.3	
	Concentration	64.0	22.0	14.0	737
	Maturation	63.0	21.3	15.7	
	Cognitive achievement	56.2	28.5	15.3	
	Global	38.8	39.9	21.3	
IV (1967–68)	Authority acceptance	74.5	12.8	12.7	
	Social contact	71.0	17.5	11.5	
	Concentration	61.2	20.4	18.4	732
	Maturation	60.4	21.6	18.0	
	Cognitive achievement	56.7	28.3	15.0	
	Global	34.8	42.8	22.4	

Note: Results for each cohort are based on the population of children in control schools early in first grade.

† 0 = adapting within minimal limits; 1 = mildly maladapting; 2 + 3 = moderately + severely maladapting.

control schools in the falls of 1964, 1965, 1966, and 1967. At the time of the first community-wide assessment in 1964, the six control schools did not differ on TOCA from the other six schools. In subsequent years, however, early first-grade ratings from intervention schools were affected by their prior involvement in the intervention program; therefore, frequency rates for control schools only are presented here. Table 12 shows also the rank order of the six scales each year, from that with the largest percent of children adapting to that with the smallest percent adapting. *These rank orders were the same all four years for both control and intervention schools.*

In each cohort, the most frequent problems were maladaption on the maturation scale and on the concentration scale. Each year the early first-grade ratings showed the *smallest* percents of children maladapting on the authority acceptance scale and the social contact scale, in that order. The global scale, because it is based on frequencies of the other scales, always showed the lowest percent of adapting children and the highest percent of maladapting children.

In summary, over a four-year period about two-thirds of the children were rated maladapting on at least one scale each year. Of these, one-third were moderately or severely maladapting on the global scale.

Clustering TOCA Scales

Table 12 tells us the frequency of a given problem in the view of teachers. It tells us nothing about the combinations of problems that occur. The question of whether shyness (social contact) occurs in combination with other difficulties, or whether difficulty in accepting authority occurs alone or is linked with other problems, is an important line of investigation.

The correlations among the TOCA scales, shown in table 13, indicate that there are some relationships. It should be noted that all correla-

TABLE 13. CORRELATIONS AMONG THE TOCA SCALES

TOCA Scales	Social contact	Authority acceptance	Maturation	Cognitive achievement	Concentration
Social contact	1.00				
Authority acceptance	0.23	1.00			
Maturation	0.50	0.51	1.00		
Cognitive achievement	0.41	0.44	0.54	1.00	
Concentration	0.32	0.64	0.65	0.53	1.00

Note: This population consisted of Cohort I children early in first grade (N = 2010).

tions are positive, ranging in strength from 0.23 to 0.65. Most of the associations are moderately strong, except those between social contact and authority acceptance (0.23), and between social contact and concentration (0.32). Therefore, our five scales of maladaptation are not independent and appear to show varying degrees of interrelationship, but no two scales were identical. These results indicated that a factor analysis could clarify the relationships among the scales as well as the relative importance of their combinations in explaining variation in TOCA ratings.

A number of studies which include factor analyses of children's behavior have shown that shyness and trouble accepting authority tend to occur in different factors (Peterson 1961; Spivak and Spotts 1965;

Achenbach 1966; Conners 1970). When we factored the ratings obtained on each of the TOCA scales, our results were similar. Social
contact and authority acceptance consistently appeared in different
factors. In each of the factor solutions in table 14, these two scales sort
out as central to the two most important factors.

TABLE 14. COMPARISON OF 2, 3, AND 4 FACTOR SOLUTIONS IN
THE FACTOR ANALYSIS OF TOCA

TOCA	Rotated Factor Loadings				
Scales	Factor 1	Factor 2	Factor 3	Factor 4	Communality
Social contact	.08	.94			.89
Authority acceptance	.88	.05			.78
Maturation	.64	.57			.73
Cognitive achievement	.56	.53			.60
Concentration	.85	.25			.79
Sum of squares	2.23	1.55			3.78
Social contact	.26	.93	.11		.94
Authority acceptance	.90	-.08	.02		.81
Maturation	.73	.45	.14		.75
Cognitive achievement	.49	.20	.85		.99
Concentration	.88	.09	.12		.80
Sum of squares	2.43	1.11	.76		4.29
Social contact	.08	.96	.17	.20	.99
Authority acceptance	.93	.09	.18	.27	.98
Maturation	.17	.33	.23	.85	.90
Cognitive achievement	.20	.20	.92	.27	1.00
Concentration	.48	.05	.25	.74	.84
Sum of squares	1.17	1.07	1.02	1.45	4.71

Note: These results are based on the output from the Data Text Program. The
Orthogonal Varimax method of rotation was used on the factor loadings from the
principal components solution (Kaiser 1958; Harman 1967). The TOCA ratings made
early in first grade on the 2010 Cohort I children were used for these analyses.

Here we report three different factor analyses—the first seeking two
factors, the second looking for three factors, and the third looking for
four factors. In each case, the striking result was that where a factor
had a high loading on social contact it had a low loading on authority
acceptance and vice versa, indicating that these two scales are each
fairly distinct. In most cases, concentration appeared to combine with
authority acceptance, that is, where one was high, the other was also.
Authority acceptance always appeared in the first factor and social
contact appeared consistently in the second.

Since social contact and authority acceptance appeared to be the key scales in our studies, agreeing with the results from the studies just cited, we decided to cluster the TOCA data primarily in terms of these two scales. There were some children who were rated both shy and aggressive; these children were most frequently rated maladapting on all five scales. Finally, maladaptation occurring with neither shyness nor aggression seemed to be a fourth important cluster. The four clusters are listed below:

Shy—social contact occurring alone or with any other scale or combination of scales *except* authority acceptance;

Aggressive—authority acceptance occurring alone or with any other scale or combination of scales *except* social contact;

Shy-aggressive—social contact and authority acceptance occurring together with or without any or all of the remaining scales; and

Neither shy nor aggressive—maturation, cognitive achievement, and concentration, each occurring alone or in any combination with each other but *without* social contact and authority acceptance.

Table 15 presents the percents of children in each of these clusters for all four cohorts. The consistency across cohorts of the percents of children in each cluster is striking and tends to validate this particular way of clustering the data. In the tradition of epidemiology, one would be somewhat reassured by such consistency that these clusters are real and that the frequencies are valid. However, implicit in such a tradition is the assumption that the problem lies in the individual even though the causes may not. Within the social adaptational framework, this assumption is inappropriate, because SAS is a judgment in the mind or records of the natural rater, even though there is evidence that it is strongly influenced by the individual's performance.

The most frequently occurring maladaptive cluster (about 21 to 22 percent), the shy cluster, represents difficulty with making social contact but not with accepting authority. Children in this cluster may or may not have been rated as having difficulty on scales other than authority acceptance.

The next most frequent cluster contains children who were rated maladapting on the maturation, cognitive achievement, and concentration scales, but not on the social contact or authority acceptance scales. The overall frequency was about 18 to 19 percent. Most of these children were rated maladapting on the cognitive achievement scale, suggesting that this cluster includes children with learning problems not associated with shyness or aggression.

The third most frequent cluster involves maladaptation on the

TABLE 15. PREVALENCE OF TOCA MALADAPTIVE CLUSTERS

Maladaptive Clusters and Scale Combinations†	Percent of Total Population			
	Cohort I	Cohort II	Cohort III	Cohort IV
Shy cluster				
SC, M, CA, C	5.0	4.9	4.7	4.9
SC	4.5	4.0	5.5	3.9
SC, CA	3.4	4.2	3.4	3.2
SC, M, CA	3.1	4.1	4.8	5.2
SC, M	2.0	1.8	1.8	1.7
SC, M, C	1.2	0.6	0.7	0.9
SC, CA, C	0.7	1.2	1.1	1.2
SC, C	0.6	0.3	0.6	0.2
Total Shy	20.5	21.1	22.6	21.2
Neither shy nor aggressive cluster				
CA	5.0	5.3	4.3	4.3
M, CA, C	3.2	2.3	3.4	3.1
C	3.1	2.3	1.6	2.3
M	2.3	1.9	2.4	2.5
CA, C	2.1	2.3	2.7	2.7
M, CA	1.6	1.8	2.2	3.1
M. C	1.4	1.8	1.7	1.2
Total NSNA	18.7	17.7	18.3	19.2
Aggressive cluster				
AA, M, CA, C	6.1	7.8	6.7	6.2
AA, CA, C	2.3	1.6	2.8	1.9
AA, C	2.1	1.1	1.7	1.5
AA, M, C	2.0	2.0	1.7	2.0
AA	1.4	1.3	1.2	1.0
AA, CA	1.0	1.0	0.6	0.9
AA, M	0.5	0.4	0.3	0.7
AA, M, CA	0.3	0.3	0.2	0.3
Total Aggressive	15.7	15.5	15.2	14.5
Shy-aggressive cluster				
SC, AA, M, CA, C	10.9	12.7	8.3	9.6
SC, AA, M, C	1.1	0.9	0.4	0.6
SC, AA, CA, C	0.6	0.5	0.7	0.6
SC, AA, M, CA	0.4	1.2	0.9	0.8
SC, AA	0.4	0.1	0.3	0.1
SC, AA, CA	0.3	0.4	0.3	0.2
SC, AA, C	0.1	0.2	0.2	0.1
SC, AA, M	0.1	0.1	0.3	0.2
Total shy-aggressive	13.9	16.1	11.4	12.2
Percent Adapting	30.7	29.7	32.7	32.6
Total N	2010	1983	1742	1603

Note: These results are based on TOCA ratings early in first grade.
† SC = Social contact; AA = Authority acceptance; M = Maturation; CA = Cognitive achievement; C = Concentration.

authority acceptance scale but not on the social contact scale. Again, these children may or may not have been seen as maladapting on other scales. Difficulty with accepting authority occurred most often in combination with difficulty concentrating. In addition, trouble on the authority acceptance scale rarely occurred alone. Although not shown here, there were considerably more boys than girls in this cluster, with approximately 15 percent of the total population represented.

The shy-aggressive cluster, with frequencies ranging from 11 to 16 percent, consists of children who had received maladaptive ratings on both the social contact and the authority acceptance scales. Note that, in all four cohorts, three-quarters of these children were rated maladapting on *all five* scales, and all but a small fraction were rated maladapting on at least four scales. Boys were, again, more numerous in this cluster.

The most severe ratings, as indicated by the mean ratings shown in table 16, occurred in the shy-aggressive cluster, which included both the

TABLE 16. A CRUDE COMPARISON OF SEVERITY OF TOCA MALADAPTIVE CLUSTERS BY MEAN TOCA RATINGS EARLY IN FIRST GRADE

Maladaptive Clusters	Mean Rating	N
Shy-aggressive	2.01	284
Aggressive	1.83	318
Shy	1.64	412
Neither shy nor aggressive	1.44	378

Note: The means for each cluster were calculated as follows: the ratings on each scale on which a child was rated maladapting were added together and then divided by that number of scales. The mean for the cluster was then calculated from these individual means. This population consisted of Cohort I children.

social contact and the authority acceptance scales. While the shy-aggressive cluster included a somewhat smaller number of children than any of the others, all five categories of social adaptational tasks were involved. The mean ratings of children in this cluster were higher than those of children in other clusters. Therefore the shy-aggressive cluster appears to encompass an important group of children.

Interpretation of Results

Returning now to the issue of adaptation versus maladaptation in the classroom, let us consider how to explain the large numbers of children seen as performing inadequately. Scott has indicated that when there is incongruity between social behavior and social norms in a particular setting, the causes can be expected to lie in one or more of three possible areas (1958).

First, there may be a kind of hiatus in which the norms reflect neither the needs of the children nor those of society; thus the children may view these norms as irrelevant and perform indifferently, and/or the teachers may consider the norms unachievable and expect less yet rate in accord with a different standard.

A second possibility is poor correspondence between the manifest and latent functions within the social structure of the schools. One may conjecture that the broader society does not intend these norms to be achieved by these particular students but rather seeks to isolate and limit their achievement by not providing adequate resources.

A third possibility, according to Scott, is that the lack of social adaptation is derived from defensive psychological processes within the participating individuals. This would suggest that the maladapting children suffer conflict concerned with achievement in school, such as conflict with family values or with peer group norms. In our view, an alternative source of the high rates of social maladaptation for many children may be their self-image, in which they see themselves not as potential students but as potential failures.

It is clear that these SAS data reflect the school's view of a child's status and are not completely objective measures of the children. Society appoints teachers as natural raters in the classroom, and their validity as raters is derived from this appointment. The teachers' personalities and other characteristics that influence their ratings are obviously important. Table 17 contains some general characteristics of the first-grade teachers in Woodlawn at the time of the initial assessment, and a notation as to whether a given characteristic was significantly associated with maladaptation on the global scale.

Whether the teaching appointment was tenured or temporary had no association with the severity with which children were rated on the global scale. On the other hand, being married and a parent, being under forty years old, being black, holding only a bachelor's degree, and being an inexperienced teacher were each associated with rating the children more severely. However, the number of teachers in this population was insufficient to determine if age, experience, race, educational level, and parental status were independent of each other in their effect upon ratings.

Three hypotheses may account for these findings. The first is that the severity with which a teacher rated her students was in some way dependent on these characteristics; the second is that teachers with

TABLE 17. RELATIONSHIPS OF FIRST-GRADE TEACHER CHARACTERISTICS
TO SEVERITY OF GLOBAL TOCA RATINGS

Teacher Characteristics	Number of Teachers (Total N = 57)	Teacher Characteristics Associated with Most Severe Ratings†
Marital-parental status		
Single, never married	9	
Presently or previously married parent	36	Presently or previously married parent
Presently or previously married nonparent	12	
Type of appointment		
Regular	44	Neither
Full-time substitute	13	
Age		
Under 31	18	
31–40	23	40 and under
Over 40	16	
Race		
Black	46	Black
White	11	
Education		
BA/BS only	38	BA/BS only
BA/BS + graduate work	19	
Teaching experience		
0 - 5 years	16	
6 - 10 years	22	0 - 5 years
11 or more years	19	
First-grade teaching experience		
Less than 1 year	12	
1 - 3 years	21	0 - 3 years
4 years of more	24	
Experience at present school		
Less than 1 year	10	
1 - 2 years	24	1 - 2 years
3 years or more	23	

† Based on significant (0.10 level) t tests comparing all possible pairs of characteristics within each group on early TOCA Global ratings, Cohort I.

these characteristics (e.g., being black or young) tended to be assigned to classrooms where children were less well adapted to the social adaptational tasks; the third is that children may have had more trouble adapting in classrooms in which the teachers had these characteristics. Our conjecture is that all these processes were operating.

Looking at these results overall, the center's board had a very clear-cut response: Why is the system allowed to go on undereducating black children? They felt that if anyone cared, the system would be made to work. Even though the board wanted to see school curricula that were more appropriate for the needs of black children, they also wanted such curricula to be high-achievement oriented. And they wanted the social system of the school to complement the values, aspirations, and talents of black children.

The Results of
Other Investigators

We have examined, with some difficulty, the extent to which the frequency rates of maladaptation among Woodlawn first-graders, as measured by TOCA, compare with rates from studies of children in other communities and among other kinds of populations. Most studies reported in the literature make no distinction between social adaptational behaviors, such as shyness or fighting in class, and psychiatric symptoms, such as manifest anxiety or bizarre behavior. In addition, there is a lack of similarity in sampling and measureing methods. Often there is a lack of systematic description of the total study population. The literature, of course, covers various age groups, whereas our studies were restricted to first and third grades.

Despite these limitations, we felt it useful to compare our findings with those of other investigators. We were particularly interested in comparing the frequency rates of different kinds of behavior which, in our frame of reference, would be called maladaptive behavior in the classroom. Haggerty found that teachers rated 51 percent of the 801 children in one Minneapolis public elementary school as exhibiting "behavior of an undesirable character more or less frequently" (1925). Wickman conducted a study in which he investigated, among other variables, the frequency of problem behaviors among 874 children in one Cleveland elementary school (1928). He found that approximately 51 percent of the children were exceptionally well adjusted, while 42 percent had minor behavior problems. These figures were based on the judgments of teachers using criteria which, for the most part, we would term social adaptational, rather than symptomatic, behaviors.

MacClenathan surveyed one elementary school in California and found that teachers rated 19.6 percent of the 625 children enrolled as having behavior difficulties of some importance or as having extremely serious behavior problems (1934). She did not report the percentage of children with minor difficulties or the percentage with ratings of "well adjusted."

Rogers found that 30 percent of 1,524 children in a cross-section of Cleveland elementary schools appeared to have moderately serious problems, and another 12 percent had serious problems (1942). Rogers used a complex system of ten indexes of social maladaptation which included test results, teacher ratings of various kinds, and indexes of disparity between the child and peers.

Ullmann (1952), Andrew and Lockwood (1954), Glidewell et al. (1959), Bower (1960), and Goldfarb (1963) did surveys of children in various kinds of school settings. The rates of children having moderate or serious behavior difficulties did not vary so much as one could expect, considering the differences which existed in orientation, the years in which the studies were conducted, the ages of the children studied, and the types of populations sampled. The range of rates varied approximately from 10 percent to 35 percent.

If the method of data collection is changed drastically and teachers are asked to rate only their most severely troubled children, the results are very different. Frequency rates from studies of this kind ranged from 2 percent severely troubled or problem children to as high as 10 percent (Hildreth 1928; McClure 1929; Martens 1932; Young-Masten 1938; Fisher 1934; Snyder 1934; Lewis 1947). The lower frequencies derived from this method may be the result of an unintentional implication that not all children are likely to be severely disturbed. Another difficulty of this method is that the selection process by which teachers determine which children are most severely troubled is unclear. Were the children cited in these studies the most troubled children, the most troublesome children, or the children that the teacher felt a clinic would accept most readily? It would seem that some of these difficulties could be eliminated by using a total survey method—one that assesses all the children in the classroom rather than relying on the teacher to comment on only those she sees as having difficulty.

Human service workers, particularly in the area of community mental health, who are interested in developing prevention and early treatment programs, would benefit greatly from the results of prospective studies on the longitudinal course of children having difficulty in school. Do such children continue to have trouble at later periods in their school careers? What are the chances that children who are trouble-free at one point in school will develop problems later? These appear to be important questions, and we attempted to gather some information in these areas in our studies of Woodlawn first-graders.

Longitudinal Studies of
Social Adaptation of First-Graders

The first two-year follow-up assessment of social adaptational status was conducted in 1967 with Cohort I. There were three more follow-up assessments of successive first-grade cohorts. The percentages of child-

ren from the original populations still in Woodlawn schools at the time
of the follow-up in third grade was roughly the same (about one-half)
from cohort to cohort. These results pertain, then, to the more stable
population.

Table 18 compares TOCA ratings made early in first grade on Cohort
I control schoolchildren to end-of-first-grade ratings; table 19 compares early ratings to those at the end of third grade (or long-term) for
the same children. The short-term relationships were relatively strong,
with gammas of 0.6 to 0.7. The long-term relationships showed a
tendency for some decrease in strength and for some drift toward the
middle over the course of time—from both the adapting and the
maladapting ends of the scale. The regression to the mean phenomenon may partly account for this drift (see note 1).

Mean ratings on all six scales worsened by the end of third grade for
all cohorts except Cohort I, where the mean ratings for the maturation,
concentration, and global scales showed no significant change. (See
table 20.) This result occurred among both boys and girls, but boys seem
to have been affected more. This may reflect a difference in the base
lines of third-grade teachers, or, more probably, it is part of the same
process involved in the deterioration in IQ test performance. Table 21
contains data on the mean change in IQ scores from first grade to third
grade in three cohorts of control schoolchildren. Note the consistent
trend toward lower scores. This trend was evidenced by boys as well as
girls, although girls had slightly better scores to begin with. This
decrease in IQ scores from first grade to third grade was not confined
to Woodlawn but was a general phenomenon in Chicago public
schools.[3]

Among the longitudinal studies of children conducted by other investigators, Robins carried out important follow-up studies of children
referred to the Child Guidance Clinic in St. Louis (1966). She found
that children who had been referred for antisocial behavior (truancy,
burglary, forgery, lying, sexual difficulties, false fire alarms, etc.) had a
high risk of social maladjustment thirty years later in almost every
context examined. For example, as adults these children had poor army
records, marital and family difficulties, and few friends. Thus these
adults had a greater risk of social maladjustment than adults who, as
children, had been referred either for non-antisocial reasons or who
had been in a matched control group.[4] This study tends to support the
importance in later life of social adaptation in early childhood and
suggests a need for additional research into the relationships among
early maladaptation, later social maladaptational status, and psychiatric symptoms.

TABLE 18. RELATIONSHIPS OF EARLY FIRST-GRADE TOCA RATINGS TO THOSE AT END OF FIRST GRADE

Social contact — Gamma = 0.61

Early \ End	0	1	2	3	Early total %
0	76.3	17.6	3.9	2.2	69.4
1	37.8	41.7	15.0	5.5	16.3
2	31.1	34.4	18.0	16.4	7.9
3	34.0	18.0	24.0	24.0	6.4
End total %	63.7	22.9	8.1	5.3	100.0

Authority acceptance — Gamma = 0.73

Early \ End	0	1	2	3	Early total %
0	78.5	13.6	5.7	2.2	71.8
1	32.1	29.6	23.5	14.8	10.4
2	26.9	26.9	26.9	19.2	10.0
3	16.7	15.0	23.3	45.0	7.7
End total %	63.7	16.7	11.1	8.5	100.0

Maturation — Gamma = 0.63

Early \ End	0	1	2	3	Early total %
0	68.7	20.0	7.5	3.8	58.0
1	35.5	41.6	14.1	8.7	19.2
2	18.0	33.7	28.1	20.2	11.5
3	13.6	20.5	27.3	38.6	11.3
End total %	50.3	25.7	13.4	10.6	100.0

Cognitive achievement — Gamma = 0.59

Early \ End	0	1	2	3	Early total %
0	63.1	24.6	8.8	3.4	52.4
1	33.2	41.8	21.9	3.1	25.2
2	13.7	33.3	40.2	12.8	15.1
3	8.8	26.3	42.1	27.8	7.3
End total %	44.1	30.4	19.3	6.2	100.0

TABLE 18 (cont.)

Concentration — Gamma = 0.66

End Early	0	1	2	3	Early total %
0	74.6	15.6	7.1	2.7	57.8
1	44.5	29.9	18.2	7.3	17.6
2	19.2	31.3	36.4	13.1	12.7
3	18.5	13.0	25.0	43.5	11.8
End total %	55.6	19.8	14.9	9.7	100.0

Global — Gamma = 0.69

End Early	0	1	2	3	Early total %
0	55.2	37.9	6.5	0.4	31.9
1	15.1	56.5	24.0	4.5	37.6
2	7.6	41.7	35.4	15.3	18.5
3	1.1	25.8	39.8	33.3	12.0
End total %	24.8	44.1	22.4	8.6	100.0

Note: This population consisted of Cohort I children who were in control schools from early to end of first grade. N = 777.

TABLE 19. RELATIONSHIPS OF EARLY FIRST-GRADE TOCA RATINGS TO THOSE AT THE END OF THIRD GRADE

Social contact — Gamma = 0.29

Third Early	0	1	2	3	Early total %
0	66.8	19.4	7.5	6.3	68.5
1	53.2	27.8	8.9	10.1	17.0
2	58.1	7.0	16.3	18.6	9.2
3	32.0	36.0	8.0	24.0	5.4
Third total %	61.8	20.6	8.6	9.0	100.0

Authority acceptance — Gamma = 0.41

Third Early	0	1	2	3	Early total %
0	64.6	21.5	8.8	5.0	72.7
1	56.8	22.7	11.4	9.1	9.4
2	42.9	20.4	18.4	18.4	10.5
3	26.5	17.6	20.6	35.3	7.3
Third total %	58.8	21.2	10.9	9.0	100.0

TABLE 19 (cont.)

Maturation — Gamma = 0. 26

Third Early	0	1	2	3	Early total %
0	52.3	29.7	10.9	7.1	57.1
1	48.3	25.8	15.7	10.1	19.1
2	41.4	34.5	13.8	10.3	12.4
3	22.6	28.3	20.8	28.3	11.4
Third total %	46.8	29.4	13.3	10.5	100.0

Cognitive achievement — Gamma = 0.26

Third Early	0	1	2	3	Early total %
0	46.9	31.4	14.6	7.1	51.3
1	39.3	30.8	17.1	12.8	25.1
2	27.0	28.4	16.2	28.4	15.9
3	30.6	27.8	13.9	27.8	7.7
Third total %	40.6	30.5	15.5	13.5	100.0

Concentration — Gamma = 0.31

Third Early	0	1	2	3	Early total %
0	56.7	27.8	10.6	4.9	56.4
1	48.2	30.6	12.9	8.2	18.2
2	39.3	34.4	11.5	14.8	13.1
3	28.1	24.6	22.8	24.6	12.2
Third total %	49.4	28.8	12.7	9.2	100.0

Global — Gamma = 0. 36

Third Early	0	1	2	3	Early total %
0	30.6	52.4	15.6	1.4	31.5
1	26.6	47.5	16.4	9.6	38.0
2	12.9	38.8	24.7	23.5	18.2
3	14.0	29.8	28.1	28.1	12.2
Third total %	23.8	45.3	19.1	11.8	100.0

Note: This population consisted of Cohort I children who were in control schools from early to end of first grade and who were present in any of the Woodlawn schools at third-grade follow-up. N = 466.

TABLE 20. TRENDS IN TOCA FROM FIRST TO THIRD GRADE

TOCA Scales	Cohort I		Cohort II		Cohort III		Cohort IV	
	Mean Change in TOCA (LT† minus Early)	t (N=466)	Mean Change in TOCA (LT minus Early)	t (N=422)	Mean Change in TOCA (LT minus Early)	t (N=359)	Mean Change in TOCA (LT minus Early)	t (N=324)
Social contact	0.13	2.46*	0.24	4.27**	0.16	3.47**	0.09	1.58 ns
Authority acceptance	0.18	3.41**	0.29	6.09**	0.19	3.69**	0.25	4.39**
Maturation	0.09	1.60 ns	0.26	4.57**	0.11	1.92(*)	0.11	1.68(*)
Cognitive achievement	0.22	3.75**	0.41	6.90**	0.30	5.10**	0.34	4.97**
Concentration	0.01	0.11 ns	0.28	5.17**	0.15	2.70**	0.12	1.92(*)
Global	0.08	1.49 ns	0.38	7.56**	0.18	3.49**	0.13	2.19*

Note: The mean change in TOCA (LT minus early) was calculated for populations that had TOCA ratings both early in first grade and at long term. These populations were in control schools from middle to end of third grade.
LT† indicates long-term, end of third grade.
** indicates significant at the 0.01 level of probability.
* indicates significant at the 0.05 level of probability.
(*) indicates significant at the 0.10 level of probability.
ns indicates not significant at the 0.10 level of probability.

TABLE 21. TRENDS IN IQ FROM FIRST GRADE TO THIRD GRADE

Cohort	IQ Mean†		Mean Drop (1st minus 3d)	N
	1st grade	3d grade		
I	97.8	94.6	3.2	318
II	99.5	96.6	2.9	334
III	100.5	98.9	1.6	203

Note: In order to avoid confounding the results with the impact of intervention, these results were based on populations that remained in control schools during the first-grade intervention program. Only children in public schools were included, because parochial schools do not give IQ tests in the first and third grades. All the mean drop figures were significant by t test at the 0.01 level of probability.

† These means were calculated from the scores obtained on the Kuhlmann-Anderson Intelligence Tests.

Social Adaptational Status: Its Meaning and Usefulness

The concept of the natural rater in the context of a specific social field is the essential characteristic of social adaptational status which differentiates it from prior efforts to assess social functioning as a dimension of health. The interaction between the child and teacher will have a particular quality in a Woodlawn first-grade classroom because of the characteristics of this particular local community and its relationships to the city of Chicago and to the broader society. While others, such as Blum (1962) and the World Health Organization (1960), have suggested the importance of social functioning as a criterion of mental health, implicit in their definition is a view of social function which tends to treat it as if it were a characteristic of the individual. In determining the adequacy of the individual's performance, social adaptational status focuses on the interaction between the individual and the natural rater in a specific social context. Ultimately, SAS exists in the mind or the records of the natural rater, although its determinants may be multidimensional.

Social adaptational status needs to be clearly distinguished from the labeling perspective which views societal reaction to deviant behavior as the main determinant of what has traditionally been called mental illness (Scheff 1966; Spitzer and Denzin 1968). This view puts the entire causation of mental illness outside the individual and places it in society. Szasz, who holds this view, maintains that mental illness is merely a social label applied by society (1960). The labeling theorists stress, as we do, the importance of the social context and the societal reaction to an individual. SAS, however, in contrast to the labeling view, allows the causation to stem from the individual as well as from society and emphasizes the interactional process between the individual and the natural rater. Thus it allows the causes of a problem to stem from biological and psychological processes as well as social processes. When the SAS of four consecutive first-grade populations of Wood-lawn children was measured, it was found that teachers using TOCA rated large numbers of children socially maladapted. Longitudinal studies of social adaptational status revealed a degree of stability in SAS ratings from early first grade to the end of third grade, indicating the persistence of early success or failure in school.

Grades and IQ and achievement test scores were found to be associated with, but not identical to, social adaptational status ratings made by teachers. Age, sex, change of teacher, change of school, and other variables were associated with SAS. Many of these characteristics or events were beyond the control of the child and appeared to stem from the family, the school, or broader societal processes.

All of these considerations led us to the conclusion that social adaptational status is a useful and measurable concept. An important question concerns the kinds of factors that contribute to an individual's social adaptational status. One has to distinguish between the locus of the assessment itself, which is in the natural rater (or his or her records), and the determinants of SAS, which may be in the individual, in the natural rater, in the interaction between the two, as well as in the immediate social field and/or the broader society. There was evidence that part of the determinism of SAS is in the individual; there was also evidence that part of the determinism lay in the natural rater. Indeed, the interplay between the two appeared to be a vital part of the process beginning with the defining of the social tasks, followed by the social adaptational response of the child, and resulting in social adaptational status by the teacher.

From the mental health perspective, social adaptational status appears to be a critical interface between man and society. While we have emphasized the interplay between the teacher and the child in the Woodlawn studies, it is equally important to see these results in the context of the community of Woodlawn, the city of Chicago, and the broader society, and the relationships of each of these to the others.

The interaction between teacher and child in the Woodlawn first-grade classroom, and the resultant SAS of the child, took place in this context. The assignment of teachers to the schools, the school budget, and the policies regarding parent roles in the school were all manifestations of the contextual processes. The social adaptational response of the child in the classroom was also mediated through familial, community, city, and broader societal factors. The range of issues related to both the setting of tasks in the classroom and the child's response is likely to be far-reaching and include a number of more general issues, such as the social class and ethnic and racial background of both the teacher and the child, as well as specific aspects of the structure and function of the school and the family, and, of course, the individual psychologies of the child and teacher.

How the other children and their adaptational responses influence the specific response of an individual first-grade child is a major area for future investigation. While these data were being gathered and while the children were being extensively observed in the classroom, the processes in this area seemed intense and appeared to influence the style and mode of an individual child's social adaptive response.

Measuring Psychological Well-Being

We have proposed that it is useful to view mental health as consisting of two major dimensions. The first is society's view of the individual's social adaptational status in his or her major social fields. The second is the state of the individual's psychological well-being.

In reviewing the literature in terms of the ways mental health has been defined, Scott (1958) and Blum (1962) indicate that there is a need for empirical research into the relationships among the various measures of mental health. Blum places emphasis on the need to investigate the relationships between social adaptational status and psychological well-being. From the theoretical standpoint, such investigations would enhance our knowledge of the origins of mental health and illness by helping to determine how social adaptation is related to the presence or absence of psychological well-being. The findings would have practical application in programming and in evaluation by defining the most useful criteria for setting program goals and for establishing base line and outcome measures.

Having examined the social adaptational status of children in the first-grade classroom, we shall look now at various measures of the children's psychological well-being. We shall also consider the kinds and strengths of relationships between measures of psychological well-being and measures of social adaptational status. Before describing these aspects of our work in Woodlawn, we had better examine the definition of psychological well-being used in these studies.

We have defined psychological well-being as that area of inner good feeling and self-esteem which has been the traditional concern of mental health clinicians. Its absence is distinguished by a set of feelings and/or behaviors traditionally termed "symptoms." One may ask why, in our research with children, we chose to consider symptoms rather than more complex diagnoses such as neuroses and psychoses. As the World Health Organization pointed out, symptoms are more easily counted (1960). Their report goes on to say that "Child psychiatrists are generally dissatisfied with the existing child diagnosis classifications (p. 9)." While there has been some improvement in this situation since that report, child diagnostic classifications are still far from easy to use in standardized community-wide assessments, and, in our view, their use in clinical work is still problematic.

However, the measurement of symptoms is not problem-free either. Even though symptoms presumably may be counted with greater reliability and validity than syndromes, such as neuroses or psychoses, the difference is one of degree. Clinicians view anxiety, depression, bizarre behavior, and so on, as symptoms and look upon them as components of mental illness. Experience teaches, however, that in some instances such feelings or behaviors are considered "normal." At what point such behaviors become pathological is often difficult to discern clinically and very difficult to define conceptually.

These difficulties, and the fact that labeling someone symptomatic often does not help in understanding or treating an individual's problem, have led some mental health experts to suggest that viewing disturbed behavior as symptoms of mental illness may even be harmful (Albee 1967; Szasz 1960). This issue, however, needs more conceptual and empirical research before a considered conclusion can be reached. The concept of symptoms is still widely used by clinicians and investigators in a variety of fields, and we have chosen to retain it for purposes of research.

Blum summarizes the difficulties of reliability and validity in identifying symptoms (1962). To a large extent, these problems stem from the vagueness of the concept. For example, if one considers content validity—which is concerned with the proper sampling of the universe of content—how does one determine whether a specific instrument actually samples the universe of symptoms properly if the definition of *that universe* is unclear? Blum points out how difficult it is to arrive at an agreement about diagnostic categories, regardless of whether the determination is being made by clinicians in interviews or by other methods. Leaving aside the specific diagnoses, we also find it very difficult to achieve agreement as to whether an individual is sick or not; but in reviewing the research in this area, Blum infers that this is more easily accomplished, with a greater degree of reliability.

While certain categories of behavior are traditionally termed symptomatic—particularly when used by clinicians—which behaviors are essential for diagnosis is obscure. For example, what are the manifestations of anxiety, and what quantity or severity of behaviors is necessary for rating of symptomatic anxiety? Ultimately, we fall back on the clinician for a judgment. For all these reasons, it is not surprising that achieving interrater agreement is a problem. Criterion-related validity is crippled by the imprecision of the symptom concept also. Other than the judgments of clinicians, there are no traditional standards for determining whether an instrument is valid.

Construct validity as it applies here is concerned with whether an instrument designed to measure the symptom concept is actually doing so. A reasonable test of construct validity would be to design an experiment in which the results are clearly predictable from the concept being measured. To the extent that this occurs, the instrument has construct validity. For example, investigators sometimes test a new symptom measure by comparing the symptom ratings of children seen at mental health clinics with those of children from a suitable control population. The prediction is that higher symptom levels lead to higher use of mental health clinics. In Woodlawn, there were no such clinics available; therefore this test could not be made. Even when there are clinics, variables other than symptoms may be responsible for bringing a child to a clinic, so that use of such clinics may not be a good indication of the frequency of symptoms.

If one accepts a common assumption among clinicians, an alternative test for construct validity may be the capacity of a symptom measure to show that the social adaptational status of a child with symptoms is lower than that of a child who is symptom-free. The assumption is that there should be an association between symptoms and lower social adaptational status. Blum suggests such a test (1962); however, careful examination of the symptom concept reveals that there is no explicit justification for expecting social adaptational status to be low in the presence of symptoms.

In reports of research, such as the Midtown Manhattan and Stirling County studies, and theoretical statements, such as those of the World Health Organization, social maladaptation is considered to be evidence of more severe symptomatology (Srole et al. 1961; Langner and Michael 1963; Hughes et al. 1960; A. Leighton 1959; D. Leighton et al. 1963; World Health Organization 1960). This implies that these authors feel that symptomatology can exist in mild forms without social maladaptation. On the other hand, many teachers and educators generally consider the presence of psychiatric symptoms to be a mea-

sure of more severe social maladaptation. Thus these two groups differ
not only in their vantage points but in their conceptualization of
"symptoms" and the relationship of symptoms to social maladaptation.
The empirical question—whether symptoms and social maladaptation
are related and, if so, in what ways—remains. In summary, construct
validity requires a greater ability to predict the consequences of the
concept under study than current concepts of symptoms and social
maladaptation allow. The symptom concept does, however, vaguely
suggest the hypothesis that social maladaptation and symptoms are
somehow related.

   The goal of the studies reported in this section was to explore the
nature and measurement of the symptom concept. At this stage in our
understanding, it is too early to call such investigations validity studies;
however, the more investigations of this sort are done, the less this will
be the case.

   Our primary effort centered around the clinicians' judgment. We
attempted to structure this judgment to a minimal degree by making a
group of very general scales, derived from a handful of traditional
symptom categories, and then designing a method in which clinicians
make judgments of children on those symptom scales. We also attempted to study clinicians' judgments as distinct from social adaptation measures and from other methods of measuring symptoms. One
conceptual problem concerns the degree to which such ratings remain
clinical judgments when information about social adaptational status
and clinical history is kept from the clinician because of research
requirements. In addition, the problem of translating the clinical assessment procedure from the office to the site of community-wide assessment would seem inevitable to distort what is traditionally thought of
as clinical judgment. Yet we need to develop and study community-
wide assessment procedures based on clinical judgment if we are going
to develop community-wide first-line services which are deeply involved
with the community's institutions and populations. Such first-line
assessment and services will need to address a range of mental health
problems, among which serious emotional disorder must be included.
This will require that clinical judgment be part of the assessment
procedures—at least in this early stage of research.

   In an effort to measure symptom status, various investigators have
used inventories with long lists of behavior, sometimes correlated with
patient status in psychiatric clinics. We used such an instrument with
mothers of first-graders as another measure (in addition to the clinical
assessment) of symptom status in first-grade children. The specific

items of behavior (see table 24) bring to mind Scott's remarks concerning the lack of a basic theoretical concept which could explain why many such behaviors be considered symptoms (1958).

Another method of examining psychological well-being is self-rating by an individual of his or her own feelings of sadness, nervousness, and so on, and we employed this technique too. But even here the definition of the symptomatic state is ambiguous, for it is assumed that the presence of sadness and tension is symptomatic. Jahoda points out that happiness is not equal to mental health, nor is sadness necessarily mental illness (1958).

In light of these problems, our use of the terms "symptom" and "symptom status" must be considered operational and heuristic. Until such a time as we understand more fully the interrelationships among symptom measures and their relationships to social adaptational measures, and until we know more about the causes of each, these terms will continue to be imprecise. This imprecision is a core problem in mental health programming; because of it, the goals of intervention programs—both community and traditional—remain somewhat vague. Yet if programs designed on the basis of assessments of need use one or more of these criteria, and systematic evaluation is done on the same measures, it will be an important step toward solving the problem. Knowing what kinds of treatment alter what kinds of behaviors or feelings will help clarify both the impact of treatment and the importance of various behaviors themselves. When we know how flexible symptom states are, how they behave over time, and how amenable they are to one or another kind of intervention, we shall have learned more about their nature.

Before we discuss the methods we used to assess symptom status among Woodlawn first-graders, it is important to describe briefly the role of the citizen board. The leadership provided by the board, particularly in developing sanction for white psychiatrists and psychologists to make clinical judgments of black children, cannot be overemphasized. We had great difficulty obtaining qualified clinical raters of any race; black clinical raters were almost impossible to locate. Of the nineteen clinicians who participated across all five studies, only one was black.

On the other hand, all the interviewers involved in getting mothers' ratings of the symptom behaviors of their children were black. Still, if board members had not been deeply involved in supporting the assessments in their community organizations, there is little doubt that neither the clinical teams nor the interviewers could have carried out the procedures successfully. Board members saw the symptom assessment procedures as potentially beneficial to the children of Woodlawn, and on that basis they worked tirelessly to develop not only support but enthusiasm for this undertaking.

Methods of Assessing Symptom Status

Three different rating methods were used to assess symptom status among Woodlawn children:

1. *Direct clinical observation (DCO)*, ratings by two clinicians who had observed the children in a standardized group setting in school;
2. *Mother symptom inventory (MSI)*, ratings made by the mother of each first-grader during a home interview; and
3. *How I feel (HIF)*, self-ratings by the students.

These methods were not intended to be screening techniques. Complete psychiatric assessment could require a synthesis of observations from all three of these vantage points as well as others. In order to prevent biased ratings, none of the three groups of raters—clinicians, mothers, and children—were told about the ratings obtained from the group using other methods.

The direct clinical observation procedure was the most independent of the teacher's view of the child's behavior in the classroom, the personal attitudes of the teacher, and the attitudes of the mother in regard to the child. While DCO is not exactly what one thinks of as clinical judgment, it enabled us to examine several key aspects—that is, the frequency with which clinical judges using standardized procedures observe symptomatology, the severity of the observed symptoms, and the levels of agreement between clinical judges.

The direct clinical observation procedure (DCO). The first step was to draw up a list of categories of symptoms commonly used by clinicians—*flatness of affect, depression, anxiety, hyperkinesis,* and *bizarre speech and behavior.* When excessive, these feelings or behaviors are viewed generally by clinicians as symptoms. A six-point scale was constructed for each symptom category and for an overall, or global, rating of symptoms. Clinicians were instructed that if a child was rated symptomatic on one or more of the other five DCO scales, the child was to be rated symptomatic on the global scale. However, the severity of the rating on the global scale was left to the discretion of the clinical rater.

The levels of each scale ranged from within normal limits at one end (a rating of zero) to the most severe symptom state at the other (a rating of 5). At each level, behavioral cues were provided as guidelines in making a rating. The scales were designed to be used by two independent raters observing groups of children for a period of about one hour. These scales are presented in Appendix C; a summary description of the behaviors included in each scale is given in figure 4.

FIGURE 4. SUMMARY DESCRIPTIONS OF BEHAVIORS INCLUDED IN THE DCO SYMPTOM SCALES

DCO Scales	Description of Behaviors
Flatness	Bland fixed expression; "zombie-like" behavior; emotional unresponsiveness; autistic; distant; "walled off."
Depression	Sad face; motor retardation; slumped posture; crying without obvious reason.
Anxiety	Fearful face; excessive startle reaction; tremulousness; tics; rocking; anxiety posture, etc.
Hyperkinesis	Excessive motion implying difficulty in self-control of movement; acts as if driven to keep moving.
Bizarreness	Grimacing, posturing; unusual and weird body movements, behavior and speech.

The raters were psychologists or psychiatrists who had had various kinds of clinical experience with children. Most were doctoral students in psychology. Before each community-wide assessment, raters received three to four weeks of training, so that all of them learned to use the scales similarly. In order to improve interrater agreement, great emphasis was placed on restricting judgments to manifest behavioral cues, for example, requiring evidence before rating a child as depressed, and so on. The raters were not informed about the research questions, the nature of the intervention, or which schools were intervention schools.

During each community-wide assessment, teams of clinical raters were used.[5] Each team consisted of one male and one female rater. In order to guard against systematic bias, the male and female members of each team were rotated so that each possible pair worked together an equal number of times. Teams were randomly assigned to all twelve schools, thereby insuring that each rater worked in each school about as much as every other rater. We did not test race of rater as a significant factor, since, as mentioned earlier, only one of the participating raters was black.

Early in the first-grade year, a random sample of children, stratified by sex, was selected from each first-grade classroom. The children were assigned to groups of ten comprising five boys and five girls. Generally, two such groups were available from each classroom. Thus about 50 percent of Cohort I and about 60 percent of Cohort III received early DCO ratings.

With each group of ten children, the first phase of assessment consisted of observation by two clinical raters who were interacting with the children during a 10- to 15-minute group discussion. The raters were instructed to focus equal attention on each child as nearly as possible. During the second phase, there was a period of unstructured play, lasting about half an hour. The third phase consisted of more group discussion, similar to that in phase one but with a little more focus on how the play had gone. Then, independently, each clinician rated each child zero to 5 on each symptom scale. The clinicians then compared ratings and, following discussion, arrived at a consensus rating of each child's behavior.

We examined the following combinations of ratings for each scale. One clinician rated the child symptomatic (i.e., a rating other than zero) while the other rated the child nonsymptomatic; after discussion, the child was rated nonsymptomatic. This sequence was coded as SNN (symptomatic, nonsymptomatic, nonsymptomatic). In a second combination, clinicians—after initial disagreement—rated the child symptomatic after discussion, or SNS. In the third combination, both clinicians, in independent judgments, rated the child symptomatic even before discussion. This was coded as SSS. The fourth combination—in which both clinicians agreed independently that the child was nonsymptomatic—was by far the most frequent. In very rare cases, both clinicians independently rated a child nonsymptomatic but decided after discussion to give a consensus rating of symptomatic. These few were considered symptomatic in the frequencies presented in table 22. Agreement among clinicians will be discussed again later in relation to severity of symptoms.

Children from the original sample of Cohort I and Cohort III who were still in Woodlawn schools at the end of first grade were rated again by clinicians at that time. When there were insufficient numbers of the original sample present for reassessment, the groups were completed by adding children who had early TOCA ratings but not early DCO ratings. Thus the population on which *reassessment* was completed comprised children who were still living in Woodlawn and were therefore more stable than children who were rated early but were not available for follow-up. The early ratings of Cohorts I and III therefore

TABLE 22. PREVALENCE OF DCO SYMPTOMS IN FIVE DIFFERENT
ASSESSMENTS

DCO Symptom Scales	Cohort I Percents			Cohort III Percents	
	Early 1st Grade (N=1000)	End 1st Grade (N=1000)	End 3d Grade (N=1350)	Early 1st Grade (N=1080)	End 1st Grade (N=1120)
Flatness					
Mild	1.0	0.4	1.2	1.0	0.8
Moderate or worse	0.0	0.0	0.1	0.1	0.1
Total symptomatic	1.0	0.4	1.3	1.1	0.9
Total nonsymptomatic	99.0	99.6	98.7	98.9	99.1
Depression					
Mild	1.0	1.0	0.4	0.5	0.6
Moderate or worse	0.5	0.2	0.0	0.1	0.2
Total symptomatic	1.5	1.2	0.4	0.6	0.8
Total nonsymptomatic	98.5	98.8	99.6	99.4	99.2
Anxiety					
Mild	2.8	3.3	0.8	2.1	1.7
Moderate or worse	0.0	0.1	0.0	0.3	0.1
Total symptomatic	2.8	3.4	0.8	2.4	1.8
Total nonsymptomatic	97.2	96.6	99.2	97.6	98.2
Hyperkinesis					
Mild	1.6	1.3	0.7	0.7	1.3
Moderate or worse	0.1	0.0	0.2	0.1	0.2
Total symptomatic	1.7	1.3	0.9	0.8	1.5
Total nonsymptomatic	98.3	98.7	99.1	99.3	98.5
Bizarreness					
Mild	2.4	2.1	0.9	0.9	1.7
Moderate or worse	0.5	0.3	0.1	0.4	0.1
Total symptomatic	2.9	2.4	1.0	1.3	1.8
Total nonsymptomatic	97.1	97.6	99.0	98.7	98.2
Global					
Mild	5.7	5.8	3.6	3.9	4.1
Moderate or worse	1.2	0.6	0.2	0.7	0.8
Total symptomatic	6.9	6.4	3.8	4.6	4.9
Total nonsymptomatic	93.1	93.6	96.1	95.4	95.1

represent true prevalences of DCO symptoms among Woodlawn first-
graders, while the subsequent assessments are representative of a
somewhat more stable population.

While the phrase "true prevalence" sounds precise, the actual calculating of the prevalence of symptomatic children could be done in a

variety of ways, each resulting in different frequencies. The major question concerned the children who should be included in the symptomatic population—whether to include only those children who both clinicians agreed independently were symptomatic, whether to include also those children who both clinicians agreed were symptomatic only after discussion, and, finally, whether to include those children rated symptomatic by only one clinician who then agreed to a consensus rating of nonsymptomatic after discussion with the other clinician. Our decision was to include all children rated symptomatic, even the last group, in the prevalence tables and analyses reported here. According to Dohrenwend and Dohrenwend (1969), children of this age have been found to have relatively lower rates of psychiatric symptoms than at later stages of life. In the Woodlawn population of children, no matter how we calculated prevalences, we found the rates indeed low. The fact that rates for children begin low but become much larger suggests that even the less obvious symptoms may have important relations to symptoms at later stages of life and to social adaptational status.

We compared the three levels of agreement of DCO clinicians in terms of the teachers' ratings of classroom adaptation. The numbers of children were small, but an impression can be obtained by examining these distributions. The children who were rated symptomatic by only one clinician with no consensus ratings of symptomatic had TOCA ratings similar to the children who clinicians agreed had a symptomatic rating. However, these results were not significant, probably because of the small numbers (see note 1). In all of the analyses involving DCO, the symptomatic population will include all three levels of agreement because of the small numbers of symptomatic children at each level.

This decision is in keeping with community-wide assessment of other health problems, where the goal involves assessing the broadest population at risk. It is important to keep in mind, however, that when we are talking about symptomatic children as rated by the DCO procedure, the large proportion of children are only mildly symptomatic, with about one-third of these mildly symptomatic children being rated so by only one clinician, who later agreed to a nonsymptomatic rating. The results of our analyses, however, will bear out the importance of including even mildly symptomatic children in the studies of relationships to social adaptational status and of the outcome of the intervention program.

The prevalences of symptomatic children are contained in table 22. The table includes the percentages of children rated mildly symptomatic (child got no rating worse than 1), moderately or worse (at least one rating of 2 to 5), the total percentage of symptomatic children, and the total percentage of nonsymptomatic children (no rating other than zero).

When examining this table, one notices first the small numbers of children rated symptomatic by even one clinician in any of the five community-wide studies. Frequency rates for the global scale, for example, vary from 4.6 to 6.9 percent of first-grade children if mildly symptomatic children are included as well as those with more severe ratings. There were slight differences in the prevalence rates for boys and girls, with boys again at a disadvantage. For girls, the figures were 3.7 to 6.2; for boys, they were 5.3 to 8.3. In the case of the moderate and worse children, the percentages range from 0.6 to 1.2 percent on the global scale. The percentages for third-graders were 3.8 mild or worse and 0.2 moderate or worse. These results indicate that the manifest symptomatology that is observable in this kind of standardized setting, using a method such as DCO, is infrequent. This finding stands in sharp contrast with frequencies of difficulties in accomplishing school tasks as rated by the teacher using TOCA.

Another contrast to teacher ratings of social adaptational status is the frequency with which DCO symptom ratings could be grouped in combinations of scales. Among those children rated symptomatic on DCO, roughly two-thirds of the ratings were confined to one scale. Only about one-third of the symptomatic children were rated symptomatic on two scales, and fewer than 5 percent were rated symptomatic on three scales. Boys had a greater tendency than girls to be rated symptomatic on more than one scale. Consequently, we have not presented DCO data as clusters of symptom scales; each scale is considered separately in order to determine what relationships, if any, each has to other measures of symptoms and to the measures of social adaptational status.

There were very few significant differences in DCO frequency rates between control and intervention groups, nor were there differences in the association between DCO and TOCA in the ratings of control and intervention groups. Therefore, given the small numbers of children rated symptomatic on DCO, both the results from DCO and the analyses of the associations between DCO and measures of social adaptational status are reported for the combined control and intervention populations.

The levels of agreement between clinical raters and the relationships of these levels of agreement to the levels of severity of the symptom ratings were the next concern. Table 23 contains the results of studies conducted early in first grade, at the end of first grade, and at the end

TABLE 23. DISTRIBUTION OF AGREEMENT BETWEEN CLINICIANS
BY LEVELS OF SEVERITY

DCO Scales	Cohorts I and III Early First Grade (N = 2080)		Cohorts I and III End First Grade (N = 2120)		Cohort I End Third Grade (N = 1350)	
	Mild†	Moderate or worse‡	Mild	Moderate or Worse	Mild	Moderate or Worse
Flatness						
SNN	10	0	2	0	2	0
SNS	9	1	6	0	9	0
SSS	0 (0.0)§	0 (0.0)	5 (38.5)	1 (100.0)	6 (35.3)	1 (100.0)
Depression						
SNN	5	1	8	0	3	0
SNS	6	2	4	0	1	0
SSS	2 (15.4)	3 (50.0)	5 (29.4)	4 (100.0)	2 (33.3)	0
Anxiety						
SNN	20	0	14	0	4	0
SNS	22	1	24	1	7	0
SSS	6 (12.5)	2 (66.7)	14 (26.9)	1 (50.0)	0 (0.0)	0
Hyperkinesis						
SNN	11	1	7	0	3	0
SNS	8	0	10	0	3	1
SSS	2 (9.5)	1 (50.0)	11 (39.3)	2 (100.0)	4 (40.0)	1 (50.0)
Bizarreness						
SNN	11	0	6	0	1	0
SNS	15	5	16	1	6	1
SSS	7 (21.2)	4 (44.4)	17 (43.6)	3 (75.0)	5 (41.7)	0 (0.0)
Global						
SNN	31	0	20	0	10	0
SNS	41	4	26	0	18	0
SSS	26 (26.5)	16 (80.0)	56 (54.9)	15 (100.0)	21 (42.9)	3 (100.0)

SNN = Rated symptomatic by one rater, nonsymptomatic by the other rater,
    nonsymptomatic on consensus.
SNS = Rated symptomatic by one rater, nonsymptomatic by the other rater,
    symptomatic on consensus.
SSS = Rated symptomatic by both raters and on consensus.
  † = Rated 1 on 0–5 scale.
  ‡ = Rated 2, 3, 4 or 5 on 0–5 scale.
  § = Percent SSS of total symptomatic for each scale and for each level of severity.

of third grade. Cohorts I and III were combined for early first grade
and for end of first grade in order to increase the number of symptomatic children in the cells. The bottom row of the table indicates that
the level of agreement between clinicians was high when the level of
severity was high. For example, independent agreement on the global
scale varied from 80 to 100 percent for the moderate or worse children,
and from 27 to 55 percent for mildly symptomatic children.

The percent of independent agreement for each of the other DCO scales is presented also, but the reader should use caution in interpreting these data, since the number in most cells is small. The consistency of the relationships between greater severity and greater agreement is important, however. Increased agreement can be assumed to be a reflection of the increased observability of symptom behavior. Increased agreement also seems to be related to increased severity, since of the children in the SNN group only two had a rating greater than mild in any of the five assessments. This suggests that the symptom concept, while extremely vague in many respects, does have a clear base in reality. If there had been no increase in agreement with more severe ratings, we would have been forced to consider that the symptom concept was so vague, at least as measured by DCO, as to have meaning only to the individual clinician, with no common basis for agreement among clinicians.

Table 22 shows that about 5 percent of all the children were rated mild, while 1 percent or fewer were rated worse than mild. These results are important for several reasons. If there are many times as many mildly symptomatic people in a community-wide assessment as there are more severely troubled people, this may account for the low reliability which characterizes many epidemiological studies of mental health (Scott 1958; World Health Organization 1960; Blum 1962). Of course, there is an assumption here that ratings of mild symptoms are associated with low interrater agreement. Although this was the case in our studies, there is a clear need for replication using other symptom measures.

We were impressed by differences among the DCO scales in regard to the relationship between severity of symptoms and agreement among clinicians. The number was too small to allow us to be more than intrigued, but certain scales seemed to have higher levels of agreement for mild symptoms than for more severe symptoms, and other scales had low agreement at the mild level but reached high agreement at the moderate or worse level of severity. These are important areas for further study. The question is, are there some symptoms which are more reliably observable than others? If so, does this observability relate to their relative importance?

The relatively large proportion of symptomatic children rated mild as compared to those rated worse raises the question of how important the mild ratings are. Are there different corollaries or even causes—social, psychological, and organic—of mild symptoms as compared to more severe symptoms? The small number of DCO symptomatic children in each level of severity or in each level of agreement made it very difficult to take these two factors into account in the studies that follow. Accordingly, we pooled the different levels of agreement and the mild plus moderate or worse children into a total DCO symptomatic population.

The mother symptom inventory (MSI). This instrument offered an opportunity to examine the frequency with which mothers reported the occurrence of such behaviors as enuresis, bizarreness, fears and worries, and nervousness—traditional symptomatic behaviors in the view of most mental health investigators. These ratings were then studied in relation to DCO symptom ratings and ratings of social adaptational status. They were also studied in relation to the evaluation of the intervention program.

Extensive family life interviews were conducted with the mothers or mother-surrogates of Woodlawn first-graders, and the MSI was administered as part of these interviews. The mothers of the same 50 percent sample (N = 1,000) of Cohort I children who had been assessed by DCO were scheduled to be interviewed at the end of the 1964–65 school year. Of the 934 families whose children were still in Woodlawn schools at the end of the first grade, 863 were located and interviewed. Only three mothers refused to participate. This was one of the lowest refusal rates ever achieved by the National Opinion Research Center.[6] The low number of refusals may be attributed in part to the strong support given the project by members of the center's board. The remaining sixty-eight scheduled interviews could not be conducted for a variety of reasons—families had moved away, extended absences (e.g., in hospital), families could not be located, and so on.

Early in the summer of 1967, all 1,687 mothers of Cohort III first-graders were scheduled for interviews and 1,392 interviews were completed. Again, the refusal rate was very low—less than 2.5 percent. The other interviews could not be completed for reasons similar to those encountered with Cohort I.

For both Cohort I and Cohort III, end-of-first-grade TOCA ratings of children whose mothers could not be interviewed were compared with those of children whose mothers had been interviewed. In both cohorts there was a tendency for children of mothers who could not be interviewed to be more maladapting. This finding is consistent with those reported earlier in which children who changed schools between kindergarten and first grade and those who changed schools during first grade were likely to be rated more maladapting than other children in the stable population. Even though the children of mothers who were interviewed differed on TOCA ratings from the children whose mothers were not interviewed, the results should be considered fairly representative of the first-grade population, since the number of mothers interviewed was so large compared to those not interviewed. Interviews were conducted in the privacy of each mother's home by trained black female interviewers and required about an hour and a half to complete. The information obtained was meant to facilitate the study of the relationship between the children's adaptational status in the classroom, their symptom status, and their family life. The interview schedule contained about 400 precoded questions and a few open-ended questions organized into twelve areas representing various categories of human needs. Six of these areas concerned the child in relation to the family; the other six concerned the family and the community.

The mother symptom inventory was part of the interview. Most of the symptom items on the inventory were selected from a list developed by Conners[7] for use in a study comparing a population of clinic children with a sample of children of PTA members in Baltimore schools (1970).[8] We added some items for the Woodlawn project, but most of the items represent behaviors which have been used in many studies of psychiatric symptoms in children (Macfarlane, Allen, and Honzik 1954; Lapouse and Monk 1958; Glidewell et al. 1959). The MSI is presented in Appendix D.

The thirty-eight items of the MSI are not necessarily independent of one another; in fact, some symptoms may be expected to show an inverse relationship, while others may overlap conceptually. The individual items were grouped into thirteen categories, based mainly on the groupings Conners found after factor analysis.

We intended the MSI items to reflect symptomatic feeling and physiological reactions rather than social maladaptive behaviors, since social adaptational status was to be measured by different methods. As a result, our inventory contains fewer items on problems with authority and other areas of social maladaptation than similar inventories developed by other investigators who did not make this distinction between symptoms and social adaptational status. There are several items on the MSI, however, which are ambiguous in whether they reflect social maladaptation or symptoms, for example, those in the childish or immature category. These have been included because they are interesting in their own right, even though in our conceptual framework they are more appropriately measures of social adaptational status.

The MSI required the mothers to answer, for each item, "How true is this of your child?" Mothers chose their responses from among those presented on a four-point scale: zero = not at all; 1 = just a little; 2 = pretty much; 3 = very much.

The frequencies of symptomatic and nonsymptomatic responses for both Cohort I and Cohort III are contained in table 24 and are grouped by categories of symptoms. These data are remarkable in the consistency of the frequencies across two separate cohorts. The Cohort III replication done two years after the Cohort I study involved different mothers, different children, and different interviewers, yet the frequency rates are quite similar. The wide range of frequencies across different behaviors is notable also. This stability in the rates of each symptom and the variation in the frequency with which different symptoms were reported lend credibility to the frequencies. These frequencies differed by sex, with girls showing slightly more symptomatology than boys.

Approximately 28 and 35 percent of the children in the two cohorts received ratings indicating that they had no problems at all or were no worse than "just a little." About 42 and 37 percent of the children were given a rating of "pretty much" or "very much" on one or two of the items, and about 30 and 28 percent were rated as having "pretty much" or "very much" trouble on three or more items in Cohort I and Cohort III respectively.

This kind of data on normative behavior is extremely helpful in understanding the range of behaviors to be expected from children in a given community. There have been a number of investigators who have studied frequencies of normative behaviors among children as reported by mothers (Macfarlane, Allen, and Honzik 1954; Lapouse and Monk 1958; Beller and Neubauer 1963; Ryle, Pond, and Hamilton 1965; Mensh et al. 1959; Wolff 1967). These studies provide information as to what one may expect the frequencies of such behaviors to be in total populations. In order to determine the importance of these behaviors to an overall assessment of a child's mental health, we must know whether they are associated with other symptom measures and/or with social adaptational status in the classroom and elsewhere.

Mothers' reports of symptoms have been used by several investigators to compare children attending a psychiatric clinic with a group of nonclinic children. Both Wolff (1967) and Conners (1970) conducted such studies. One of the main purposes of the Wolff study was to determine whether children attending a psychiatric clinic differ in regard to symptoms from other children in the same community.

TABLE 24. MSI FREQUENCY RATES BY SYMPTOM

MSI Items Grouped by Categories of Symptoms	% Nonsymptomatic (0)		% Symptomatic (2+3)	
	Cohort I	Cohort III	Cohort I	Cohort III
Bizarre behavior				
Looks stony-faced	84.7	84.1	3.0	2.0
Has weird, odd, or strange movement or looks	89.9	90.5	1.4	1.4
Says weird, odd, or strange things	80.7	82.5	3.5	2.3
Sad and worried				
Worries about illness and death	82.0	83.2	4.8	4.9
Looks sad	69.7	74.4	2.9	3.7
Cries and sobs for unexplained reasons	77.1	80.0	6.8	5.5
Fears				
Afraid of new situations	71.6	70.7	4.1	4.2
Afraid of people	90.9	87.9	0.8	1.6
Afraid of being alone	62.3	58.0	10.9	12.9
Afraid to go to school	93.9	91.8	1.2	1.9
Trouble with feelings				
Keeps anger to himself	72.7	70.3	6.3	8.3
Lets himself get pushed around by other children	49.1	50.4	15.0	17.5
Muscular tension				
Muscles get stiff and rigid	92.0	93.1	1.3	1.3
Twitches and jerks, etc.	84.9	88.1	4.1	3.3
Body shakes	94.5	95.3	1.5	1.1
Nervous habits				
Bites or picks nails	77.1	77.6	7.6	7.6
Chews on clothing, etc.	84.9	84.3	3.9	4.7
Picks at things, such as hair, clothes, etc.	72.6	74.1	7.1	7.7
Sleep problems				
Restless or awakens at night	79.6	80.1	3.4	4.6
Has nightmares	81.3	79.6	2.6	3.4
Complaints of symptoms when doctor finds nothing wrong				
Headaches	70.8	69.6	4.0	3.8
Stomachaches	58.7	55.5	5.5	6.0
Vomiting	84.5	82.5	1.5	1.8
Aches and pains	84.1	83.7	2.5	2.1
Loose bowels	88.8	88.7	1.2	1.2
Toilet problems				
Runs to bathroom constantly	78.4	79.9	7.0	5.6
Wets bed	86.7	82.9	8.4	11.0
Wets self during the day	96.5	95.8	1.1	2.3
Had accidents with bowel movements in last year	90.8	90.9	2.3	1.7

TABLE 24 (cont.)	% Nonsymptomatic (0)		% Symptomatic (2+3)	
MSI Items Grouped by Categories of Symptoms	Cohort I	Cohort III	Cohort I	Cohort III
Childish or immature behavior				
Sucks thumb	85.0	85.1	9.5	10.8
Clings to parents or other adults	63.8	63.9	10.9	13.5
Speech problems				
Stutters	85.5	87.7	3.2	2.6
Does not speak clearly other than stuttering	72.6	75.1	7.8	6.7
Eating problems				
Picky and finicky about food	37.5	36.6	23.7	26.9
Underweight	72.2	72.6	6.2	5.7
Overweight	92.4	91.1	1.0	2.6
Sex				
Plays with own sex organs	86.9	85.6	5.0	6.5
Involved in sex play with other children	92.6	91.9	1.9	2.4

Note: These populations consist of intervention and control schoolchildren in Cohorts I (N=863) and III (N=1391). The percentages differed significantly (p<.10) for only three items with Cohort I and only five items with Cohort III. Chi square tests were used for these comparisons.

Conners investigated mothers' reports of symptoms to see if they could be used to distinguish psychiatric outpatient children from normal children and hyperkinetic children. Both investigators found that many of the symptom behaviors did discriminate between clinic and non-clinic populations.

Most of the thirty-eight symptom behaviors on MSI are items taken from the Conners instrument. The two instruments are similar not only in the items but in scaling. The procedures for administration differed, however; MSI was administered by personal interview while Conners used a questionnaire. Conners offered us his data so that we could compare symptom frequencies and see whether those from MSI differed from those of his clinic and control populations. Table 25 presents the comparison of MSI results for Cohort I and the Conners data broken down by socioeconomic level and race. Data for Cohort III in Woodlawn are not presented, since frequencies were so similar to those of Cohort I.

In order to match Conners's population and our Woodlawn children as closely as possible, we used his data for the six- to eight-year-old group. Unfortunately for our purposes, Conners did not have a large number of black lower- or middle-class clinic children at this age range, although he did have an adequate number of white lower- and middle-class clinic children. However, we felt it would still be useful to

TABLE 25. COMPARISON OF PERCENTAGES OF WOODLAWN CHILDREN
RATED SYMPTOMATIC ON MSI VERSUS CONNERS'S EAST BALTIMORE
POPULATION SUBGROUPS

MSI Items Grouped by Categories of Symptoms	Wood-lawn Cohort I N=863	Clinic White Lower N=38	Clinic White Middle N=73	Control White Lower N=45	Control Black Lower N=38	Control Black Middle N=48
Sad and worried						
Worries about illness and death	18.0	34.2*	47.2*	24.4	28.9	12.5
Fears						
Afraid of new situations	28.4	63.2**	67.1**	40.0	47.4*	43.7*
Afraid of people	9.1	28.9**	32.9**	22.2**	2.6	16.7
Afraid of being alone	37.7	64.9**	57.5**	42.2	42.1	41.7
Afraid to go to school	6.1	25.0**	20.5**	13.3	5.3	4.2
Trouble with feelings						
Keeps anger to himself	27.3	26.3	17.8	22.2	31.6	27.1
Lets himself get pushed around by other children	50.9	42.1	42.5	57.8	52.6	47.9
Muscular tension						
Muscles get stiff and rigid	8.0	39.5**	21.9**	15.6	15.8	2.1
Twitches and jerks, etc.	15.1	39.5**	31.5**	22.2	13.2	12.5
Body shakes	5.5	15.8*	13.7*	13.3(*)	13.2	4.2
Nervous habits						
Bites or picks nails	22.9	52.6**	37.0*	37.8*	47.4**	16.7
Chews on clothing, etc.	15.1	36.8**	26.0*	20.0	23.7	14.6
Picks at things, such as hair, clothes, etc.	27.4	42.1(*)	21.9	28.9	47.4*	27.1
Sleep problems						
Restless (or awakens at night)	20.4	65.8**	54.2**	48.9**	18.4	14.6
Has nightmares	18.7	31.6(*)	36.1**	33.3*	28.9	18.7
Complaints of symptoms when doctor finds nothing wrong						
Headaches	29.2	28.9	28.8	22.2	26.3	10.4**
Stomachaches	41.3	36.8	32.9	28.9	44.7	18.7**
Vomiting	15.5	5.3	4.1*	11.1	21.1	16.7
Aches and pains	15.9	26.3	28.8**	26.7(*)	26.3	8.3
Loose bowels	11.2	5.3	8.2	0.0*	5.3	2.1(*)
Toilet problems						
Runs to bathroom constantly	21.6	26.3	23.3	24.4	23.7	22.9
Wets bed	13.3	23.7	31.5**	15.6	26.3*	25.0*
Has had accidents with bowel movements in past year	9.2	23.7**	9.6	2.2	13.2	6.2

TABLE 25 (cont.) MSI Items Grouped by Categories of Symptoms	Wood- lawn Cohort I N=863	Clinic White Lower N=38	Clinic White Middle N=73	Control White Lower N=45	Control Black Lower N=38	Control Black Middle N=48
Childish or immature						
Sucks thumb	15.0	13.2	19.2	8.9	5.3	22.9
Clings to parents or						
other adults	36.2	57.9*	54.8**	33.3	52.6(*)	39.6
Speech problems						
Stutters	14.5	10.5	6.8	13.3	36.8**	8.3
Doesn't speak clearly						
other than stuttering	27.4	45.9*	30.1	11.1*	31.6	29.2
Eating problems						
Picky and finicky						
about food	62.5	65.8	65.8	71.1	65.8	70.8
Overweight	7.6	10.5	4.2	4.4	5.3	14.6
Sex problems						
Plays with own						
sex organs	13.1	28.9*	50.0**	15.6	28.9*	6.2
Involved in sex play						
with other children	7.4	7.9	21.9**	4.4	18.4*	0.0(*)

Note: For each symptom item the ratings of Woodlawn children and East Baltimore children were divided into "not at all" (0) and "a little bit," "pretty much," and "a lot" (1+2+3). Chi square tests were applied to compare the relative frequency of a given symptom in the Woodlawn population and the frequency of that symptom in the various groups in Conners's population.
** indicates significant at the 0.01 level of probability.
 * indicates significant at the 0.05 level of probability.
(*) indicates significant at the 0.10 level of probability.

compare Woodlawn children to Conners's clinic and control children if we kept these sampling limitations in mind.

Among Conners's control children, three populations were sufficiently large to warrant comparison: the white lower class, the black lower class, and the black middle class. The control white middle-class sample was too small to include.

In about two-thirds of the symptoms, frequencies for the Woodlawn population were lower than those for Conners's populations and generally similar to those of his control populations. For example, the percentage of Conners's two clinic populations that were rated symptomatic by their parents on the item "worries about illness and death" was significantly higher than that of the symptomatic population of Woodlawn children or those of either of Conners's three control populations. This was true also of items in the MSI fears category. Items in the category trouble with feelings did not reveal significant differences between any of the East Baltimore populations and the Woodlawn children. On all of the muscular tension items, symptomatic ratings were more frequent in the East Baltimore clinic population than in Woodlawn.

One of the interesting aspects of these data was revealed in the category called speech problems. Here the highest frequency of stuttering was in Conners's black lower-class control children who were significantly worse than any other population, including the Woodlawn children. There should be further study to determine why this particular population exhibited such a high frequency of stuttering and why this symptom was not particularly prevalent in the clinic children.

The other item under speech problems, "not speaking clearly or being hard to understand" (phrasing on the Conners instrument was somewhat different from MSI), showed that the white lower-class *clinic* children had the highest frequency of this symptom, while the white lower-class control children were better off than any other population. This suggests that unclear speech is an important behavior in the referral of white lower-class children to the clinic.

Overall, these results suggest that Woodlawn frequencies were more similar to Conners's control populations and showed less symptomatology than his clinic population. However, differences in class, race, and community characteristics between Woodlawn and East Baltimore seemed to play a role in the presence of symptoms. The importance of these factors appeared to vary for different symptoms. The data suggest that many of the symptom behaviors described in the MSI items are meaningfully related to clinic referral, but that many symptoms are also related, in ways not clearly understood, to the social and cultural contexts in which they occur. It is important to remember also that conjecture about what these data say concerning the importance of these symptoms must take into account the fact that the criteria used to refer and admit children to the clinic probably are not based only on the symptoms of the child but may also be based on class and race as well as other factors. For example, Shepherd, Oppenheim, and Mitchell (1966) found in a community study that one factor which played an important role in the referral of children to a clinic was the parental reaction to symptomatic behavior.

How I feel (*HIF*). This self-rating instrument was administered to Cohort III and Cohort IV students in third grade, and it was the one direct assessment of the child by the child himself. The HIF contained eight questions; two pertained to "symptoms" and the other six to social adaptational status, that is, how the child thought he or she was doing at the tasks included in TOCA. The six social adaptation questions are not reported here, since they are not germane to this discussion. See Appendix E for the HIF.

One of the two symptom questions asked the student to rate whether he felt sad almost not at all (zero), a little (1), pretty much (2), or a lot (3). The other question asked the student to use the same four levels to rate whether he felt nervous.

In Cohort III, the HIF was administered in a standardized procedure in the classroom to groups of twenty children randomly chosen from each of Woodlawn's forty-four third-grade classrooms. It was administered to all Cohort IV children in third grade. Frequencies of sad and nervous ratings for both cohorts are contained in tables 26 and 27. These tables show the frequencies of children in both cohorts who rated themselves as sad or nervous, both sad and nervous, or neither.

TABLE 26. CROSS-TABULATION OF COHORT III RESPONSES ON HOW I FEEL

		Sad			
		0	1	2+3	Total
Nervous	0	11.3	13.6	6.8	31.7
	1	16.3	7.7	12.4	36.4
	2+3	8.0	13.2	10.7	31.9
	Total	35.6	34.5	29.9	100.0

N=750.

TABLE 27. CROSS-TABULATION OF COHORT IV RESPONSES ON HOW I FEEL

		Sad			
		0	1	2+3	Total
Nervous	0	10.5	11.0	6.2	27.6
	1	9.7	12.4	11.9	34.1
	2+3	6.1	17.3	15.0	38.3
	Total	26.3	40.7	33.0	100.0

N=956.

Note: These populations included both control and intervention children as well as some third-graders who had not been in Woodlawn in first grade. Had we followed the usual procedure of restricting the analyses to control schools only, we would have been describing a more stable population. See table 48 for a comparison of control and intervention schools.
0 = not at all; 1 = a little; 2 = pretty much; 3 = a lot.

In Cohort III, a total of 51 percent rated themselves very sad (2+3) or very nervous, with 11 percent of all children rating themselves as both very sad and very nervous. In Cohort IV, these percents were slightly higher, with 56 percent very sad or very nervous, and 15 percent rating themselves both.[9] In addition to their importance as self-ratings, these ratings are of interest also because they were found to be related to a variety of aspects of school performance, even as far back as first grade. These relationships are discussed in the section that describes relationships between different symptom and adaptation measures.

The Persistence of Symptom Status

The most direct data on the longitudinal course of symptom status in Woodlawn first-graders came from Cohort I children who received DCO ratings early in first grade, at the end of first grade, and at the end of third grade, and Cohort III children who received ratings early in first grade and at the end of first grade.[10] Cohort III did not receive DCO ratings at the end of third grade.

The DCO results for Cohort I indicated that children who were rated symptomatic on the global scale early in first grade had a greater risk of being rated symptomatic on the global scale again at the *end* of first grade than children who had been rated nonsymptomatic early in the year. In spite of this statistical significance, most children (about 85 percent) did not retain their symptoms—even from early to end of first grade. See table 28 for these results. Studies of early and end-of-first-grade ratings for Cohort III revealed no significant results. Of the thirty-eight children rated symptomatic early in first grade, only four were still symptomatic at the end of first grade.

By third grade, twenty-nine children in Cohort I who had been rated symptomatic early in first grade were still in Woodlawn schools and were rated on DCO. Only three of these were again rated symptomatic at the end of third grade, and this result was not statistically significant. Other than the early to end-of-first-grade global ratings for Cohort I, DCO results revealed no significant persistence of symptoms. We found that being rated anxious, bizarre, and so on early in first grade was not associated with a higher risk of being rated symptomatic later on. However, these results may be due to the fact that, over the two-year period, some of the few children who had been rated symptomatic on any one scale early in first grade were no longer in Woodlawn schools, leaving very small numbers of symptomatic children.

Studies of children who were absent on the day of DCO assessment or who were no longer in Woodlawn schools revealed that there may have been more to the persistence of symptoms than was obvious. Absenteeism on the day of DCO assessment at end of first grade was greater among children who had been rated bizarre early in first grade. Significantly fewer of these children were still in Woodlawn schools at the end of third grade. (See table 29.) None of the other DCO scales

TABLE 28. PERSISTENCE OF SYMPTOMATIC RATING ON DCO

DCO Rating Early in First Grade	Cohort I End First grade		Cohort III End First grade		Cohort I End Third grade	
	Nonsymptomatic on Global Scale	Symptomatic on Global Scale	Nonsymptomatic on Global Scale	Symptomatic on Global Scale	Nonsymptomatic on Global Scale	Symptomatic on Global Scale
Nonsymptomatic on global scale	727	47 (6.1%)	746	36 (4.6%)	440	18 (3.9%)
Symptomatic on global scale	45	8 (15.1%)	34	4 (10.5%)	26	3 (10.3%)
Significance level	*		ns		ns	

Note: These results are based on chi square tests (with Yates correction for continuity) on the 2x2 tables of symptomatic vs. nonsymptomatic ratings early in first grade and symptomatic vs. nonsymptomatic ratings at the end of first grade and, for Cohort I, at the end of third grade also. Early in first grade, Cohort I N = 1000 and Cohort III N = 1080.
* indicates significant at the 0.05 level of probability.
ns indicates not significant at the 0.10 level of probability.

TABLE 29. RELATIONSHIP BETWEEN BIZARRE RATINGS ON DCO
EARLY IN FIRST GRADE AND BEING ABSENT OR NO LONGER IN
WOODLAWN SCHOOLS FOR DCO ASSESSMENT AT END OF FIRST AND
END OF THIRD GRADES

	End of First Grade			End of Third Grade		
Rated Early in First Grade	Present for DCO	Absent for DCO	No Longer in Woodlawn Schools	Present for DCO	Absent for DCO	No Longer in Woodlawn Schools
Number of children rated nonbizarre	807	97	67	479	77	415
Number of children rated bizarre	20	6	3	8	2	19
Significance level		(*)	ns		ns	*

Note: These results are based on chi square tests (with Yates corrections for continuity)
on 2x2 tables comparing bizarre vs. nonbizarre ratings early in first grade and
number of children present for reassessment vs. number of children absent or no longer
in Woodlawn schools for reassessment at the end of first or end of third grade. Early in
first grade, Cohort I N = 1000.
* indicates significant at the 0.05 level of probability.
(*) indicates significant at the 0.10 level of probability.
ns indicates not significant at the 0.10 level of probability.

were associated with either absenteeism or having left Woodlawn
schools.

The children who did retain the symptomatic status may be an
important population to follow in the interest of defining the relationship of early symptoms to adult mental health. Those who were rated
bizarre early and who later disappeared from the study population may
be particularly important.

Relationships between
Different Symptom Measures

When the frequencies of symptoms were compared across the different
measurement methods, rates varied widely. It is important to keep in
mind that factors such as who the observers were, what symptoms they
looked for, the span of time over which judgments were made, and the
situation in which the children were judged may have influenced the
ratings in ways of which we are unaware. The number of children rated
symptomatic on DCO was small, even when the mild ratings were
included. With the MSI, almost all the children were rated by their
mothers as showing "just a little" of at least one symptom. When we
counted only those children who were rated "pretty much" or "very
much," we found that two-thirds of the children received such ratings
on at least one symptom item. The HIF ratings showed that roughly

half of the children rated themselves as very nervous, very sad, or both; if the mild ratings are included, this percentage climbs to 90.

Children who were assessed symptomatic on MSI or HIF far outnumbered those rated symptomatic on DCO, and the MSI and HIF frequencies differed also. One question is whether the instruments assessed children differently in terms of severity. Did DCO pick out the most severely symptomatic children, while MSI picked out the moderate and severe children and HIF the mild, moderate, and severe? Or did the symptom concept being measured by each of the instruments differ from one instrument to the next, so that the populations designated symptomatic by each instrument were unrelated to each other?

This line of questioning led us to ask whether the children designated as symptomatic on DCO were also rated symptomatic on MSI. We did not pursue this with HIF, since it was administered two years after the DCO and MSI assessments. The numbers of children rated symptomatic on DCO were so small that, for these studies, a child was included in the symptomatic group even if he or she was rated only mildly symptomatic by one clinician—even if, after discussion, the two clinicians agreed to rate the child nonsymptomatic.

To simplify our examination of the relationship of MSI and DCO, a summary rating was computed for each of thirteen MSI categories along with an overall MSI rating. These summary ratings for each of the separate categories and for the overall MSI were calculated by summing the number of items on which a child was rated "pretty much" (2) or "very much" (3) on MSI.

For each of the thirteen categories, two classifications were used. A child was considered nonsymptomatic if he or she got no rating of 2 or 3 in that category, and symptomatic if he or she got one or more ratings of 2 or 3. For the studies of overall MSI, a child was considered nonsymptomatic if he or she received no ratings of 2 or 3, mildly symptomatic if he or she received one or two ratings of 2 or 3, and most symptomatic if he or she received three or more ratings of 2 or 3. The resulting frequencies for each category and for the overall MSI are presented in table 30.

The percentage of children rated by clinicians on each DCO scale who were also rated by their mothers in a MSI category are shown in table 31, as are the frequencies for each MSI category found in the total populations of children rated on DCO and MSI. Thus the frequency with which DCO symptomatic children were rated symptomatic in each MSI category can be compared with the frequency with which the total population of children was rated symptomatic in the same

TABLE 30. THE NUMBERS AND PERCENTAGES OF CHILDREN RATED SYMPTOMATIC AND NONSYMPTOMATIC ON MSI ON THE THIRTEEN CATEGORIES AND OVERALL

MSI Categories	Cohort I (N = 863)		Cohort III (N = 1391)	
	Nonsymptomatic	Symptomatic	Nonsymptomatic	Symptomatic
Bizarre behavior				
Number	812	51	1325	66
Percent	94.1	5.9	95.3	4.7
Sad and worried				
Number	757	106	1225	166
Percent	87.7	12.3	88.1	11.9
Fears				
Number	739	124	1160	231
Percent	85.6	14.4	83.4	16.6
Trouble with feelings				
Number	698	165	1077	314
Percent	80.9	19.1	77.4	22.6
Muscular tension				
Number	815	48	1327	64
Percent	94.4	5.6	95.4	4.6
Nervous habits				
Number	744	119	1181	210
Percent	86.2	13.8	84.9	15.1
Sleep problems				
Number	820	43	1304	87
Percent	95.0	5.0	93.8	6.3
Psychosomatic				
Number	775	88	1251	140
Percent	89.8	10.2	89.9	10.1
Toilet problems				
Number	732	131	1164	227
Percent	84.8	15.2	83.7	16.3
Immature behavior				
Number	699	164	1080	311
Percent	81.0	19.0	77.6	22.4
Speech problems				
Number	785	78	1280	111
Percent	91.0	9.0	92.0	8.0
Eating problems				
Number	629	234	960	431
Percent	72.9	27.1	69.0	31.0
Sex problems				
Number	809	54	1288	103
Percent	93.7	6.3	92.6	7.4

TABLE 30 (cont.)	Cohort I			Cohort III		
OVERALL	A	B	C	A	B	C
Number	302	322	239	393	581	417
Percent	35.0	37.3	27.7	28.3	41.8	30.0

Note: For each of the 13 MSI categories, a child was considered "symptomatic" if he had a rating of 2 or 3 on at least one of the items in the category; otherwise he was considered "nonsymptomatic." For the overall MSI, A means that a child had no ratings of 2 or 3 on any of the 38 items; B means that he had ratings of 2 or 3 on one or two items; C means that the child had ratings of 2 or 3 on three or more items.

TABLE 31A. PERCENTAGES OF CHILDREN RATED SYMPTOMATIC ON MSI AND THOSE WHO WERE ALSO RATED SYMPTOMATIC ON DCO

| MSI Categories | Total Populations§ | | Symptomatic on DCO | | | | | |
| | | | Flat | | Depressed | | Anxious | |
	Early	End	Early	End	Early	End	Early	End
Bizarre behavior								
Cohort I	6.0	5.8	0.0	0.0	8.3	9.1	17.4	4.2
Cohort III	3.6	4.0	12.5	12.5	0.0	16.7	4.8	7.1
Sad and Worried								
Cohort I	12.5	11.7	37.5*	25.0*	33.3	45.5*	13.0	12.5
Cohort III	10.7	11.3	12.5	0.0	0.0	16.7	4.8	7.1
Fears								
Cohort I	14.2	14.2	37.5*	25.0	25.0	18.2	8.7	12.5
Cohort III	15.6	15.0	37.5*	0.0	20.0	16.7	23.8	7.1
Trouble with feelings								
Cohort I	19.1	19.1	25.0	75.0*	0.0	18.2	21.7	16.7
Cohort III	23.7	23.2	37.5	0.0	0.0	33.3	28.6	28.6
Muscular tension								
Cohort I	5.6	4.8	0.0	0.0	8.3	9.1	17.4	0.0
Cohort III	3.8	4.1	12.5	0.0	0.0	0.0	9.5	14.3
Nervous habits								
Cohort I	13.9	13.9	25.0	25.0	25.0	18.2	21.7	25.0
Cohort III	14.1	14.2	0.0	0.0	0.0	16.7	9.5	21.4
Sleep problems								
Cohort I	5.0	4.6	0.0	0.0	8.3	0.0	0.0	8.3
Cohort III	5.9	5.6	25.0*	0.0	0.0	0.0	19.0	0.0
Psychosomatic								
Cohort I	10.1	9.4	12.5	75.0*	8.3	27.3*	8.7	20.8*
Cohort III	9.0	9.2	37.5*	0.0	0.0	0.0	9.5	7.1
Toilet problems								
Cohort I	15.4	15.5	12.5	0.0	8.3	9.1	21.7	4.2
Cohort III	15.2	15.8	37.5	0.0	60.0*	16.7	19.0	14.3

TABLE 31A (cont.) MSI Categories	Total Populations§		Symptomatic on DCO					
			Flat		Depressed		Anxious	
	Early	End	Early	End	Early	End	Early	End
Immature behavior								
Cohort I	19.1	19.1	12.5	25.0	8.3	18.2	21.7	16.7
Cohort III	23.4	22.2	37.5*	25.0	20.0	33.3	33.3*	42.9*
Speech problems								
Cohort I	9.2	8.8	0.0	0.0	8.3	0.0	17.4	0.0
Cohort III	6.5	7.2	0.0	0.0	0.0	0.0	0.0	7.1
Eating problems								
Cohort I	27.3	27.0	37.5	75.0*	25.0	63.6*	39.1	29.2
Cohort III	30.2	31.1	50.0*	0.0†	40.0	33.3	23.8	21.4
Sex problems								
Cohort I	6.4	6.0	0.0	0.0	25.0*	0.0	21.7*	8.3
Cohort III	6.3	7.2	0.0	0.0	0.0	16.7*	0.0	7.1
OVERALL								
Cohort I	65.2	64.2	75.0	100.0*	66.6	72.7*	78.3	66.7
Cohort III	71.3	70.5	100.0*	37.5†	80.0	66.6	71.5	78.6

Note: Tests of significance were based on t tests comparing the number of items rated 2 or 3 within each MSI category and overall for children rated "symptomatic" versus "nonsymptomatic" on DCO. Cohort I N = 839 for DCO early, N = 753 for DCO end, and N = 863 for MSI. Cohort III N = 782 for DCO early, N = 923 for DCO end, and N = 1391 for MSI.

* indicates that the t value was significant at the 0.10 level of probability.

† indicates that DCO symptomatic children were significantly less symptomatic on MSI.

§ indicates all of the children with DCO and MSI ratings in each of the four studies.

TABLE 31B. PERCENTAGES OF CHILDREN RATED SYMPTOMATIC ON MSI AND THOSE WHO WERE ALSO RATED SYMPTOMATIC ON DCO

MSI Categories	Total Populations§		Symptomatic on DCO					
			Hyperkinetic		Bizarre		Global	
	Early	End	Early	End	Early	End	Early	End
Bizarre behavior								
Cohort I	6.0	5.8	12.5	0.0	20.0*	5.6	15.5*	4.1
Cohort III	3.6	4.0	0.0	0.0	0.0	0.0	5.1	7.3
Sad and worried								
Cohort I	12.5	11.7	6.2	11.1	20.0	5.6	20.7*	14.3
Cohort III	10.7	11.3	16.7	14.3	8.3	0.0	7.7	9.8
Fears								
Cohort I	14.2	14.2	18.7	11.1	12.0	5.6	19.0	12.2
Cohort III	15.6	15.0	0.0	0.0	33.3*	7.1	25.6*	4.9†
Trouble with feelings								
Cohort I	19.1	19.1	6.2	11.1	12.0	5.6	13.8	14.3
Cohort III	23.7	23.2	33.3	7.1	41.7	21.4	30.8	17.1

| TABLE 31B (cont.) | Total Populations§ | | Symptomatic on DCO | | | | | |
| MSI Categories | | | Hyperkinetic | | Bizarre | | Global | |
	Early	End	Early	End	Early	End	Early	End
Muscular tension								
Cohort I	5.6	4.8	6.2	0.0	16.0*	0.0	12.1	2.0
Cohort III	3.8	4.1	0.0	14.3	0.0	0.0	5.1	7.3
Nervous habits								
Cohort I	13.9	13.9	6.2	11.1	16.0	16.7	19.0	16.3
Cohort III	14.1	14.2	0.0	14.3	16.7	21.4	7.7	17.1
Sleep problems								
Cohort I	5.0	4.6	12.5	11.1	12.0	5.6	8.6	4.1
Cohort III	5.9	5.6	0.0	0.0	25.0*	14.3*	17.9*	4.9
Psychosomatic								
Cohort I	10.1	9.4	0.0	11.1	4.0	27.8	6.9	20.4*
Cohort III	9.0	9.2	0.0	7.1	8.3	0.0	10.3	4.9
Toilet problems								
Cohort I	15.4	15.5	25.0	0.0	24.0	11.1	20.7	6.1
Cohort III	15.2	15.8	50.0*	7.1	0.0	0.0	25.6*	4.9†
Immature behavior								
Cohort I	19.1	19.1	6.2	33.3	16.0	16.7	13.8	18.4
Cohort III	23.4	22.2	33.3*	21.4	41.7*	42.9*	33.3*	31.7
Speech problems								
Cohort I	9.2	8.8	12.5	0.0	8.0	0.0	10.3	0.0†
Cohort III	6.5	7.2	0.0	7.1	16.7	7.1	5.1	4.9
Eating problems								
Cohort I	27.3	27.0	31.2	33.3	44.0*	33.3	37.9*	34.7
Cohort III	30.2	31.1	16.7	21.4	33.3	35.7	25.6	22.0
Sex problems								
Cohort I	6.4	6.0	12.5	0.0	20.0*	0.0	15.5*	4.1
Cohort III	6.3	7.2	0.0	0.0	0.0	7.1	0.0	4.9
OVERALL								
Cohort I	65.2	64.2	75.0	66.6	72.0	77.8	72.4*	67.3
Cohort III	70.3	70.5	83.4	50.0	58.4	71.5	74.3	58.6

Note: Tests of significance were based on t tests comparing the number of items rated 2 or 3 within each MSI category and overall for children rated "symptomatic" versus "nonsymptomatic" on DCO. Cohort I N = 839 for DCO early, N = 753 for DCO end, and N = 863 for MSI. Cohort III N = 782 for DCO early, N = 923 for DCO end, and N = 1391 for MSI.

* indicates that the t value was significant at the 0.10 level of probability.

† indicates that DCO symptomatic children were significantly less symptomatic on MSI.

§ indicates all of the children with DCO and MSI ratings in each of the four studies.

category on MSI. In order to obtain an estimate of statistical significance, t tests were calculated to see whether MSI scores of children rated symptomatic on DCO differed from those of children rated nonsymptomatic on DCO.

These results should not be given too much importance, because of the small numbers of children rated symptomatic on DCO. They do, however, represent a very crude measure of the distribution of DCO symptomatic children across the MSI categories. Given this caution, it is of interest that of the fifty significant associations shown in table 31, only five were in the wrong direction, that is, symptomatic children on DCO being less symptomatic on MSI than children who were rated nonsymptomatic on DCO. This indicates some degree of association between DCO and MSI ratings.

Studies of the relationships between DCO and MSI involved DCO ratings of Cohort I and Cohort III made early in first grade and at the end of first grade. The MSI ratings were done at the end of the year, but they represented the mother's assessment of symptomatic behavior in her child over several preceding weeks. DCO ratings were obtained during a very limited time period—exactly one hour of observation. Therefore one could expect both early DCO ratings and those made at the end of first grade to have some relationship to MSI, even though MSI was done only once in each cohort. Table 30 presents data based on the four DCO assessments compared to the two MSI assessments.

One would expect that children rated symptomatic on a specific DCO scale would be rated symptomatic by mothers on those MSI scales which are conceptually similar. For example, children rated depressed by clinicians could be expected to be rated symptomatic in the MSI sad and worried category by mothers, and those rated as bizarre by clinicians would be expected to be rated bizarre by mothers. On the other hand, some of the symptoms would appear to be less likely to be related to one another. For example, we would have less reason to expect hyperkinetic children to be seen by mothers as having trouble with feelings—that is, trouble expressing anger or as getting pushed around by other children. The expectation that there would be associations assumes that children have similar symptomatic behaviors in different social fields and that these behaviors are viewed similarly by mothers and clinicians. In addition, predictions could not be made about many of the possible relationships of DCO and MSI, owing to a lack of a theoretical or empirical basis for such specific predictions.

In looking at the results, we find that the relationships which did exist between DCO and MSI ranged from low to moderate in strength as reflected in the percent differences. While one would expect most of the children who were rated depressed by clinicians to be rated sad and worried by their mothers, this did not occur. The range of DCO depressed children rated sad and worried by their mothers was from zero in one study to 45 percent in another, while the range of children rated sad and worried in the total population was from 11 to 12.5 percent. In other words, while there was significant overlap between the two instruments, DCO symptomatic children could not be considered as a subpopulation of the MSI population. What the results show are associations between specific DCO scales and specific MSI items, only a few of which occurred repeatedly and none of which occurred in all four studies.

Seven significant associations between specific DCO scales and MSI items occurred more than one time out of the four studies. Other associations occurred but were not replicated, indicating the fluidity of the relationship between ratings by clinicians and ratings by mothers. We should keep in mind that evaluation of these results must take into account the small numbers of children who were involved.

DCO flatness vs. MSI. Children who were rated flat on DCO had a tendency to be rated more symptomatic than the nonflat children in several MSI categories. The number of children rated flat on DCO ranged from between four in one study to eight in the other three studies.

In the MSI categories sad and worried, fears, and psychosomatic problems, children rated flat on DCO were rated significantly more symptomatic on MSI than DCO nonsymptomatic children in two of the four studies.

In spite of the small numbers of children rated flat on DCO, there were fifteen associations between that instrument and MSI, and only two were in the wrong direction. With such small numbers and the general lack of replications, it is difficult to generalize about specific associations; yet the overall impression is one of moderate relatedness between being rated flat on DCO and being rated symptomatic on MSI.

DCO depression vs. MSI. Children who were rated symptomatic on the DCO depression scale were also relatively few. The numbers ranged from five in one study to a maximum of twelve in another. In two of the four studies these children were rated significantly more symptomatic on sex problems than DCO nonsymptomatic children. One would have expected depression and sad and worried to be consistently related to each other; there was only one significant relation between the two. Judging from the lower number of associations, it appears that the depressed children were seen by their mothers on MSI as troubled less consistently than the flat children. It is of interest that depression on DCO showed the strongest relationship with sex problems, conceivably because of guilt and its association with depression. We shall see that DCO depression behaved quite differently from either MSI or HIF in relation to social adaptational status.

DCO anxiety vs. MSI. The numbers of children rated anxious on DCO ranged from fourteen to twenty-four. Children who were seen as anxious on DCO were rated symptomatic in the immature behavior category in two of the studies. Again, a relationship between anxiety as rated by clinicians and nervous habits and/or fears as rated by mothers might have been expected, but they did not occur. The anxious children were seen by their mothers as even less troubled than the depressed children. The association with immaturity suggests that the anxious child appeared regressed to the mother. The question this raises is whether the mother misinterpreted anxiety as immaturity, or whether the child actually acted immature at home as a way of assuaging anxiety. If the latter is true, the source of the anxiety may be in the demand on the child to perform school tasks. Behaving immaturely at home (i.e., psychological regression) could therefore be a psychological defense against the stress felt in school.

DCO hyperkinesis vs. MSI. Six to fourteen was the range of numbers of children rated symptomatic on the DCO hyperkinesis scale. This scale was significantly associated with only two MSI symptom categories and no associations were replicated. Apparently these children did not appear troubled to their mothers on the items which were included in the inventories. In retrospect, the MSI did not ask mothers to rate behaviors which are thought to reflect hyperkinesis. For example, mothers were not asked to rate their children's concentration.

DCO bizarreness vs. MSI. The number of children rated bizarre on DCO ranged from twelve to twenty-five in four studies. In two studies, these children received more symptomatic ratings than nonbizarre children in sleep problems and immature behavior. An association between the clinicians' ratings of bizarreness and the mothers' ratings of bizarre behavior could have been expected, and it did occur once. Other associations with bizarreness occurred, but they were not consistent from one study to the next. If one uses the number of MSI categories rated as a measure, bizarre children were seen by their mothers as very troubled—similar to the findings with flat children.

Bizarreness and flatness appear to be important symptoms producing a
variety of troubled behaviors.

DCO global vs. MSI. The number of children rated symptomatic on the
DCO global scale was higher, of course, than the number rated symptomatic on the individual symptom scales. The range was from thirty-
nine in one of the four studies to fifty-eight in another. We found
symptomatic ratings on the DCO global scale to be positively associated
with nine MSI categories plus the overall MSI, and negatively associated with three MSI categories. Neither the positive nor the negative
associations were replicated. The global ratings made by clinicians
could have been expected to be strongly associated with the overall
rating on MSI. The two were associated in one of the studies.

In summary, the studies of the relationships between DCO and MSI
were limited by the small numbers of children in each of the DCO symptomatic cells. In spite of these limitations, these studies gave us a crude
approximation of the relationship between the two instruments, and
they revealed limited but interesting areas of overlap between children
rated symptomatic on DCO and those rated symptomatic on MSI. This
overlap was by no means total; many more children were rated symptomatic on MSI than on DCO, and all of the DCO symptomatic
children were not rated symptomatic on MSI. It is noteworthy that all
of the replicated associations and almost all of the other associations
were in a positive direction, that is, more symptoms on DCO were
associated with more symptoms on MSI.

While the results indicate some similarity between the symptom
concepts being measured by the two instruments, there are clearly
differences in what each of them measures. This suggests that views of
mothers and those of clinicians cannot be used as substitutes for one
another. The DCO was a direct observation of symptom behavior made
by clinicians. The Mother Symptom Inventory, on the other hand,
asked mothers to rate behaviors which have been traditionally thought
to reflect symptoms. According to the results, many of the behaviors
rated by mothers do not consistently relate to the symptom behaviors
seen by clinicians. There was not much concordance between what
mothers and clinicians were asked to rate. Mothers rated concrete
behaviors, while clinicians were asked to observe behavior, then make a
rating of symptoms on the basis of the observed behavior. In addition,
mothers and clinicians observed behaviors in different social fields and
the children's behavior may have differed in these two fields.

The lack of a clear theoretical basis for the MSI is revealed by the relatively nonspecific nature of the associations with each of the DCO symptom scales. Even so, the children who were rated flat and bizarre on DCO appeared to exhibit more MSI symptom behaviors with more or less expectable patterns than did the other DCO symptomatic children. It was striking that hyperkinetic children did not show MSI symptom behaviors. However, they did have worse social adaptational status in terms of specific social tasks, as will be shown in the next section.

Let us turn now to studies of the relationships between psychological well-being and social adaptational status.

Relationships between
Psychological Well-Being and
Social Adaptational Status

Understanding the relationship between the individual's psychological well-being and his social adaptational status is centrally important to understanding the nature of mental health and its relationship to the social system. Accordingly, we set out to examine the associations between psychiatric symptoms and social adaptational status.

The four TOCA maladaptive clusters (shy, aggressive, shy-aggressive, neither shy nor aggressive) provided one way of grouping the maladapting children and enabled us to compare the frequencies of symptoms among children in each maladaptive cluster to those among adapting children. We also compared children who were rated maladapting on the TOCA global scale to the adapting children in regard to the relative frequency with which the two groups were rated symptomatic.

Many significant associations were found to exist between the TOCA maladaptive clusters and the DCO, MSI, and HIF ratings done around the same time or (concurrently) as well as longitudinally. In each case, there were scales which were not associated with TOCA. However, where significant relationships occurred, symptomatic ratings were nearly always associated with maladaptive ratings rather than with adaptive ratings.

Relationships between DCO
and TOCA

Four concurrent studies were conducted investigating the relationships between TOCA and DCO ratings made early in and at the end of first grade for Cohort I and Cohort III. The results of these studies are contained in table 32. The percentages of children adapting on TOCA who were rated symptomatic on each of the DCO scales are shown, and the ratings of these children are contrasted with those in each of the maladaptive TOCA clusters separately, and with those maladapting on the TOCA global scale. The percentages of the various maladapting children rated symptomatic on DCO are also included.

Shy-aggressive cluster vs. DCO. Early in the year, children in the TOCA shy-aggressive maladaptive cluster were more frequently rated anxious on DCO—significantly so in one of the four studies, with a tendency in that direction in the other three. In one study, these children also received significantly more frequent ratings of symptomatic on the DCO bizarreness scale. In all of the studies, children in the TOCA shy-aggressive cluster were more often rated hyperkinetic than the adapting children, significantly so in one of the four. Shy-aggressive children showed a significantly greater tendency to be rated symptomatic on the DCO global scale in two of four studies.

Shy cluster vs. DCO. In all four studies, children in the TOCA shy maladaptive cluster were rated symptomatic on the DCO flatness scale more frequently than adapting children, significantly so in two of the four studies. In all of the studies, these children were more frequently rated symptomatic on the DCO depression scale, significantly so in one out of four studies. There was a similar result in the relationship of the shy cluster to the DCO anxiety scale. It was striking that no children in this maladaptive cluster were rated hyperkinetic. *Overall, however, children in this cluster seemed to have the strongest risk of being rated symptomatic on DCO.*

Aggressive cluster vs. DCO. In all four studies, children in the TOCA aggressive cluster showed a tendency to be rated anxious on DCO more frequently than the adapting children—significantly so in one study. In two studies, there were significant associations between this cluster and the DCO hyperkinesis scale, with children in this cluster being rated hyperkinetic more frequently than adapting children in all four studies. The percentages approximate those of children in the shy-aggressive cluster who were rated hyperkinetic on DCO. Children whose TOCA ratings placed them in the aggressive cluster were more frequently rated symptomatic than adapting children on the DCO global scale in two of the four studies.

TABLE 32. CONCURRENT STUDIES OF PERCENTAGES OF CHILDREN RATED ADAPTING OR MALADAPTING ON TOCA WHO WERE SYMPTOMATIC ON DCO

| | TOCA Maladaptive Clusters | | | | | | | | | | | |
| | TOCA Global Adapting | | Shy-Aggressive | | Shy | | Aggressive | | Neither Shy nor Aggressive | | TOCA Global Maladapting | |
DCO Scales and Assessment Time†	I	III	I	III	I	III	I	III	I	III	I	III
Flatness												
Early	0.4	0.5	0.0	0.0	3.8*	3.8**	0.5	0.6	0.0	0.0	1.2	1.4
End	0.0	0.5	0.6	0.6	1.6	2.3	0.0	0.5	0.0	1.2	0.5	1.1
Depression												
Early	1.2	0.3	2.0	0.0	3.8	1.7	0.5	0.0	0.0	0.5	1.6	0.7
End	1.3	0.5	1.1	0.0	1.6	2.8*	1.2	0.0	0.7	1.2	1.2	1.0
Anxiety												
Early	2.3	1.6	3.9	3.4	4.3	3.8	3.3	1.9	0.5	2.1	3.0	2.8
End	0.0	1.0	6.8**	2.5	3.3*	1.7	3.6**	2.6	3.9**	2.4	4.3**	2.3
Hyperkinesis												
Early	0.4	0.5	3.3(*)	1.7	0.0	0.0	3.3*	1.9	2.6	0.5	2.2	0.9
End	0.4	1.4	2.3	1.9	0.0	0.0	2.8(*)	2.1	0.7	2.4	1.6	1.6
Bizarreness												
Early	1.9	1.4	5.3	0.0	2.9	3.4	4.4	0.6	1.0	0.0	3.3	1.3
End	0.9	2.2	5.1*	0.6	1.6	1.1	2.4	2.6	2.6	1.8	2.9	1.6
Global												
Early	4.2	3.6	9.2(*)	3.4	10.0*	9.2**	8.8(*)	3.8	3.6	2.6	7.9(*)	5.2
End	2.2	4.3	9.6**	4.3	4.9	6.2	8.5**	4.7	7.2*	5.9	7.6**	5.3

Note: Chi square tests were calculated (with Yates's correction for continuity) on 2x2 tables comparing adapting on TOCA versus each maladaptive cluster and DCO symptomatic versus nonsymptomatic. Ns: Cohort I early=995, end=992; Cohort II early=1071, end=1116; Cohort III early=995, end=992; Cohort III early=1071, end=1116.

** indicates significant at the 0.01 level of probability.
  * indicates significant at the 0.05 level of probability.
(*) indicates significant at the 0.10 level of probability.
† "Early" refers to assessments (both TOCA and DCO) made early in first grade. "End" refers to assessments (both TOCA and DCO) made at end of first grade.

NSNA cluster vs. DCO. The reader will recall that the neither shy nor aggressive maladaptive cluster (NSNA) contained children who were rated as having no difficulties on the authority acceptance scale or the social contact scale, but who did have difficulties on the maturation, cognitive achievement, or concentration scales. Many children in the other maladaptive clusters which indicated troubles with shyness or aggressiveness also had troubles with maturation, cognitive achievement, or concentration. In one study, NSNA was significantly associated with the DCO anxiety scale and the DCO global scale.

Global TOCA vs. DCO. While it is true that, taken together, children who were rated maladapting on the TOCA global scale showed more symptoms on all of the DCO scales than did adapting children, they received significantly more symptomatic ratings only on the DCO anxiety scale (one out of four studies) and on the global scale (two out of four studies).

Overall, the percentages of children rated symptomatic on DCO were generally higher among children rated maladapting on TOCA than among adapting children. This can be seen by looking at the table as a whole and comparing the percentages in the adapting columns to those in the maladapting columns. It is also noteworthy that anxiety, as measured by DCO, is characteristic of all the TOCA maladaptive clusters.

To summarize the association of DCO to individual TOCA clusters: there are basically two symptom profiles which relate to the maladaptive clusters. *One profile is anxious, hyperkinetic, and possibly bizarre, and occurs with the shy-aggressive and aggressive maladapting clusters.* This suggests that it is the aggressive component of these two maladaptive clusters that entails the risk of these three specific DCO symptoms. *The other profile is flat, depressed, and anxious, and occurs with the shy maladaptive cluster.* In concurrent studies, children in the NSNA cluster seemed less prone to being rated symptomatic on DCO than children in any of the other clusters.

Relationship between
Early Social Adaptation
and Later Psychological Well-Being

What happens to children rated maladapting early in first grade in regard to their relative risk of being rated symptomatic at the end of first grade and at the end of third grade? Table 33 contains the results of two studies with Cohort I and one study with Cohort III. The DCO

TABLE 33. LONGITUDINAL STUDIES OF PERCENTAGES OF CHILDREN RATED ADAPTING OR MALADAPTING ON TOCA EARLY IN FIRST GRADE WHO WERE SYMPTOMATIC ON DCO AT END OF FIRST GRADE AND END OF THIRD GRADE

DCO Scales and Assessment Time†	TOCA Early Global Adapting	TOCA EARLY MALADAPTIVE CLUSTERS				TOCA Early Global Maladapting
		Shy-Aggressive	Shy	Aggressive	Neither Shy nor Aggressive	
Flatness						
I End	0.0	0.7	1.5	0.0	0.0	0.6
III End	0.0	0.0	2.6**	0.6	1.0	1.3(*)
I L.T.	0.4	1.0	2.7(*)	0.0	0.6	1.2
Depression						
I End	0.7	1.3	2.9	0.0	1.0	1.4
III End	0.6	0.0	1.7	0.0	1.6	1.0
I L.T.	0.4	0.0	0.0	0.0	1.8	0.5
Anxiety						
I End	0.0	6.7**	3.9**	5.3**	3.6**	4.7**
III End	1.4	1.8	0.4	5.1*	2.1	2.2
I L.T.	0.0	0.0	2.2(*)	1.5	0.6	1.2
Hyperkinesis						
I End	0.0	3.4*	0.5	1.2	2.6*	1.8(*)
III End	1.1	1.8	0.9	3.2	2.1	1.9
I L.T.	0.4	1.9	0.5	0.0	4.2*	1.7
Bizarreness						
I End	0.7	4.7*	2.4	2.3	3.1	3.1(*)
III End	2.2	0.9	1.7	2.6	1.0	1.6
I L.T.	0.0	1.9	2.7*	0.0	1.2	1.5(*)
GLOBAL						
I End	1.5	10.7**	7.3**	7.6**	8.2**	8.3**
III End	4.1	3.6	5.6	7.1	5.2	5.5
I L.T.	1.1	4.8(*)	7.1**	1.5	6.7**	5.3**

Note: These results are based on chi square tests (with Yates's correction for continuity) on 2x2 tables comparing adapting on TOCA early in first grade versus each maladapting cluster, and DCO symptomatic versus nonsymptomatic. Ns: Cohort I end = 992, L.T. = 855; Cohort III end = 1056.
** indicates significant at the 0.01 level of probability.
 * indicates significant at the 0.05 level of probability.
(*) indicates significant at the 0.10 level of probability.
† "End" refers to DCO assessments made at end of first grade. "L.T." refers to long-term assessments made at end of third grade.

assessment was repeated twice with Cohort I, at the end of first grade and at the end of third grade. Cohort III did not receive DCO ratings at the end of third grade.

Table 33 contains the frequencies of symptomatic ratings among the children rated adapting on TOCA early in first grade. It also shows the frequency of symptomatic ratings among children in each of the maladaptive clusters, as well as the frequency of symptomatic children who were maladapting on the TOCA global scale. The results of these longitudinal studies of the relationships between DCO and TOCA indicate five points. (1) The percentages of symptomatic children were higher among maladapting children than among adapting children. This result is clearly reflected in the data presented in both tables 32 and 33. (2) Anxiety, as measured by DCO, is characteristic of all the social maladaptive clusters. (3) Children in the shy-aggressive cluster were more frequently rated symptomatic on the DCO anxiety, hyperkinesis, and bizarreness scales, while children in the shy cluster were rated more flat, somewhat more depressed, and more anxious than adapting children. However, the aggressive cluster was not so similar to the shy-aggressive cluster as it was in the concurrent studies. (4) Children who were in the aggressive cluster early in first grade did not show so strong a risk of hyperkinesis and bizarreness later on as they did in concurrent studies. (5) Compared to the risk they faced in first-grade concurrent studies, children in the NSNA cluster early in first grade showed a greater risk of anxiety and hyperkinesis as well as a greater risk of being rated symptomatic on the DCO global scale later on.

In summary, TOCA was related to DCO both concurrently and longitudinally such that social maladaptation to the classroom was related to a higher risk of symptoms—a risk that, in the case of NSNA, was low early in first grade, as compared to other clusters, but increased as the school career progressed. The risk for children in the shy-aggressive and shy clusters was much higher early in their school career and remained so at least until the time of long-term assessment in third grade, with the shy cluster involving somewhat greater risk than the shy-aggressive cluster. Children in the aggressive cluster seemed to have a higher risk earlier but a decreased risk of symptoms over time.

There was an important finding in regard to the risk of symptoms among the adapting children. *Frequencies of symptoms among these children dropped as their school careers progressed, suggesting that a successful early start reduced the risk of later symptoms.* The next step was to see whether these results held up when other symptom measures were studied in relation to social adaptational status.

Relationships between
Other Symptom Measures and TOCA

Let us look now at the relationship between MSI ratings and the TOCA maladaptive clusters. The population considered is restricted to the control schoolchildren, since the numbers in this population were sufficiently large. The results of studies conducted with the intervention schoolchildren differed somewhat from the control results (see note 1). These differences are discussed in chapter 4.

Table 34 contains the frequencies with which the Cohort I and Cohort III children who were rated adapting early and at the end of first grade were rated symptomatic on each MSI category and overall. A child was considered symptomatic if he was rated 2 or 3 on any items in a MSI category and on any of the thirty-eight items for overall; these frequencies are compared to the frequencies of children in each of the maladaptive clusters. The last column in this table presents the frequencies with which children who were maladapting on the TOCA global scale (i.e., all of the children from the four maladaptive clusters) were rated symptomatic in each of the MSI categories and overall.

TABLE 34A. PERCENTAGES OF CHILDREN RATED ADAPTING OR MALADAPTING ON TOCA WHO WERE SYMPTOMATIC ON MSI

MSI	TOCA		TOCA MALADAPTIVE CLUSTERS			
	Global Adapting		Shy-Aggressive		Shy	
Categories	Early	End	Early	End	Early	End
Bizarre behavior						
Cohort I	5.7	4.5	3.9	6.6	5.5	6.2
Cohort III	3.8	2.8	7.0	4.8	5.6	7.4
Sad and worried						
Cohort I	12.4	13.5	19.6	18.0	11.0	12.5
Cohort III	8.1	10.6	9.3	11.3	15.6*	7.4
Fears						
Cohort I	14.3	12.4	13.7	18.0	13.7	13.7
Cohort III	15.2	15.6	7.0	21.0*	16.7	21.0
Trouble with feelings						
Cohort I	15.2	14.6	23.5	31.1*	26.0*	25.0
Cohort III	17.1	20.2	23.3	21.0	18.9	24.7
Muscular tension						
Cohort I	3.8	3.4	7.8	11.5*	5.5	3.7
Cohort III	1.9	2.3	2.3	4.8	3.3	2.5
Nervous habits						
Cohort I	11.4	13.5	11.8	14.8	12.3	11.2
Cohort III	12.4	11.5	23.3	21.0*	13.3	12.3
Sleep problems						
Cohort I	1.9	3.4	15.7*	13.1	6.8	3.7
Cohort III	6.7	6.4	4.7	4.8	3.3	3.7
Psychosomatic						
Cohort I	7.6	5.6	13.7	18.0*	13.7*	15.0*
Cohort III	10.0	10.6	9.3	16.1	11.1	6.2

TABLE 34A (cont.) MSI Categories	TOCA Global Adapting		TOCA MALADAPTIVE CLUSTERS			
			Shy-Aggressive		Shy	
	Early	End	Early	End	Early	End
Toilet problems						
Cohort I	13.3	12.4	21.6	14.8	9.6	12.5
Cohort III	7.1	11.5	25.6*	14.5	15.6*	17.3
Immature behavior						
Cohort I	23.8	13.5	9.8	19.7	26.0	27.5*
Cohort III	16.2	15.1	16.3	17.7	17.8	23.5
Speech problems						
Cohort I	5.7	3.4	9.8	9.8*	5.5	11.2*
Cohort III	6.7	8.2	9.3	6.5	6.7	6.2
Eating problems						
Cohort I	28.6	23.6	25.5	26.2	24.7	27.5
Cohort III	34.8	30.7	23.3	32.3	33.3	35.8
Sex problems						
Cohort I	5.7	4.5	5.9	9.8	11.0	7.5
Cohort III	6.2	6.9	4.7	6.5	7.8	4.9
OVERALL						
Cohort I	60.9	51.7	64.7	72.2*	60.3	66.2*
Cohort III	67.6	65.6	72.1	75.8*	68.9	70.4

Note: These results are based on t tests comparing TOCA adapting cluster versus each maladaptive cluster on the number of items rated "pretty much" or "a lot" in each of the 13 MSI categories and overall. The populations consisted of children who were in control schools from early to end of first grade for Cohort I and from middle of first grade to end of first grade for Cohort III. Ns: Cohort I early = 369, end = 369; Cohort III early = 519, end = 562.
* indicates significant at the 0.10 level of probability.
† indicates adapting children were significantly more symptomatic on MSI.

TABLE 34B. PERCENTAGES OF CHILDREN RATED ADAPTING OR MALADAPTING ON TOCA WHO WERE SYMPTOMATIC ON MSI

MSI Categories	TOCA Global Adapting		TOCA Maladaptive clusters				TOCA Global Maladapting	
			Aggressive		NSNA			
	Early	End	Early	End	Early	End	Early	End
Bizarre behavior								
Cohort I	5.7	4.5	4.2	2.6	2.9	3.2	4.2	4.6
Cohort III	3.8	2.8	2.5	5.8	7.2	6.1	5.5	6.1
Sad and worried								
Cohort I	12.4	13.5	11.3	11.7	11.6	8.1	12.9	12.5
Cohort III	8.1	10.6	15.2	8.7	13.4*	19.4	13.9*	11.9
Fears								
Cohort I	14.3	12.4	8.5	9.1	15.9	14.5	12.9	13.6
Cohort III	15.2	15.6	17.7	9.7†	17.5	14.3	15.9	15.7
Trouble with feelings								
Cohort I	15.2	14.6	21.1	18.2	23.2*	19.4	23.5*	23.2
Cohort III	17.1	20.2	20.3	18.4	23.7	18.4	21.4	20.3

TABLE 34B (cont.) MSI Categories	TOCA Global Adapting		TOCA Maladaptive clusters				TOCA Global Maladapting	
			Aggressive		NSNA			
	Early	End	Early	End	Early	End	Early	End
Muscular tension								
Cohort I	3.8	3.4	5.6	6.5	5.8	3.2	6.1	6.1
Cohort III	1.9	2.3	3.8	1.0	4.1	6.1	3.6	3.5
Nervous habits								
Cohort I	11.4	13.5	15.5	13.0*	13.0	11.3	13.3	12.5
Cohort III	12.4	11.5	19.0*	18.4*	12.4	16.3	15.9	16.9
Sleep problems								
Cohort I	1.9	3.4	2.8	5.2	2.9	1.6	6.4	5.7
Cohort III	6.7	6.4	6.3	5.8	4.1	6.1	4.5	5.2
Psychosomatic								
Cohort I	7.6	5.6	9.9	7.8	14.5*	12.9	12.9*	13.2*
Cohort III	10.0	10.6	15.2	10.7	9.3	12.2	11.3	11.0
Toilet problems								
Cohort I	13.3	12.4	11.3	14.3	20.3	21.0	15.2	15.4
Cohort III	7.1	11.5	17.7*	16.5*	18.6*	14.3	18.4*	15.7
Immature behavior								
Cohort I	23.8	13.5	16.9	20.8	24.6	25.8*	20.1	23.6*
Cohort III	16.2	15.1	26.6*	24.3*	22.7	21.4	21.4*	22.1*
Speech problems								
Cohort I	5.7	3.4	7.0	5.2	10.1	8.1	8.0	8.6*
Cohort III	6.7	8.2	5.1	6.8	7.2	5.1	6.8	6.1
Eating problems								
Cohort I	28.6	23.6	22.5	22.1	29.0	33.9	25.4	27.1
Cohort III	34.8	30.7	29.1	32.0	24.7	28.6	28.2	32.0
Sex problems								
Cohort I	5.7	2.5	4.2	5.2	5.8	6.5	6.8	7.1
Cohort III	6.2	6.9	8.9	4.9	8.2	11.2	7.8	7.0
OVERALL								
Cohort I	60.9	51.7	60.6	62.4	69.5	66.2	63.7	66.5*
Cohort III	67.6	65.6	79.7*	79.6	72.2	70.5	73.2*	74.2

Note: These results are based on t tests comparing the TOCA adapting cluster versus each maladaptive cluster on the number of items rated "pretty much" or "a lot" in each of the 13 MSI categories and overall. The populations consisted of children who were in control schools from early to end of first grade for Cohort I and from middle of first grade to end of first grade for Cohort III. Ns: Cohort I early = 369, end = 369; Cohort III early = 519, end = 562.
* indicates significant at the 0.10 level of probability.
† indicates adapting children were significantly more symptomatic on MSI.

The data revealed a fair degree of relateness between the TOCA maladaptive clusters and symptomatic ratings on MSI. In studies by Mitchell and Shepherd (1966) and Rutter and Graham (1966), children who were rated by parents as being deviant on a questionnaire similar to the MSI were more likely to be rated as having behavior disorders in school by the teacher than children who were not rated as deviant by the parents. However, as in our study, the overlap between the two instruments was far from total. The relationships we found between social maladaptation and being symptomatic on MSI are summarized below by maladaptive cluster, and the number of studies out of four that yielded significant associations are indicated in parenthesis.

Shy-aggressive cluster vs. MSI. The following MSI categories were associated with this cluster: fears (1); trouble with feelings (1); muscular tension (1); nervous habits (1); sleep problems (1); psychosomatic (1); toilet problems (1); speech problems (1); and overall (2).

Shy cluster vs. MSI. The comparison between children in the shy cluster and adapting children in regard to MSI ratings yielded the following significant associations: sad and worried (1); trouble with feelings (1); psychosomatic (2); toilet problems (1); immature behavior (1); speech problems (1); and overall (1).

Aggressive cluster vs. MSI. Children whose ratings on TOCA placed them in the aggressive maladaptive cluster were rated symptomatic significantly more frequently than adapting children on the following MSI scales: nervous habits (3); toilet problems (2); immature behavior (2); and overall (1). The table shows that, on three out of four occasions (one of which was significant), there was a tendency for children in this cluster to be rated *less fearful* on MSI than adapting children. This was the *only* occasion when being rated maladapting was associated with less risk of being rated symptomatic on MSI.

NSNA cluster vs. MSI. The study of the association of this cluster to symptom ratings on MSI recalls the general lack of relationship found in concurrent studies of NSNA and DCO. While there were some associations between this cluster and MSI, MSI overall was not significantly higher for children maladapting on the NSNA cluster than for children who were adapting. The significant associations were: sad and worried (1); trouble with feelings (1); psychosomatic (1); toilet problems (1); and immature behavior (1).

A review of these results indicates that the relationships between MSI and the TOCA maladaptive clusters were similar to those between DCO and TOCA. The shy-aggressive and shy clusters were related to more categories on MSI than the other maladaptive clusters, as was the case with these two clusters and DCO. Children in the aggressive cluster were rated symptomatic on MSI in fewer categories than children in the shy or shy-aggressive clusters; but the relationships were replicated more frequently and appeared more specific, as was the relationship between the aggressive cluster and DCO.

Children in TOCA's aggressive cluster showed a lower risk of being symptomatic on the MSI fears category than adapting children. The items in this category concerned problems such as "afraid of being alone," "afraid of people," and "afraid of new situations." While these children were rated on MSI as having significantly fewer fears, they had significantly more symptoms in the MSI nervous habits category. This is an interesting result, particularly in view of the fact that these children had a greater risk of being rated anxious on DCO. The DCO-TOCA ratings also revealed that children in the aggressive cluster were more likely to be hyperkinetic on DCO than adapting children, as were the shy-aggressive children. Thus these aggressive children seem genuinely more anxious, rather than fearful of places and people.

In summary, MSI was related to TOCA such that social maladaptation to the classroom was associated with a greater risk of being symptomatic, and this finding corroborated our results from studies of DCO and TOCA.

TOCA maladaptive clusters vs. HIF. The third symptom measure to be examined in relation to TOCA was the self-rating instrument How I Feel (HIF) on which Cohort III and Cohort IV children rated their feelings of nervousness and/or sadness in third grade. The HIF ratings were examined to determine their longitudinal relationships to first-grade TOCA done two and a half years earlier, and their concurrent relationships to third-grade TOCA.

We concluded that these studies showed only a weak relationship between the control children's self-ratings on HIF and teachers' ratings of these children on TOCA (see note 1). There were more relationships between the intervention children's HIF ratings and TOCA. However, control children's ratings on HIF were associated with other measures of social adaptational status such as IQ, grades, and achievement test scores.

The points to be summarized from the results of the HIF-TOCA studies can best be made in the section on evaluation of the impact of intervention, since they are intricately related to differences between intervention and control. One point can be made here, however. The TOCA aggressive cluster was not significantly related, concurrently or longitudinally, to ratings of sadness or nervousness in either Cohort III or Cohort IV. This finding contrasts with the results of the MSI-TOCA studies and the DCO-TOCA studies, where the aggressive maladaptive cluster was associated with symptoms of nervous habits and anxiety. Apparently, children who were in the TOCA aggressive cluster in first grade, or who were in the aggressive cluster in third grade—in spite of looking anxious to others—did not confide their feelings of anxiety in their self-ratings on HIF, or they denied such feelings. This result adds to the view of the child in the aggressive cluster as not being fearful of specific things or people, being aggressive with others, having trouble sitting still and concentrating and learning, appearing anxious to others but not feeling anxious himself, and not necessarily lacking in test-taking capacity as on IQ tests.

*Relationship between
Early Psychological Well-Being
and Later Social Adaptation*

What about the children who were symptomatic early in first grade? What was the risk of their maladapting later on? Early first-grade ratings on each DCO scale were examined for Cohort I and Cohort III in relation to the ratings on individual TOCA scales made at both the end of first grade and end of third grade.

Table 35 presents gamma values and indicates the significant associations (by chi square) between early symptom ratings and end-of-first-grade and end-of-third-grade TOCA ratings for Cohort I and Cohort III. The gamma values give an indication of the strength of associations in terms of the likelihood of predicting order in a second variable on the basis of order in the first, that is, how much you can tell about the level of TOCA rating by knowing that a child was symptomatic rather than nonsymptomatic. The highest strength is plus 1 or minus 1, the lowest is zero.

Flatness early in first grade was strongly related to shyness at end of first grade and was still strongly related to shyness by the end of third grade. Early depression was also related to shyness, particularly at the end of first grade. Recall the concurrent relationship of the shy maladaptive cluster to flatness and depression (table 32) and the relationship of the shy cluster early in first grade to later flatness (table 33).

The association of early anxiety to later maladaptation was weak. All of the results concerning anxiety suggest strongly that school failure is

TABLE 35. GAMMA VALUES FOR THE RELATIONSHIPS OF DCO RATINGS EARLY IN FIRST GRADE TO TOCA RATINGS AT END OF FIRST GRADE AND THIRD GRADE

| | TOCA SCALES | | | | | | | | | | | |
| | Social Contact | | Authority Acceptance | | Maturation | | Cognitive Achievement | | Concentration | | Global | |
DCO Scales	End	L.T.†	End	L.T.	End	L.T.	End	L.T.	End	L.T.	End	L.T.
Flatness												
Cohort I	.71*	.81*	-.46	-.63	.29	-.08	.46	.29	-.58	-.42	.39	1.00
Cohort III	.57*	.67	.17	-.28	.44	.22	.35	.46	-.32	.18	.43	.13
Depression												
Cohort I	.51*	.36	-.16	-1.0*	.10	.21	-.28	-.55	-.31	-.42	.02	-.05
Cohort III	.65	-.09	.03	-.09	.79*	-.13	-.19	-.39	.02	-.17	.52	-.65
Anxiety												
Cohort I	.33	.28	-.21	.11	.12	.37	-.06	.28	-.28	.08	.18	.47
Cohort III	.51*	.12	.17	-.03	.51*	-.08	.12	-.21	.17	.18	.34	-.41
Hyperkinesis												
Cohort I	-.19	-.12	.73*	.05	.13	.61	.17	.44	.40	.57	.64	.49
Cohort III	.41	.54	.73*	1.00*	.85*	1.00	.16	1.00	.73*	1.00	1.00*	1.00
Bizarreness												
Cohort I	.37*	.41	.18	.36	.24	1.00*	.24	.05	-.15	.42	.36	1.00
Cohort III	.20	.11	.14	-.20	.33	.35	.23	-.20	-.23	-.28	.00	.04
Global												
Cohort I	.33*	.26	.11	-.12	.16	.35*	.03	.20	-.13	.11	.33	.36
Cohort III	.37*	.22	.19	-.03	.49*	.11	.19	-.10	.14	.06	.31*	-.23

Note: The results of significance are based on chi square tests (with Yates's correction for continuity) on 2x2 tables of DCO symptomatic versus nonsymptomatic and TOCA adapting (1) versus maladapting (1+2+3). The gamma (which is the same as Q in this case) values are based on the same 2x2 tables. A positive gamma indicates symptoms are associated with maladaptation.

Ns: Cohort I, end first grade = 926, third grade = 567. Cohort III end first grade = 946, third grade = 529.

* indicates chi square significant at the 0.10 level of probability.

† indicates end of third grade.

partly the cause of anxiety in these children. This inference is based on
results that showed that children who were anxious early in first grade
may have been maladapting then but had no greater risk than
nonanxious children of maladapting later. However, children rated
anxious in third grade had histories of early maladapting in first
grade. This conclusion—that school failure generates anxiety in some
children—is further borne out in the following sections.

Ratings of hyperkinesis early in first grade were associated with the
authority acceptance, maturation, and concentration scales on TOCA
—difficulties which continued at least as far as the end of third grade.
This combination of symptoms and social maladaptation is discussed
later in terms of the hyperactivity syndrome, a clinical problem of
major importance.

In the concurrent studies, we noticed that ratings of hyperkinesis
were characteristic of aggressive children, that is, those children in the
aggressive and shy-aggressive clusters; in the longitudinal studies of
relations of early TOCA ratings to later symptoms, hyperkinesis was
associated with the NSNA cluster. These are children who have learning difficulties but do not have trouble with shyness or authority. All of
these findings indicate that early hyperkinetic children are an important group who have concurrent and potential problems in most areas
of social maladaptation.

This difference—between children who began school with symptomatic ratings and demonstrated a higher risk of social maladaptation,
and children who were rated maladapting early in their school careers
and had a continuing or growing risk of being rated symptomatic—
provides an interesting opportunity for conjecture regarding the causes
in each instance. It is possible that children who were rated symptomatic early in school had been seen by their parents as maladapting at
home before the children entered school. If such a child succeeded at
the social tasks set in school by his teacher, his or her early symptoms
would be likely to decrease as the importance of school success
increased and confidence in succeeding in school was strengthened. In
contrast, the child who was rated socially maladapting in school early in
first grade would be likely to feel bad, particularly if the child had been
maladapting at home in the view of his or her parents. The child would
thus continue to perform poorly and reinforce low self-esteem. As a
result, there would be a decreased expectation on the part of the
teacher, reinforcing still further the child's low self-esteem and a
higher risk of symptoms.

This formulation is conjecture not proved by our studies; but it is in keeping with the data presented thus far and other data to be presented. It suggests a causal interplay between SAS and symptoms that is highly related to specific social fields. We are not suggesting that this interplay is the sole cause of either social maladaptation or symptoms; we are hypothesizing about the nature of the relationship between these two dimensions of mental health.

Relationships between
Psychological Well-Being and IQ,
Readiness, Reading Achievement,
and Grades

The preceding discussion has dealt with the relationships between the symptom measures and TOCA. We shall now consider the relationships between these same symptom measures and other social adaptational measures, that is, first- and third-grade IQ, first-grade readiness test performance, third-grade reading achievement, and first- and third-grade subject grades.

DCO vs. other adaptational measures. The results of investigations of the relationships between DCO and other measures of social adaptational status are presented first. These results should not be interpreted too specifically, because of the small number of children rated symptomatic on each DCO scale. There were, however, significant relationships which clearly indicate that children rated symptomatic and nonsymptomatic on DCO differed in their performance on IQ, readiness, and reading achievement tests and grades.

In order to increase the number of symptomatic children in the DCO cells, we again employed the broad definition of symptomatic used earlier—namely, all children who were rated symptomatic by at least one clinician, even if, after discussion, both clinicians rated the child nonsymptomatic. The results show this definition of symptomatic to be meaningful. In addition, the DCO intervention and control populations were combined so that we could study the largest possible number of symptomatic children. The differences between intervention and control in regard to relationships with these other adaptational measures were minimal, thus justifying their being combined.

The relationships of Cohort I and Cohort III DCO made early in first grade and at the end of third grade (or long-term) to the respective social adaptational measures are contained in table 36. Only Cohort I received long-term ratings.

The table contains the gamma values for the strength of the

relationships between each DCO scale and each social adaptational measure; the associations that were statistically significant by t test at the 0.10 level of probability are indicated. Results were omitted if there were fewer than five children in the DCO symptomatic cell. For purposes of calculating gamma, IQ, Metropolitan Readiness Test, and Metropolitan Reading Achievement Test ranges were each divided into three parts, with the middle part including scores which were one standard deviation on either side of the mean. Grades were classified in four levels—excellent, good, fair, and unsatisfactory. DCO ratings were divided into nonsymptomatic vs. symptomatic for each scale. A positive gamma value indicates that being symptomatic on DCO was associated with worse scores on adaptational measures. A negative gamma indicates that being symptomatic was associated with better adaptational scores. The table shows that there were a number of strong positive associations and a few negative associations between DCO and the several adaptational measures.

Children assessed as flat by clinicians on DCO early in first grade were clearly less ready for school (as measured by the Metropolitan Readiness Test) than nonflat children. Their first-grade subject grades were consistently worse, yet their conduct grades were better than those of the other children. Children rated flat in third grade on DCO had worse grades in speaking. The gamma values also reveal a tendency toward worse third-grade subject grades and Metropolitan Reading Achievement Test scores. Children who were rated flat on DCO in third grade had somewhat lower IQ scores and worse subject grades in first grade.

Overall, flat children tend to be seen as performing poorly in school, except for conduct, where they have less trouble than nonflat children. They seem to have somewhat more trouble performing adequately in verbal areas. The study of the longitudinal course of children who were rated flat in first grade was hampered by the fact that, by third grade, only a small number of these children were still in Woodlawn schools. This was due partly to the usual rate of attrition over a two-year period in a group that was already small in first grade.

The DCO depression scale was not associated in the predicted direction with IQ, readiness, reading achievement, or grades either in first or third grade. In fact, the results were in the other direction; *there was a tendency for depressed children to receive better grades than nondepressed children in both first and third grade, longitudinally as well as concurrently.* In contrast to flatness, depression was associated with being seen as performing better. As in the case of flatness, the

TABLE 36. GAMMA VALUES FOR THE RELATIONSHIPS OF DCO RATINGS EARLY IN FIRST GRADE AND END OF THIRD GRADE TO PERFORMANCE ON IQ, READINESS, AND READING ACHIEVEMENT TESTS AND GRADES

DCO Scales and Assessment Time	IQ		MRT	MAT	First Grade Grades							Third Grade Grades				
	1st Gr	3d Gr	1st Gr	3d Gr	Reading	Oral Lang.	Handwriting	Soc. Sci.	Arithmetic	Science	Conduct	Reading	Mathematics	Speaking	Writing	Spelling
Flatness																
Cohort I Early	.20	—	.68*	—	.62*	.71*	.33	.59*	.62*	.45	-.54*	—	—	—	—	—
Cohort III Early	—	—	.71*	—	.41	.63*	.42	.48*	.45*	.19	-.47*	—	—	—	—	—
Cohort I LT†	.27	-.02	.04	.51	.07	.44	.31	.31	-.16	.02	.21	.26	.27	.75*	.37	.24
Depression																
Cohort I Early	.32	—	.11	.13	-.17	.29	-.41*	-.10	-.04	-.06	-.61*	-.78	-.75*	-.31	-.63	-.82*
Cohort III Early	—	—	.03	—	—	—	—	—	—	—	—	—	—	—	—	—
Cohort I LT	—	-.25	—	-.32	—	—	—	—	—	—	—	.00	-.48	-.58	-.72*	-.39
Anxiety																
Cohort I Early	.09	.14	.26	-.53*	.09	.34	.14	.02	-.10	.12	-.19	.10	.16	.31	.20	-.02
Cohort III Early	.05	.67	.19	.36	.15	.12	.13	.42*	.14	.39*	.00	.27	.09	.04	.29	.27
Cohort I LT	—	.29	—	.64*	.75*	.73	.55*	—	.71*	—	.38	.83*	.95*	.87*	.74*	.93*

Hyperkinesis																
Cohort I Early	.06	.43	.20	-.57*	-.03	-.24	.03	.36	-.02	.17	.53*	-.03	.61	.00	.03	.04
Cohort III Early	-.16	—	.34	—	.36	.36	.29	.31	.42	.32	.38	—	—	—	—	—
Cohort I LT	-.02	—	.71	—	.75*	.39	.68*	.88*	.50*	.68*	.55*	—	—	—	—	—
Bizarreness																
Cohort I Early	-.22	—	-.02	—	.12	.13	-.07	-.07	.03	-.15	.05	-.19	.16	-.02	-.14	-.17
Cohort III Early	.16	.81*	.31	.16	.27	.14	.41*	.26	.19	.06	-.01	.40	.49*	.42	.11	.15
Cohort I LT	.19	-.02	.34	.42	.06	.39	-.01	.10	.37	.02	-.18	.08	-.11	.07	.19	-.09
Global																
Cohort I Early	.03	.11	.29	-.33*	.12	.24*	-.01	.17	.07	.13	.10	-.02	.16	.19	.08	-.09
Cohort III Early	.10	.55*	.34*	.11	.20	.23*	.22*	.31*	.19	.22	.00	.30	.30*	.25	.19	.24
Cohort I LT	.06	-.02	.41*	.40*	.31*	.39*	.26*	.39*	.27*	.25	.17	.28*	.24*	.34*	.14	.15

Note: These populations consist of children in public schools only. The early samples that received DCO ratings were Cohort I early, N=1000; Cohort III early, N=1080; Cohort I third grade, N=1350. The other scores were unavailable for many children for a variety of reasons. The gamma values for DCO versus IQ, Metropolitan Readiness Test (MRT), and Metropolitan Achievement Test (MAT) are based on 2 x 3 tables of the two DCO levels (symptomatic and nonsymptomatic) for each scale and three IQ and MRT or MAT levels, the middle levels of which include scores within one standard deviation of the mean of each score; the other two levels are those scores below and those above this range. The DCO versus grades results are based on 2 x 4 tables of the two DCO levels and the four grade levels of excellent, good, fair, and unsatisfactory.

— indicates that gamma was not calculated because of very small numbers in at least one of the marginals. A positive gamma indicates that symptoms were associated with poor performance.

* indicates that the symptomatic and nonsymptomatic children differed significantly by t tests (p<0.10) on the corresponding adaptational measure.

† End of third grade.

conduct grades of these children tended to be better than those of other children. Ratings on the DCO anxiety scale also showed very interesting results. In both cohorts, children who were rated anxious in first grade did not perform very differently than their nonanxious classmates in regard to IQ, readiness, reading achievement (in Cohort I they did even better than nonanxious children), or grades. The most striking results concerned the relationship between ratings of anxiety on DCO in third-grade and first-grade subject grades; third-grade reading achievement; and third-grade subject grades. Anxiety in third grade was clearly associated with having performed worse than nonanxious children in first grade as well as in third grade. *Anxiety was increasingly tied, then, to prior and current poor performance in school.*

Hyperkinesis showed a pattern somewhat similar to anxiety in its relation to these measures of social adaptation, although the relationships of this scale to the conduct grade were somewhat stronger than those of the anxiety scale, even in first grade. While there was some tendency for hyperkinetic children in first grade to receive worse grades, children rated hyperkinetic in third grade *had received even worse grades in first grade two years before* than had the nonhyperkinetic third-graders. Thus hyperkinesis in third grade also seems to stem partly from early school failure. However, we showed earlier that early hyperkinesis leads to later poor school social adaptational status. Therefore, school failure and hyperkinesis are mutually reinforcing.

Bizarreness revealed still another pattern. The relationship of this DCO symptom to these SAS measures was not at all impressive. In first grade, children rated bizarre appeared to have trouble with handwriting, and later on in third grade, these same children performed less well on IQ tests and in mathematics. These results suggest the possibility of some form of difficulty with understanding and expressing symbols—but this is very much a conjecture. Overall, there does not appear to be much relationship between ratings of bizarreness and these social adaptational measures.

The scores of children rated symptomatic on the DCO global scale early in first grade yielded somewhat mixed results, which was not unexpected given the very specific patterns of relationships between the social adaptational measures and each DCO symptom scale. Overall, studies of these relationships indicate that different symptoms have different patterns, with some apparently stemming partly from school failure (anxiety and hyperkinesis) and some, such as flatness, being strongly associated with poor performance from the start. Depression was

associated with better performance, suggesting that these children not
only cared about school performance but generally could perform
better than other children. Bizarreness remained a mystery, with little
association to school performance except for a hint that this symptom
might have some relationship to difficulties with symbols.

MSI vs. other adaptational measures. These studies were conducted
using MSI ratings from Cohort I and Cohort III. Recall that MSI
ratings were made at the end of first grade in both cohorts, but in each
case mothers were asked to assess their children's behavior over the
preceding several weeks. First-grade IQ tests and readiness tests were
given during first semester. Grades were given at the end of first
semester in first grade and in third grade. The third-grade IQ and
reading achievement tests were given approximately two years after the
MSI symptom ratings, in the second semester of third grade.

Only the data for control schoolchildren are presented in table 37.
Again, gamma values are included to give an indication of the strength
of association and a statistically significant association is indicated.
There were a number of significant differences in the results for
intervention children and control children (see note 1); we shall discuss
these differences in chapter 4.

The children rated by mothers as bizarre on MSI performed worse
than nonbizarre children on first-grade IQ and readiness tests, but in
at least one cohort, they had slightly better grades. The MSI sad and
worried category was not strongly related to the adaptational measures
in Cohort I; in Cohort III, however, children rated symptomatic in this
category received somewhat worse grades in first grade and did
significantly less well on the first-grade readiness test.

These mothers' ratings of sad and worried behaviors did not show
the same relations to school performance as did the clinicians' ratings
of depression—which were associated with better performance. The
difference in results of DCO and MSI in relation to school performance may be due to differences in the two variables—sad and worried
on MSI, and depression on DCO. The differences in the relations of
depression and sadness and worry provide evidence that clinically
assessed depression is different from sadness and worry as viewed by
mothers. This conclusion is supported further by the minimal relationship between these two symptom measures found in studies discussed
earlier. We shall see that HIF self-ratings of sadness were associated
with poor social adaptational status, particularly in the intervention
schools. Mothers' ratings of sad and worried were also associated with

TABLE 37. GAMMA VALUES FOR THE RELATIONSHIP BETWEEN MSI AND PERFORMANCE ON IQ, READINESS, AND READING ACHIEVEMENT TESTS AND GRADES

	IQ		MRT	MAT	First Grade							Third Grade				
MSI Categories	1st Gr.	3d Gr.	1st Gr.	3d Gr.	Reading	Oral Language	Handwriting	Soc. Sci.	Arithmetic	Science	Conduct	Reading	Mathematics	Speaking	Writing	Spelling
Bizarre behavior																
Cohort I	-.24	.00	.08	.09	-.04	.05	-.18	-.59*	-.12	-.40	-.07	.03	.09	-.17	-.27	-.02
Cohort III	.48*	.19	.32*	-.45	.01	.12	-.06	-.20	.06	-.34	-.49*	.00	.34	.13	-.08	.25
Sad and worried																
Cohort I	-.06	.18	.43	-.14	.05	.09	.14	.00	.15	-.03	.11	.00	-.04	-.03	-.36*	.06
Cohort III	-.11	.29	.31*	-.01	.21*	.21*	.19*	.29*	.21*	.09	-.08	-.06	.25	.31*	.11	.11
Fears																
Cohort I	-.06	-.08	-.14	-.35	-.02	-.01	-.19	-.09	-.08	-.34*	-.19	-.24	-.08	-.20	-.21	-.15
Cohort III	.52*	.08	.31*	.04	-.02	.11	.19*	.02	.14	-.09	-.01	-.20	.09	.03	.17	.13
Trouble with feelings																
Cohort I	.31	.00	.32*	-.17	.18	.21*	.14	.25*	.13	.22*	.23*	.25*	-.08	-.33*	-.25	-.16
Cohort III	.25*	.27	.18*	-.24	.17*	.17*	.06	.13	.22*	.02	.02	.03	-.05	.13	-.02	.10
Muscular tension																
Cohort I	.43*	.34	.41	.12	-.07	.35	.07	.03	-.10	-.40	.29	.03	-.06	.13	.13	-.02
Cohort III	-.20	.69	.33	-.30	.57*	.51*	.29	.09	.34*	.35	-.13	.36	.18	.59*	.01	.25
Nervous habits																
Cohort I	.18*	.17	-.03	.11	.04	.14	-.01	-.04	.03	-.12	.08	-.22	-.07	.08	-.20	-.13
Cohort III	.24*	-.17	.13	-.17	.10	.06	.02	-.01	.05	.05	.07	.07	-.04	.28*	.03	.16

	1	2	3	4	5	6	7	8	9	10	11	12	13	14	15	16
Sleep problems																
Cohort I	.11*	.56	.31	.12	.38*	.30	.09	.19	.09	.12	.46*	-.28	.00	-.21	-.34	.01
Cohort III	-.06	.29	.02	.29	-.02	.01	-.11	-.19	-.08	-.16	-.07	.28	.27	.25	.06	.06
Psychosomatic																
Cohort I	.27	.18	.06	.48	.22	.22	.25*	.19	.24*	.17	.06	.06	-.07	.13	.08	.17
Cohort III	.05	.21	-.06	-.02	.18	.01	.20	.11	.25*	.07	.01	-.11	.19	.11	-.15	-.08
Toilet problems																
Cohort I	-.09	-.07	.15	.01	.10	.05	.01	.16	.03	.08	.40*	.31	.06	.07	.15	.08
Cohort III	-.21	.01	.25	.49*	.34*	.24*	.36*	.29*	.28*	.22*	.16	.26*	.34*	.54*	.28*	.36*
Immature behavior																
Cohort I	.06	.15	.19	-.09	.20*	.16	.10	.05	.10	.06	.06	-.21	-.04	-.34*	-.46*	-.28*
Cohort III	.38*	-.06	.20*	.13	.05	.13	.26*	.00	.18*	.07	-.15	.21	.21*	.29*	.25*	.13
Speech problems																
Cohort I	.08	.36	.16	.31	.26	.33*	.02	.06	.07	.03	.06	-.05	-.08	.39	.09	.07
Cohort III	.03	.20	.31*	.29	.29*	.36*	.11	.10	.12	.05	.23	.36	.20	.44*	.02	.26
Eating problems																
Cohort I	-.04	.10	.03	.03	-.01	.10	-.18*	-.14	.00	-.21	.11	-.18	.02	.13	-.08	.03
Cohort III	-.09	-.27*	-.02	-.16	-.01	.14	.11	.10	.10	.15	.03	-.08	-.06	.00	-.13	-.11
Sex problems																
Cohort I	-.09	-.23	.26	-.04	.19	.31	.13	.11	-.01	-.06	.14	.00	-.14	.09	-.22	-.20
Cohort III	.06	.46	.32*	.10	.03	.13	.18	-.17	-.03	-.24	.03	.03	.11	.43*	-.04	-.05
Overall gamma																
Cohort I	.23	.21	.18	-.04	.14	.20	.10	.14	.11	.06	.25	-.06	.10	-.04	-.09	.00
Cohort III	.18	.16	.19	.04	.19	.23	.26	.18	.23	.16	.05	.14	.19	.26	.16	.17
Overall MSI																
B vs. A (t-test)																
Cohort I		*	*			*	*		*				*		*	
Cohort III															*	*

TABLE 37 (cont.)

MSI Categories	IQ		MRT	MAT	First Grade							Third Grade				
	1st Gr.	3d Gr.	1st Gr.	3d Gr.	Reading	Oral Language	Handwriting	Soc. Sci.	Arithmetic	Science	Conduct	Reading	Mathematics	Speaking	Writing	Spelling
Overall MSI **C vs. A** (t-test)																
Cohort I	*				*	*										
Cohort III	*			*	*	*	*	*	*	*	*	*	*	*	*	*
Overall MSI **C vs. B** (t-test)																
Cohort I	*				*	*										
Cohort III				*	*	*		*	*		*		*	*		

Note: This population consisted of children in public schools who were in control schools during the first-grade intervention program. The samples that received MSI ratings and contained children who were in control schools numbered 369 for Cohort I and 562 for Cohort III. The other scores were unavailable for many children for a variety of reasons.

In each of the 13 MSI categories, a child was considered "symptomatic" if he or she had a rating of "pretty much" or "very much" on at least one item in the category; otherwise, the child was considered "nonsymptomatic." Gamma values were calculated using the two levels of each of the 13 MSI categories. Three levels of IQ, MRT, and MAT were used such that the middle levels include scores within one standard deviation of the mean; the other two levels include scores above and below this range. For grades, the four levels of excellent, good, fair, and unsatisfactory were used.

For the overall MSI score, a child was considered "nonsymptomatic" or (A) if he or she had no ratings of "pretty much" or "very much" on any of the 38 items. If a child received one or two ratings of "pretty much" or "very much" on any of the 38 items, the child was considered "mildly symptomatic" or (B); if a child received three or more ratings of "pretty much" or "very much," the child was considered "severely symptomatic" or (C).

For MSI overall, there is only one gamma value corresponding to three significance results because gamma was calculated using all three levels, whereas t tests compared each possible pair of levels.

A positive value of gamma indicates that MSI symptom ratings were associated with poor performance on these social adaptational measures.

* indicates that the nonsymptomatic and symptomatic children differed significantly by t-test ($p < 0.10$).

poor adaptational status, although not specifically in intervention schools. On the other hand, clinical ratings of depression are associated with better school performance.

If one considers the symptom concepts involved, if one sees oneself as not performing in the eyes of others, sadness may be a way of eliciting needed support, while clinical depression may be an internal process of a different kind—one associated with caring about task performance in a driving, self-energizing way associated with succeeding. Sadness, in other words, would be more related to an interactional process between the child and others, particularly the natural rater; depression rated by clinicians would be more of an intrapsychic process in which the child, having accepted the social tasks in the classroom as important, then experiences internal conflict around giving up earlier roles while feeling inexorable pressure to perform the new roles. One child uses the outward appearance of sadness to reduce the pressure; the other child keeps the conflict internal, experiences some depression, but drives toward success.

The MSI trouble with feelings category was related to the social adaptational measures being considered here. First-grade IQ, readiness, and grades were significantly worse in children who were rated symptomatic in this category; but by third grade, these children were either performing on a par with others or somewhat better. The muscular tension category on MSI showed a few such relationships. In both cohorts, nervous habits were associated with lower IQ performance. In Cohort III, children rated symptomatic in the MSI toilet problems category showed associations with performance on the adaptational measures (mainly grades), but this was not true in Cohort I.

The overall MSI revealed more impressive relationships to the adaptational measures than any of the thirteen MSI symptom categories. Here there was no ambiguity. Children who received no MSI symptomatic ratings of "pretty much" or "very much" did better than children who received one or more ratings of "pretty much" or "very much," and children who received one or two ratings of "pretty much" or "very much" did better than children who received three or more such symptom ratings. These relationships were both concurrent and longitudinal for third-grade grades but not for third-grade IQ or reading achievement.

As we saw with DCO, the various symptom categories differed in their relationships to the various adaptational measures. Generally, the higher the overall MSI, the worse the grades and scores on these measures.

HIF vs. other adaptational measures. The associations between HIF, and first- and third-grade adaptational scores, and grades are presented in table 38 for control schoolchildren. The results for intervention schoolchildren differed (see note 1). These results and others which differ for intervention and control children are discussed in the next chapter.

TABLE 38. GAMMA VALUES FOR THE RELATIONSHIPS BETWEEN HIF AND PERFORMANCE ON IQ, READINESS AND READING ACHIEVEMENT TESTS, AND GRADES

HIF	IQ 1st Gr.	IQ 3d Gr.	MRT 1st Gr.	MAT 3d Gr.	Reading	Oral Lang.	Handwr.	Soc. Sci.	Arith.	Science	Conduct	Reading	Math	Speaking	Writing	Spelling
					First Grade							Third Grade				
Nervous																
2 vs. 1	ns	ns	ns	ns	†	ns	ns	ns	ns	ns	ns	ns	ns	ns	ns	†
3 vs. 1	ns	ns	ns	ns	ns	ns	ns	ns	ns	ns	ns	*	ns	ns	ns	ns
3 vs. 2	ns	ns	ns	ns	*	*	*	ns	ns	ns	ns	*	*	ns	*	*
Gamma	-.06	.11	-.07	.13	-.01	.11	.02	.00	.04	-.02	.11	.20	.11	.14	.14	.11
Sad																
2 vs. 1	*	ns	ns	ns	ns	ns	ns	ns	ns	ns	ns	*	*	ns	*	ns
3 vs. 1	*	*	ns	*	ns	ns	ns	ns	ns	ns	ns	ns	*	*	*	ns
3 vs. 2	*	ns	ns	ns	ns	ns	ns	ns	ns	ns	ns	ns	ns	ns	ns	ns
Gamma	.31	.18	.24	.35	.09	.04	.06	.03	.09	.12	.06	.09	.37	.21	.27	.16
N	162	131	195	136	194	195	197	195	197	188	197	167	166	167	167	165

Note: This population consists of Cohort III children who were in any of the Woodlawn control schools from middle to end of first grade. Parochial schoolchildren were not included, since these schools do not give these tests at the same time as the public schools and since the subjects taught in public and parochial schools are not comparable. On each HIF scale, children were divided into "nonsymptomatic" (1), "a little bit" (2), and "pretty much" and "a lot" (3).

Gamma values were calculated using the three levels of HIF and three levels for IQ, Metropolitan Readiness Test, and Metropolitan Reading Achievement Test scores in which the middle level included scores within one standard deviation of the mean. The other two levels included scores above and below this range. For grades, the four levels of excellent, good, fair, and unsatisfactory were used. A positive value of gamma indicates that HIF symptoms were associated with poor performance. Gamma values for the nervous scale are low because nervousness is not ordinal with respect to performance scores. "A little" nervousness, for example, is better than "not at all" in terms of performance.

Results of significance are based on t tests comparing all three pairs of levels of symptomatic ratings on scores from the Kuhlmann-Anderson IQ Test in first and third grade, the Metropolitan Readiness Test in first grade, the Metropolitan Reading Achievement Test in third grade, and grades in first and third grades.

* indicates significant at the 0.10 level of probability.

ns indicates not significant at the 0.10 level of probability.

† indicates symptomatic children had better social adaptational scores.

"A little bit" of nervousness was associated with better reading grades in first grade and better spelling grades in third grade. Generally, "a little bit" of nervousness was associated with better grades than "pretty much" or "a lot" in both first and third grade, with not much difference among ratings of "not at all," "pretty much" and "a lot." These findings are similar to those found by Fein (1963). The HIF ratings were made in third grade, and the association between first-grade adaptational status and third-grade nervousness spanned a period of more than two years. Generally, what differences there were suggest that "a little bit" of nervousness was associated with somewhat better social adaptational status. This result is similar to those which showed clinical depression to be associated with better performance. Both mild self-ratings of nervousness and clinical depression could be part of internal adaptive processes associated with energizing oneself to accomplish social tasks. However, this is not the only possible explanation. Either or both of these results could represent the psychological "cost" of adapting, that is, the pain engendered by giving up earlier childhood roles and assuming more grown-up roles.

Self-ratings of sadness on HIF in third grade were associated with IQ test performance in a very striking way. Third-graders who rated themselves "not at all" sad were the same children who had achieved the highest IQ scores in first grade. The next-highest IQ scores went to the third-graders who indicated that they were "a little bit" sad. The worst first-grade IQ scores were those of the third-graders who rated themselves "pretty much" or "a lot" sad. Sadness in third-graders was also reflected in lower *third-grade* IQ scores, reading achievement scores, and grades. This is in keeping with the findings in the MSI sad and worried category shown in table 38. In contrast to ratings measuring nervousness, *a little sadness was not better than no sadness.* Those relationships were even more pronounced with the intervention children.

Just as we found in the studies of DCO and MSI and their relationships to adaptational measures, the two HIF symptom scales differed in their relationships to the adaptational measures, but both scales yielded important results.

Summary of Relationships
between Social Adaptational Status
and Psychological Well-Being

In thinking about the significance of these relationships, one must keep in mind that they emerge from community-wide studies of total populations of Woodlawn first-grade children. We studied the relationships between adaptation to the classrooms in this specific community and the psychological well-being of the community's children. It is clear that the results from studies of children in other communities or other populations of children, such as those attending a second-level mental health clinic, may be different from those we obtained.

With a few important exceptions, our results indicate that social maladaptation is associated with low psychological well-being, both concurrently and longitudinally. There is some evidence that certain kinds of maladaptation early in first grade increase the risk of specific symptoms by third grade. For example, children who were shy in first grade not only showed a continuing risk of symptoms of flatness, depression, and anxiety but also an increasing risk of bizarreness by third grade. Children in the NSNA maladaptive cluster and those who had poor grades early in first grade showed an increasing risk of hyperkinesis. Poor grades and low IQ scores early in first grade led to an increasing risk of anxiety by third grade. These examples suggest that the process of adapting to the classroom plays a role in the manifestations of these symptoms in third grade. If we consider the relationship of early symptoms to later maladaptation, we find some evidence that the presence of symptoms in children early in first grade increases the risk of later poor social adaptational status, depending on the type of symptom.

An overview of the relationships between specific measures of social adaptational status and specific symptom measures is contained in figure 5. The large solid circles on this chart indicate a strong positive relationship, while the smaller solid circles indicate that the evidence of a relationship between the two variables was only moderately strong. A negative relationship is represented by an open circle.

The number of times a particular relationship was replicated was the primary criterion for assessing the strength of evidence. Where there was a clear and strong longitudinal relationship but not a concurrent relationship, or vice versa, the relationship is shown as strong. Where only moderate evidence of a relationship was found in the concurrent or longitudinal studies, a smaller circle was used.

Based on these results, the following inferences seem to be indicated:

1. The symptoms of children in the TOCA shy maladaptive cluster differed from the symptoms of children in the aggressive cluster. The shy children had a higher risk of symptoms involving less outward manifestation and a more inhibited type of symptomatic behavior. The children in the aggressive cluster, on the other hand, had symptoms which were excitatory and physically active.

2. Children in the shy-aggressive maladaptive cluster had a risk of having a number of kinds of symptoms, but the associations were moderate with no very specific pattern.
3. Children in the aggressive cluster had fewer kinds of symptoms than other maladapting children, but the specific symptoms associated with the aggressive cluster were more consistent across cohorts and across rating periods.
4. Children in the NSNA cluster did not show a risk of having as many kinds of symptoms as the children in the shy cluster or the shy-aggressive cluster; nor was the NSNA cluster related strongly to a few symptoms, as was the aggressive cluster. Children in this cluster showed an increasing risk of symptoms as the school career progressed, however.
5. Lower IQ scores and poor grades related to many symptoms. Lower readiness or reading achievement scores were related to symptoms but to somewhat fewer symptoms than IQ or grades.
6. Depression, as measured by DCO, appeared to be associated with better social adaptational status, in contrast to sadness, which seems to be a different concept and was associated with worse social adaptational status.
7. Anxiety was associated with all but one of the measures of social maladaptation. Ratings of mild anxiety were associated with better social adaptational status. The risk of anxiety increased over time for children experiencing school failure.
8. Although hyperkinesis was associated with poor classroom performance, hyperkinetic children did as well or better than nonhyperkinetic children on IQ and achievement tests. These results suggest that hyperkinetic children do not lack test-taking ability but are rather unable to sustain performance in the classroom.
9. In regard to MSI, the *eating problems* and *sex problems* categories had little or no association with social maladaptation. *Trouble with feelings, toilet problems,* and *immature behavior* were the categories most generally related to poor social adaptational status.
10. In regard to the HIF, nervousness was related to the shy and shy-aggressive clusters and to grades. Sadness was *not* related to shyness or aggressiveness in control children, but clearly was related to those school tasks directly associated with learning.

These studies were based on a concept of mental health consisting of two dimensions: social adaptational status and psychological well-being. The patterns of relationships between these two dimensions indicate that social adaptational status and psychological well-being are indeed two different concepts with specific interrelationships. There is evidence that suggests that social maladaptation has causal relationship to low psychological well-being. Both dimensions are important in obtaining a comprehensive view of mental health.

While the vagueness of the concept of symptoms continues to be a problem in assessing the interrelationships of symptoms, these results suggest that systematic community-wide studies can help clarify the concepts and that there are specific kinds of symptoms with specific patterns of relationship to social adaptation. Problems in this area range from the relatively atheoretical basis from which the MSI is derived (which hinders interpretation of results) to the difficulties in the reliability of clinical observations in the DCO procedure. The reliability of DCO was much better when the severity of symptoms was greater, but, since the number of severely symptomatic children was small, we pooled the mildly symptomatic children with children who were rated severe. Nevertheless, the studies of the interrelationships based on these DCO populations demonstrate that the children rated mildly symptomatic, even those about whom there was disagreement between clinical raters with eventual consensus of nonsymptomatic, should not be ignored.

Social Adaptational Status:
Its Relevance to Clinical Problems

Traditionally, clinicians have conceived of mental illness as being *within* the individual patient, even though the causes of illness may stem from a variety of sources, including the social context in which the individual functions. Social adaptational status has some similarity to the traditional clinical view, in that the causes of mental illness are conceived of as stemming, potentially, from many sources; but social adaptational status assumes that the social aspects of the illness may be partly *outside* the individual. On the other hand, psychological well-being—as we have conceptualized and measured it—is within the individual, even though its determinants may also stem from many sources.

This raises the question, why develop a dimension of mental health—a concept which is confusing enough as it is—which is partly outside the individual? The answer is implicit in the conceptual framework upon which this research was based. This framework postulates that there are two dimensions of mental health—psychological well-being and social adaptational status, or SAS. SAS is the

resultant of a highly interactional process between the natural rater and
the individual, a measure of the adequacy of the individual's social
function. It is in this sense that we have described social adaptational
status as the interface between the individual and society.

Clinical investigators have considered social function of the individual to be a major dimension of health, just as we have in our research.
The difference is in the degree to which investigators, in their assessment of social function, have conceived of it as a characteristic of the
individual rather than as a result of interaction between the individual
and society, highly idiosyncratic to the particular fit between natural
rater and individual in the context of a specific social field.

We suggest that taking into account that aspect of the locus of
mental health problems which lies outside the individual is a necessary
part of assessing the individual's mental health. This implies that not
only is the social adaptational aspect of an individual's mental health
considerably influenced by the natural rater and/or characteristics of
the social field but that in the "treatment" of an individual's illness, the
"illness" may usefully be viewed as potentially including other people
and processes outside the individual. The results of our studies of the
social adaptational status and psychological well-being of Woodlawn
first-graders lend support for this approach.

An example of the difference between this and the more traditional
view may be a clinician's identification of a child as hyperactive based
on referral by a teacher in the classroom. The hyperactive child is a
clinical problem that is much discussed and written about in child
psychiatry. The results of our research in Woodlawn indicate that part
of the identification of the problem lies outside the child, and that, in
order for the problem to be understood by the clinician, the clinician
must understand that potentially the locus of the problem extends
beyond the child to include the teacher and other social contextual
aspects. For instance, the problem may involve the teacher's need for
extreme order as much as the child's inability to sit still. Our
observations have been that what is considered acceptable behavior
varies greatly from one classroom to the next and from one parent to
the next, and this variation illustrates the idiosyncratic aspect of the fit
between the natural rater and the individual.

In practical terms, the clinician's consideration of the social adaptational aspect of the child's problem may mean that, instead of referring
the child to a second-level clinic as a patient, he may first request
first-level staff to visit the classroom and the family to assess the
influences on the problem and the locus of the problem itself. This is

not to say that the problem *necessarily* lies outside the child, but it is clear that the locus of the problem should be assessed—that it should not be assumed that the locus lies solely in the child.

It is not a new idea in psychiatry that the locus of the problem may extend beyond the patient and include, for example, the family. Yet clinicians (even those who hold such a view) often continue to treat the patient alone or with other family members, stopping short of assessing the problem in the classroom or other social fields in which the individual is involved.

At least in part, this practice reflects a general lack of training among clinicians to do this sort of assessment; for example, it is still not unusual for residents in child psychiatry to have no experience in the elementary school classroom throughout the course of training. Partly, the practice stems from the lack of an integrated system of mental health care such as we described earlier. In the traditional "non-system," it has not been feasible for a clinician to go into the variety of social contexts in which each of his patients is involved, and there has not been available a coordinated first-level structure with staff from whom he could request this first-level assessment. This is a striking example of how community mental health, as a broadened purview of the mental health professions, may make a major contribution toward increasing the effectiveness of mental health services. The advantages of a broader framework for viewing mental health are important not only in regard to clinical work but in regard to epidemiology and first-level assessment generally, where such a framework is, in fact, essential.

The results of the longitudinal community-wide studies of SAS and psychological well-being conducted in Woodlawn yielded a relatively clear nosology of the kinds of phenomena that can be considered clinical problems if one accepts the possibility that part of the problem may lie beyond the child. We considered four maladaptive clusters (shy, aggressive, shy-aggressive, and learning difficulties involving neither shyness or aggression) which can more usefully be called "social maladaptive modes" as long as there is the clear understanding that the problem as well as its causes may include more than the child alone. Social maladaptive modes is a particularly useful term in considering the clinical relevance of SAS, and we shall employ it throughout this discussion.

The population of adapting children provided an extremely impor-tant comparison group for studies of differences among these maladaptive modes. The modes were measured over several years and occurred with remarkably consistent frequencies from year to year. They reveal fairly specific courses over time and fairly specific risks of psychiatric symptoms as well as other characteristics which support the idea that viewing clinical problems in this manner is a useful way of assessing child mental health on a community-wide basis.

It should be stressed that this approach is not in conflict with traditional views of clinical assessment. Rather it is a broadening of previous work which appears to have two advantages: first, that options for intervention are more numerous and possibly more effective, since treatment is not limited to the patient; and second, that this approach may move us further ahead in solving the problems of developing more reliable and valid child diagnostic categories. These points can be illustrated by looking at the four maladaptive modes in regard to work done by previous investigators.

Children whose behavior exemplified the shy maladaptive mode (about 20 percent of all children in each cohort) began school with a relatively high risk of symptoms compared to children who were adapting early in first grade and to children who demonstrated other maladaptive modes. Their risk of symptoms appeared to increase slightly over time, at least as far as third grade. These results tend to support the traditional view of mental health professionals—demonstrated at least as early as 1928 by Wickman's study—that shyness is an important sign of later difficulty. However, longitudinal empirical studies by other investigators did not find a relationship between early shyness and adult mental health problems (Morris, Soroker, and Burrus 1954; Michael, Morris, and Soroker 1957; Robins 1966). Yet Anthony (1970) reports that, in a retrospective study of schizophrenics, he found evidence that shyness and withdrawal are developmental antecedents. Perhaps in some children shyness is a normal concomitant of situational factors, such as being in a new school, while in other children shyness may be a sign of pathology. In any case, our results suggest that shy children are an important group.

Children in the aggressive mode, about 15 percent across all cohorts, also suffered from problems with concentration (about 13 percent), underachievement (about 10 percent), and immaturity (about 9 percent). Children in this mode were also rated by clinicians as anxious and hyperkinetic and by their mothers as having nervous habits and toilet problems and being immature.

The complex of characteristics that make up the aggressive mode suggests an overlap with what some clinicians call hyperactivity and others call minimal brain dysfunction. The controversy over the naming of this clinical syndrome is part of the fundamental disagreement over the characteristics of the problem. For example, some investigators claim that neurological signs are the primary indicators (Conners 1967; Menkes, Rowe, and Menkes 1967); others maintain that many children with this syndrome lack neurological signs and children without the syndrome may have such signs (Morrison and Stewart 1973; Thompson 1973; Wender 1971). Wender points out that hyperactivity is not a good name because some of these children may be *hypo*active, or less active than normal. He selects minimal brain dysfunction as an appropriate name.

According to Wender (1971), the frequently occurring characteristics of minimal brain dysfunction are: (1) motor and verbal hyperactivity; (2) short attention span, poor concentration, and school underachievement; (3) learning difficulties in the areas of reading, writing, comprehension, and arithmetic; (4) low impulse control leading to low frustration tolerance, antisocial behavior, and impaired sphincter control; (5) some interpersonal relationships which are excessively independent, others which are excessively dependent; (6) increased emotional lability, hyperreactivity, low self-esteem, and increased aggressiveness.

Insofar as these characteristics were measured in our study, they seem to overlap with the characteristics of children in the aggressive mode. The prevalences of hyperactivity found in other studies range from 10 to 20 percent, with males composing 75 to 90 percent of those with problems. Our prevalence of 15 percent agrees with that of a county-wide study of all elementary schoolchildren (Bentzen 1963), and our sex ratio, while not so extreme as other studies, showed substantially more boys than girls in this mode. Many studies have found that children with minimal brain dysfunction tend to be sociopathic as adults (Robins 1966; Battle and Lacey 1972; Menkes, Rowe, and Menkes 1967; Morrison and Stewart 1973). Therefore the children in the aggressive mode represent a particularly important group for further study.

Eleven to 16 percent of all children across all four cohorts were rated as having problems with both shyness and aggression, that is, the shy-aggressive mode. While the children in this mode had the most severe TOCA ratings, their related characteristics and symptoms were in some ways similar to those of the shy mode and in other ways to those of the aggressive mode. However, the pattern of symptoms in shy-aggressive children is somewhat less clear than in the shy or the aggressive mode.

We have not been able to find a similar population described in the literature, and thus there was no opportunity to compare frequencies found in other studies or to consider the risks in adulthood that these early ratings represent. The frequencies we found and the course of these children through third grade led us to conclude that this population warrants more investigation, The next chapter presents data which suggest that this mode is particularly sensitive to intervention.

The fourth mode includes children (about 20 percent of all children) who were neither shy nor aggressive (the NSNA mode). However, these children were rated underachievers (about 12 percent), immature (about 9 percent), and as having problems with concentration (about 9 percent). They suffered primarily from learning problems, were rated hyperkinetic by clinicians more frequently than adapting children, and rated themselves as more sad. While these children did not have the problems with authority acceptance demonstrated by the aggressive mode, their pattern of difficulties suggests that some of them may be considered to have minimal brain dysfunction, if one accepts Wender's description.

In summary, the results suggest four fairly definable maladaptive modes based on the child's SAS in the classroom. Basically, these modes represent styles of maladaptive responses by first-grade children as assessed by the teacher. This approach to developing a nosology of child mental health problems is a departure from previous efforts, which have mainly attempted to define categories of symptomatic behavior rather than categories of social maladaptive responses. Our results demonstrate that the latter approach holds promise as a way of assessing child mental health. We found that the frequencies of such modes are quite stable from year to year; thus the course of the modes can be studied over time, and symptom patterns associated with each social maladaptive mode can be studied. Early in the discussion of psychological well-being, we pointed out the difficulty investigators have had in trying to develop valid and reliable categories of child mental health disorder. Perhaps much of the difficulty has come from starting with attempts to find clusters of symptoms rather than starting with attempts to categorize styles of social maladaptive responses.

As a first-level community-wide screening procedure, this approach seems quite plausible—particularly when one considers (1) the need to include social contextual aspects in the assessment procedures, and (2) the contexts in which first-level assessment takes place; the phenomena which one observes in the classroom are not basically clinical but related to social tasks.

These four social maladaptive modes seem to be reliable and valid at the first level of assessment, and they may provide a basis for examining symptom patterns—but *within* social maladaptive categories. This requires further study, of course; but it does offer us a way to proceed in child mental health nosology—one which potentially relates social contextual variables with clinical phenomena in the child.

SYMPTOM MEASURES & SCALES	TOCA MALADAPTIVE CLUSTERS				IQ	MRT or MAT	Grades
	Shy-Aggressive	Shy	Aggressive	NSNA			
D C O — Flatness		●				•	•
Depression	•						○
Anxiety	•	●	●	•			●
Hyperkinesis	•		●	●		○	●
Bizarreness	•	•		•			
M S I — Bizarre Behavior						•	•
Sad and Worried		•		•		•	•
Fears	•		○			•	•
Trouble with Feelings	•	•		•	•	●	•
Muscular Tension	•					•	•
Nervous Habits	•		●	●			
Sleep Problems	•					•	•
Psycho-somatic	•	●		•			•
Toilet Problems	•	•	●	•		•	●
Immature Behavior		●	•	•	•	•	•
Speech Problems	•	•				•	•
Eating Problems				○			
Sex Problems						•	
H I F — Nervous	•	•					•
Sad				●	●	•	•

● STRONG POSITIVE RELATIONSHIP
● MODERATE POSITIVE RELATIONSHIP
○ MODERATE NEGATIVE RELATIONSHIP

Figure 5. Summary of Relationships between Social Adaptational Status and Psychological Well-Being

4 Evaluation of the First-Grade Intervention Program

The mental health system concept discussed earlier described the first of three levels of care as consisting of programs which are community-wide, highly integrated into the social structure of the community, and designed to prevent mental illness or enhance mental health in total populations *within the community*. The program for Woodlawn first-grade children was to be a first-level program, and the goal was to help first-graders get off to the best possible start in school in terms of social adaptational status and pychological well-being.

Before discussing in detail the development of a first-level intervention program for Woodlawn's first-grade population, we should review briefly how the three levels of care function and relate to each other as part of an integrated system. Beyond the first level, where programs are rooted in the community and are concerned with both healthy and ill individuals in total populations, there is the second level that focuses on people already in need. Here specialized outpatient care functions as a closely integrated backup to first-level programs. This level is not so closely tied to the local community as the first level, nor is the emphasis on total populations of healthy as well as ill individuals. At the third level, which consists of the hospital and its variations, the primary focus is on the highly specialized needs of severely ill patients requiring hospitalization. Again, there is a close relationship between this level and the second and first levels of care. There are two key requirements for the effectiveness of such a system: (1) the first level must be rooted in the community with viable mechanisms for community participation in policy-making and goal-setting; and (2) all three levels must be highly interrelated.

In the early thinking of the Woodlawn Mental Health Center Board and staff about what kind of intervention program to design for

Woodlawn first-graders, we were mindful of the fact that a program at the first level, since it is not concerned solely with an ill population, is best not conceptualized in terms of traditional interpersonal psychotherapy or pharmacotherapies more suitable for patients already in need. Variations of such therapies are essential for the crisis response aspects of first-level care; however, concern with healthy as well as ill populations at the first level requires consideration of community-wide programming for total populations in which only a few individuals may be ill. Thus such first-level programming may utilize intervention processes which complement the normally occurring social processes in the community's various social fields, making use of the knowledge gained in more traditional interventions. The goal is to modify and develop techniques which could influence these social processes in such a way that the mental health of individuals is enhanced.

As planning got under way, the Woodlawn Mental Health Center Board collaborated closely with the staff in the development of a program design which the board ultimately sanctioned and interpreted to the community. The board, in turn, communicated to the staff the concerns of the people of Woodlawn about the program in which their young children would be participating. As the intervention part of the program evolved, it focused not only on children who were experiencing trouble in school but came to include all of the children in the first-grade population of Woodlawn along with the social processes affecting them. All first-grade classrooms in all twelve Woodlawn elementary schools were involved in the assessment of need, with the classrooms in six of the schools participating in intervention. The board and staff agreed that we had to develop intervention processes that were system-oriented, that is, that reflected the view that the problem might stem from a variety of sources—the child, parent-teacher relations, the nature of the social tasks confronting the child in the classroom, and so on.

It is important to emphasize here what the expectations of the board, the staff, community citizens, and school faculties were regarding how much benefit the program would accomplish. In general, feelings fluctuated from expecting a miraculous cure at one extreme to expecting no benefit at all at the other. The expectation that we attempted to foster, in ourselves and others, was that impact would develop gradually over several years—through deliberate commitment to periodic community-wide assessment, program design based on the results of assessment, evaluation of impact, and redesign, in that order. This process requires involvement over long periods of time and a deliberate long-range strategy. It also requires a willingness to alter intervention procedures in order to strengthen impact. These psychological orientations are not so much problems for community citizens as for staff. Perhaps understandably, mental health professionals sometimes suffer at the start of new programs from unrealistic expectations and/or an unwillingness to evaluate impact and modify intervention techniques at each stage of program evolution. We employed the long-range strategy of gradual evolution in the program for Woodlawn children. It began as a modest community-wide intervention process that was redesigned each year in keeping with both the results of the evaluation of impact and of our clinical experience.

One of the requirements for community-wide first-level programming is a community-wide assessment system which provides a basis for the original planning and design of a program and for evaluating impact. In addition, we found that the results of evaluation of the first-grade intervention program provided information relevant to the concept of mental health on which the assessment system design and the design of the first-grade intervention program were based.

While teachers' ratings of the children's social adaptation to the first-grade classroom (TOCA) formed the primary measure of social adaptational status, scores from IQ and achievement tests and grades were considered to be additional measures of social adaptational status in the social field of the classroom. To a great extent, these measures were independent of the teacher and thus offered a way of looking at impact that was less vulnerable to the possibility of teacher bias. These measures—along with TOCA ratings and the measures of psychological well-being (mainly DCO)—were interpreted as criteria of impact in evaluating the intervention program implemented in approximately half of Woodlawn's first-grade classrooms in 1965.[11] The results of evaluation presented here are for the school years ending 1965, 1966, 1967, and 1968—the four years the intervention program was in operation in six of the twelve Woodlawn schools. Results are presented also for two-year follow-up assessments.

Summary of Intervention Procedures

The twelve Woodlawn elementary schools were divided into two matched groups—intervention schools and control schools. The criteria for matching and the degree to which the two groups met these criteria are contained in the discussion in chapter 3 (section called "Results of the Initial Assessment"). The flip of a coin determined which of the two groups of schools would be intervention schools throughout the four cohorts of children reported here. However, the periodic assessment of social adaptational status and psychological well-being were carried out in all twelve schools for all four cohorts.

Conceptually, it would have been inconsistent with the system view of mental health described earlier (or with the results of studies completed later) to treat the maladapting child as if the problem resided solely in him. It became apparent that the intervention program would have to address those key social factors which influence a child's adaptation to school—the teacher, peer group, family, and school administration, as well as the interrelationships among them. Our theoretical development suggested that the intervention program should place primary focus on the classroom and the social adaptational process that goes on there. Accordingly, the intervention design provided for implementation of the program in the child's classroom—a major social field at this stage of life—and for this to be supplemented by group consultation with school staff as a way of working more directly with the key school personnel involved with first-graders. The ultimate expectation was that the administration of the program would be carried out by the teacher and other school personnel (Schiff and Kellam 1967). We thought that this kind of intervention would not only keep the child in focus but would also involve other people in the social field of the classroom who could influence both the social adaptational process and the child's psychological well-being.

Our goal then was twofold: to strengthen the child by improving his social adaptational status in the classroom as well as his psychological well-being, and to enhance the relevant aspects of the classroom, the school, and the family so that each would more effectively support the adaptational process in first-graders through a variety of group and interpersonal processes. Improving social adaptational status was not construed to mean merely conforming to the existing view of the teacher, the parents, or others involved in the subsystem of the classroom; it was taken to mean also paying equal attention to the possibility that the view of the natural raters affecting the social field of the classroom might be skewed. For instance, the teacher could need to alter the *perspective* from which the child's performance in the classroom is viewed rather than seeking to have the child alter his school performance. Other issues, such as the relationship between mother and teacher, faculty interrelationships, and administration-faculty relationships, were also of concern in planning the intervention stategy.

Three first-level community-wide procedures were defined for the intervention program in the 1964–65 school year. They were economical enough, in terms of money and manpower, to be initiated in all of the first-grade classrooms in the six intervention schools, and yet they allowed us to reach all children—particularly those rated maladapting —as well as the significant other people in the classroom subsystem. The three procedures were: (1) consultation by a mental health professional[12] from the Woodlawn Mental Health Center, including weekly staff meetings with first-grade teachers and school administrators in each intervention school; (2) weekly meetings in the classroom involving the children, the teacher, and a mental health worker from the center; (3) introductory meetings to inform parents about the program, obtain their sanction, and elicit their active support.

All intervention procedures were reviewed for modification at the end of each program year on the basis of the results of evaluation and clinical experience. For example, in the first year of the program (1964–65), only the most maladapted children were involved in the classroom meetings; subsequently, these meetings were expanded to include all the children in each intervention classroom. Finally, these meetings included the children's parents as well. In addition, there were occasions when parents from a particular classroom met with the teacher, the mental health professional, and one or more members of the board. Their purpose was to strengthen the functioning of the classroom by discussing parental roles, parent-teacher relations, and the psychological aspects of the child's adapting to the student role as these are experienced by the individual child, parents, and teachers.

In all four years reported here, the intervention program was carried out in the second semester of first grade only. The number of weekly classroom meetings varied from year to year, from a low of about eleven in the first year to a high of seventeen or eighteen meetings lasting approximately half an hour. In the first year, when the meetings included only moderately or severely maladapting children, the focus was the children's discussion of how they were doing—what their feelings were about themselves, about each other, about school, and about performing the tasks they faced in the classroom.

In the first year, the weekly classroom meetings were led by the psychiatrist assigned to each school. Both teacher and psychiatrist sat facing a small group of ten to twelve first-grade children sitting in a semicircle at the front of the classroom. This group included children who had been rated by the teacher on TOCA as moderately or severely maladapted. The arrangement was familiar, since the teacher set up small groups in this way for other purposes, such as reading sessions.

The rest of the children sat in their seats doing other kinds of work—copying stories from the blackboard or doing arithmetic; this was also in keeping with usual classroom procedure.

Meetings would usually open with the psychiatrist asking the children how things had gone during the last week. Often there was silence for some moments, and then one of the children would say "fine" and be joined by a chorus of other children in the small group. The psychiatrist would sit quietly by the teacher, waiting for the children to make another comment. Sometimes one of the children would say something like "Joey hits me." After a pause the psychiatrist would ask the child, "How do you feel about that?" The child might answer that he felt bad and, following another pause, the psychiatrist would ask the other children in the group what they thought. The meetings were half an hour long; after two or three meetings in which the psychiatrist focused on the children's feelings and the pauses were long, the children would begin to bring up one or another issue more freely. By the third or fourth meeting, when the group began to talk about problems and feelings, the children began to express ideas—such as the fact that Joey was not the only one who hit other children, and that they were worried that they would be hit. The psychiatrist would then focus on why such things were happening and what they could do about the problem—with Joey participating in the conversation.

During that first year, the children in the small groups appeared to engage with each other and with the psychiatrist and teacher haltingly. In those groups where the evaluation went reasonably well, discussions started to focus on talking about a range of problems. The children expressed fears and worries about having to grow up and face first grade and school, having to leave their mothers and their homes and familiar toys, and having to come to school. It was difficult to move to the point of discussing how growth or change could come about. Occasionally, a student who was not part of the small group would raise his hand and say something in response to an issue being discussed in the group meeting. This happened often enough to raise the possibility that the children in the rest of the class could provide important strength in the group to discuss issues of growing up and doing the tasks confronting first-graders—to examine the tasks with the teacher and feel free to ask why the tasks were expected.

During these discussions the teachers often sat as if they were merely observers—sometimes looking doubtful and interjecting comments which seemed to be directed at closing off the questions about feelings that the psychiatrist was raising with the children. Many teachers gradually became interested in the group process, while some remained distrustful or anxious over the nature of these interactions. Those who became interested seemed to evolve gradually in their understanding of the process, but others continued to feel dissatisfied about the children's performance. On the other hand, there appeared to be increasing interest in the quality of the communication between the teacher and the children, with many teachers becoming very conscious of the nature of their relationships with the students. Evidence of a new consciousness among the teachers ranged from a concern with the social tasks required of the children to a concern with how much that group was solving learning problems in the classroom as well as behavioral difficulties.

Thus the first year provided an initial experience in developing group process among the maladaptive children in the first-grade classrooms of the intervention schools. There were difficulties in initiating conversation, and often when the conversation did begin to flow, it would plateau at the point at which the children were expressing problems. It was very difficult to move on to problem-solving and talking about growing up. There were even times when the children displayed a kind of obstinacy by siding with each other to confront the teacher and psychiatrist with their unwillingness or inability to overcome the fears and sadness they felt about growing up. We recognized this phenomenon informally among ourselves and called it the Peter Pan phenomenon.

The evaluation of the first year of the program, made at the end of the school year, revealed not only that there was a lack of apparent progress but that SAS seemed to have worsened and there was no change in psychological well-being. These results are detailed later below. Actually, there was some progress; in third grade, we found that intervention children showed improvement in IQ performance, but we had no way of knowing about this impact at the end of first grade. In any case, our clinical impression of the small group was that it was too homogeneous, because it was composed entirely of children whose teachers viewed them as having difficulties with the social tasks of the classroom. We decided that, in the second year, all first-grade students in intervention schools would participate in the classroom meetings so that the strength of children who were succeeding in school could be added to the group process. We felt that this modification would help move the group process toward problem-solving and the various factors in growing up rather than merely defining problems and feelings. To some extent, the group process changed in the predicted direction; the kind and degree of benefit were revealed by the evaluation at the end of the program's second year and in the third-grade follow-up.

In the second year, a typical meeting—when it went well—consisted of the psychiatrist asking the children how things had gone during the last week, just as he had done the first year. The children, after a pause, would say, "fine." Before long one of the children would bring up something that had happened. On one occasion it was that Susie had misbehaved when the teacher left the room, with the added comment, "she almost always does." The psychiatrist focused the group discussion on whether Susie really "always" misbehaved during the teacher's absence, whether it was just Susie, whether it was really a problem, and if so, why did it happen, and what did people feel about it. Susie was a new child in the class who had transferred from another school. The other children thought that she did not know how to act in first grade.

After talking about the problem for some time, one of the children raised the possibility that Susie did not know anyone yet. Others joined in the discussion, and expressed ideas such as maybe Susie felt lonely and scared when the teacher left. This kind of group process occurred frequently with respect to a new child in the classroom. One child suggested that maybe Susie should go back to kindergarten. The psychiatrist commented that Susie was a classmate and "all of us should try to figure it out, including Susie." Another child suggested that the teacher send a note home asking Susie's mother to spank her. These seemed to be efforts to test the teacher and the psychiatrist to see if such solutions were the kind the teacher and psychiatrist wanted. Then a child said, "Maybe we should tell her our names." Spontaneously, at this point the children went to Susie one by one and told her their names. Susie smiled all the while, for the first time that anybody could remember.

Not all meetings in the second year were so expressive of feelings or so warm and recognizing of the class "groupness" as this. Sometimes, silence would last for what seemed many minutes. On occasion, the teacher would become anxious and suggest her solution to the problem under discussion, as if to guard her role as the person in control. At times, teachers still seemed to become anxious over the unfamiliarity of this kind of open-ended interaction. Frequently, teachers had to be encouraged to ask questions regarding how the children felt and then encouraged more to mean it once they had asked. There was a tendency to ask questions in a rhetorical fashion rather than being open to the expression of feelings.

By the end of the first year, in most schools the staff meetings between faculty, school administrators, and mental health professionals had evolved from a primary concern with questioning the mental health professional to test his knowledge and/or commitment to a greater focus on a mutual concern about the program's development. The active support of the district superintendent and the principals of parochial schools was an important contribution toward resolving, at least temporarily, the major problems of trust over the course of the first year and into the second. In one of the schools this evolution of trust did not occur, and that school continued to have problems between staff and the mental health professionals throughout the course of the program; this school was also one of the most economically depressed schools in Woodlawn and had less than 30 percent of its first-graders rated as adapting. The teachers and administrative staff seemed overwhelmed by the feeling that little could be done to help the students improve at their school tasks. The impact of the program in this school was less strong than in the other five intervention schools.

Although there were occasional parent meetings the second year, there was not a concerted effort to involve the parents actively in the intervention process. With the end of the second year, many of the board members and the center staff professionals, as well as some school staff members, felt that family involvement should be much more intense than it had been in the first two years. Thus, in the third year, parents were invited to attend the weekly classroom meetings. From none to eight or nine parents, mostly mothers, would be present at any particular weekly classroom meeting. These meetings were quite similar to those of the second year except that the mental health professionals encouraged parents to participate in the discussion. However, the focus continued to be mainly on getting the children to express their feelings, define problems, and contribute to the solutions.

Parents often became concerned about the conversation, particularly mothers who were raising their children without other adults in the household. They sometimes expressed grief over the need to support their children who would grow up and, eventually, leave home. Some felt that supporting the growing-up process in their children was a difficult task which for them involved a sense of personal loss as the child grew older and needed them less. They revealed intense feelings of sadness and a longing for their children to remain young.

In addition, teachers and parents frequently were anxious over the prospect of becoming more involved with each other. Some parents were very suspicious about the teacher's motives and her interest in relating to parents in a more meaningful way; and although many teachers from the very beginning expressed the view that the program would not work without parent participation, when this prospect became a reality teachers often felt very insecure about inviting parents into the classroom to take part in what went on there. The plan to invite parents into the classroom, strongly supported by the Woodlawn Mental Health Center Board, also required the active urging of school officials. The anxiety that school administrators, faculty, and parents experienced when faced with the eventuality of so close a relationship between them cannot be emphasized enough. Over the course of the third year some of this anxiety gradually abated. In fact, one of the unmeasured consequences of the program appeared to be the breaking down of the barriers between school and family with regard to collaborating in such efforts as the weekly classroom meetings.

During the second and third years, classroom meetings included all children in each first-grade intervention school classroom. In the third year, these meetings included parents as well. These modifications appeared to be effective in producing more conversation among all concerned—the children, the teacher, parents, and the mental health staff. Increasingly, the discussions dealt with the expression of feelings, the involvement of more children, the raising of a wider range of concerns and problems, and heightened interest in solving problems. The children who were less severely maladapted talked more freely about their feelings and encouraged more maladapted children to talk more freely. The children talked about their feelings about having to grow up and face first grade and about a variety of other feelings concerning involvement with the other children in the classroom.

When the children would raise a problem—for example, that one child was not able to write properly—the discussion would center on why it had been raised, how everyone felt about it, whether only one child had the problem, and why such a problem could occur. The question would then arise of what to do about it. On more than one occasion children in the classroom would suggest that the child involved sit closer to the teacher because "maybe she is lonely." The teachers, parents, and the mental health staff were often impressed with the sensitivity the children demonstrated at such times.

The focus on feelings appeared to be a new experience for the teacher, parents, and the children; in contrast, the psychiatrist was more familiar with this frame of reference than he was with curriculum material. The important matter for the psychiatrist was to realize that the curriculum was vitally important even though one could want to change it in some ways. For the teacher, there was an equally important problem; she had to learn to deal with the expression of feelings as a new frame of reference within the context of the classroom. Both these problems were an expected part of the entry process, given the fact that each professional tended to view the situation from his or her own vantage point.

Frequently the teachers asked the mental health professionals whether they really understood the problem of educating a classroom of children. Gradually, however, teachers became more adept at fostering group process in all kinds of discussion of problems, even those related to learning didactic material.

The fourth year was characterized by deliberate afforts to broaden the roles of the school administration and the classroom teacher in the administration of the program. The mental health professional began to attend only every second or third classroom meeting, although he was always available for consultation and support when problems arose. Over the four years reported here, many teachers developed a capacity to lead group meetings, incorporate sensitively group process in daily work with the children, and generally become much more open to the expression of feelings by the children themselves.

The critical question that this description raises is that of the impact of the program on the children's social adaptational status and their psychological well-being. The results of all four years of the program are presented in the following pages. The intervention process was directed at the social system, and while the first-grade classroom was the base for most of the operations, the process extended to the family, school staff, and community leaders as well. A major part of the program was devoted to efforts to influence the teacher's point of view so that she would be more open in her communication with the children—even collaborate with them in examining the kinds of tasks she required of them as students. A good deal of the work in this area took place during the weekly staff meetings with teachers and administrators when any issues related to supporting the child to grow, develop, and learn were discussed. In retrospect, the failure to include an examination of the educational aspects of curriculum design along with other aspects of the human needs of children, family members, and faculty was probably a major reason that there was not more impact from the intervention process, but more on this after a consideration of the results.

Results of Evaluation

Impact on
Social Adaptational Status

Assessments of social adaptation to the classroom were obtained periodically for children in both intervention and control schools, and ratings of the two groups were compared. Psychiatric symptom measures, achievement and intelligence test scores, and grades were compared across these two groups also. In 1964 (Cohort I), TOCA assessments were made at about the ninth week of first grade and again at the end of the year. Based on the results from Cohort I, we felt the need for an additional assessment prior to intervention. Cohorts II, III, and IV were therefore assessed additionally at mid-first grade.

Beginning with the second year, the first semester of first grade was utilized as an additional period of time for research control. Not only could we compare the ratings of children who were in the intervention program to those of children who were not; we could also compare first-semester ratings of intervention schoolchildren to those of control schoolchildren before the program was begun, *or* to the ratings of the same intervention schoolchildren after their involvement in the program. The results of the first year's evaluation had established the importance of this additional control. At the end of the first year, TOCA assessments revealed that children in intervention schools were rated less adapted than were control schoolchildren—in spite of the fact that the two groups began the year well matched on TOCA.

TOCA: The results of comparing TOCA assessments for all four cohorts early in first grade to those made at midyear, and midyear assessments to those made at the end of first grade, are shown in table 39. The results of the long-term follow-up assessments made at the end of third grade are presented in table 40.

When Cohort I early ratings were compared to those made at the end of first grade, intervention schoolchildren appeared to lose ground in relation to control schoolchildren on all TOCA scales except social contact. However, long-term follow-up of those children who were still in Woodlawn in the third grade revealed no difference in the ratings of children who had been in intervention schools and those who had attended control schools. In addition, while there was a significant drop in the IQ scores of both groups by third grade, the scores of intervention schoolchildren did not decline as much as those of control schoolchildren. (See figure 5.) For those who remained in Woodlawn schools, the seemingly adverse effect of intervention disappeared and, in fact, some benefit to IQ was apparent.

The first measured impact of the program at the end of first grade appeared to be a shift in the intervention teachers' assessments toward

TABLE 39. SHORT-TERM IMPACT OF INTERVENTION ON TOCA

Cohort and TOCA Scales	p values		N	
	Pre-intervention	Intervention Period	Intervention	Control
Cohort I				
Social contact		ns		
Authority acceptance	No midyear	.01†		
Maturation	TOCA done	ns	898	777
Cognitive achievement	for Cohort I	.05†		
Concentration		.02†		
Global		.04†		
Cohort II				
Social contact	ns	ns		
Authority acceptance	ns	.01		
Maturation	ns	.01	912	738
Cognitive achievement	ns	.01		
Concentration	ns	.01		
Global	ns	.01		
Cohort III				
Social contact	ns	.01		
Authority acceptance	ns	.04		
Maturation	ns	.01	865	620
Cognitive achievement	ns	.08		
Concentration	ns	.01		
Global	ns	.01		
Cohort IV				
Social contact	.01†	.02		
Authority acceptance	ns	.01		
Maturation	.01†	.01	746	619
Cognitive achievement	ns	.01		
Concentration	ns	ns		
Global	ns	.01		

Note: Populations consisted of children in intervention schools from middle to end of first grade and those in control schools for the same period who had TOCA ratings at early, middle, and end of first grade. There were no midyear ratings for Cohort I, so comparisons were done on early to end-of-first-grade ratings.

The p values were based on t-tests comparing change in the TOCA ratings of intervention schoolchildren to change in those of control schoolchildren for the period indicated. Unless otherwise indicated (†), intervention schoolchildren did better than their counterparts in control schools.

ns indicates not significant at the 0.10 level of probability.

† indicates that control schoolchildren did better than intervention schoolchildren.

TABLE 40. LONG-TERM IMPACT OF INTERVENTION ON TOCA

Cohort and TOCA Scales	Pre-intervention	Intervention Period	Post-intervention	Intervention (N)	Control (N)
Cohort I					
Social contact		ns	ns		
Authority acceptance		.03†	ns		
	No midyear				
Maturation	TOCA was	.06†	ns	528	466
Cognitive achievement	done for	ns	ns		
Concentration	Cohort I	.04†	ns		
Global		.05†	ns		
Cohort II					
Social contact	ns	ns	.01		
Authority acceptance	ns	.01	.06		
Maturation	ns	.01	.01	515	422
Cognitive achievement	.04	ns	.01		
Concentration	ns	.01	.01		
Global	ns	.01	.01		
Cohort III					
Social contact	ns	.06	ns		
Authority acceptance	ns	ns	ns		
Maturation	ns	.02	ns	469	359
Cognitive achievement	ns	ns	ns		
Concentration	ns	.01	ns		
Global	ns	.01	ns		
Cohort IV					
Social contact	.01†	.02	.01		
Authority acceptance	ns	.01	ns		
Maturation	ns	.01	.03	306	324
Cognitive achievement	ns	ns	.01		
Concentration	ns	ns	ns		
Global	ns	ns	.04		

Note: Populations consisted of children in intervention schools from middle of first grade to the end of third grade and those in control schools for the same period who had TOCA ratings at early, middle, and end of first grade and at the end of third grade. There were no midyear ratings for Cohort I, so comparisons were done on early minus end-of-first-grade and early minus end-of-third-grade ratings.

The p values were based on t tests comparing change in the TOCA ratings of intervention children to change in those of control children for the period indicated. Unless noted otherwise (†), intervention schoolchildren did better than their counterparts in control schools.

ns indicates not significant at the 0.10 level of probability.

† indicates that control children did better than intervention children.

harsher ratings than those made previously by teachers in either intervention or control schools. This hypothesis is supported further by the fact that in each cohort after the first, intervention schoolteachers

rated incoming first-graders more harshly early in the year than did
control schoolteachers. Cowen and his colleagues (1963) also describe
this phenomenon in a school intervention program which they implemented.

The early to mid-first-grade TOCA comparisons (the period during
which there was no intervention) indicated very little movement in
Cohorts II, III, and IV when change in intervention schoolchildren was
compared to that in control schoolchildren. The only exception was in
Cohort IV, where on two scales there was significantly greater improvement in control schools than in intervention schools. The mid-to-end
period of first grade, the time during which intervention occurred in the
six designated schools, revealed quite a different picture. Each year
after the first, intervention schools showed significant benefit over and
above control schools on almost all scales. Tables 39 and 40 include
only the early-to-end comparisons for Cohort I in the first column,
because there were no midyear ratings for this population. Table 39
results are based on the comparisons of change scores which were
calculated by subtracting midyear ratings from early ratings and
end-of-year ratings from midyear ratings. Appendix F presents a
comparison of results derived from other possible statistical methods.

Long-term TOCA results were based on the ratings of children who
had been in either intervention or control schools during the second
semester of first grade, and who were in any of the twelve Woodlawn
schools in third grade. The number of children in each cohort who were
still in Woodlawn for third-grade follow-up was somewhat over 50
percent of the original population. Thus these results are restricted to
the less mobile Woodlawn children. This smaller population generally
showed no significant differences between the ratings of intervention
schoolchildren and control schoolchildren during the intervention-free
first semester. The results of middle to end-of-first-grade comparisons
are included also, since these data could have been different for this
subpopulation than for the larger population.

Whereas the intervention program appeared to produce measurable
short-term impact consistently from middle to end-first-grade, the
third-grade follow-ups revealed impact also, but somewhat less consistently. Cohort I showed no long-term impact of intervention on TOCA;
Cohort II demonstrated long-term impact on all scales. Cohort III
showed no long-term impact on any of the scales. Cohort IV showed
impact on four of the six scales, including the TOCA global scale.

One way to get an idea of the magnitude of these changes is to
examine the change over the course of these studies in the percentages

of children rated adapting (zero) or moderately plus severely maladapting (2 plus 3) in intervention schools as compared to control schools. Tables 41 and 42 contain such data on the TOCA global scale for all four cohorts. A glance at these percentages reveals that, except for

TABLE 41. SHORT-TERM CHANGE IN TOCA GLOBAL RATINGS WITH AND WITHOUT INTERVENTION

| | End-First-Grade minus Mid-First-Grade | | | | | |
| | Change in Percentage of 0s | | Change in Percentage of 2 + 3s | | N | |
Cohort	Intervention	Control	Intervention	Control	Intervention	Control
I	-7.1	-7.1	4.4	0.5	898	777
II	6.4	2.4	-3.6	5.5	912	738
III	9.0	1.1	-8.2	1.1	865	620
IV	4.3	0.5	-5.0	1.3	746	619

Note: In each cohort the population consisted of children in intervention schools from middle to end of first grade and those in control schools for the same period who had TOCA ratings at early, middle, and end of first grade. There were no mid-year ratings for Cohort I, so comparisons were done on early minus end-first-grade ratings.

TABLE 42. LONG-TERM CHANGE IN TOCA GLOBAL RATINGS WITH AND WITHOUT INTERVENTION

| | End-Third-Grade minus Mid-First-Grade | | | | | |
| | Change in Percentage of 0s | | Change in Percentage of 2 + 3s | | N | |
Cohort	Intervention	Control	Intervention	Control	Intervention	Control
I	-8.2	-7.7	3.0	0.4	528	466
II	4.8	-10.2	4.3	17.8	515	422
III	-2.8	-5.0	-1.0	0.3	469	359
IV	-2.0	-3.2	0.6	4.3	306	324

Note: In each cohort the population consisted of children in intervention schools from middle of first grade to end of third grade and those in control schools for the same period who had TOCA ratings at early, middle, and end of first grade and end of third grade. There were no midyear ratings for Cohort I, so comparisons were done on early minus end-of-third-grade ratings.

Cohort I, there was either more gain or less loss on the part of intervention children rated adapting compared to control children. As for the children rated 2 or 3, in all cases except one there was either greater benefit or less loss among the intervention children (see note 1).

These data are, of course, the result of assessments by teachers who, in the case of first-grade teachers in intervention schools, were also participants in the intervention program. It is reasonable to suppose that these teachers had strong biases about the program, pro or con. The first measured change due to intervention (Cohort I) appears to have been a shift on the part of the intervention schoolteachers toward a harsher base line once the program was under way in the second half of the year. It is possible that the apparent benefit from the program found among intervention schoolchildren in subsequent cohorts could have been merely a shift by these same teachers back to a less harsh base line more similar to that established with the early ratings for Cohort I.

While the third-grade ratings show benefit and therefore tend to argue against this hypothesis, the possibility that the third-grade teachers were merely undoing the raised expectations of the first-grade intervention schoolteachers is a real one; therefore other measures of benefit are required. Intelligence and achievement test performance scores are less broad, but these measures are more independent in terms of biases created by the teachers' involvement in the intervention program. We judged that these quasi-social adaptational measures could be reasonably expected to reflect benefit from the program. Consequently, while the importance of the teachers as natural raters supports the theoretical importance of TOCA ratings, we also employed these additional social adaptational status measures of the program's effectiveness.

Intelligence tests. The Kuhlmann-Anderson Group Intelligence Test, 6th edition, was administered by the Chicago public schools in first grade,[13] and the test was given prior to the start of the intervention program. A third-grade version of this test was given in the second semester of third grade. First-grade scores were subtracted from third-grade scores, and the differences between intervention and control children were compared. Figure 6 shows the mean change in IQ for both intervention and control children still in Woodlawn schools in third grade. It indicates the differences in the amount of change between the two groups. For Cohorts I and II, there was less deterioration in IQ for children in intervention schools. In Cohort III there was a slight gain in the IQ scores of intervention children, while the IQ scores of control schoolchildren continued to deteriorate, although less so than in previous years.

In order to eliminate bias on the part of the school board testers, third-grade Kuhlmann-Anderson IQ tests and Metropolitan Achievement Tests were administered by a group of outside testers hired by the center to a random sample of twenty children in each of the forty-four

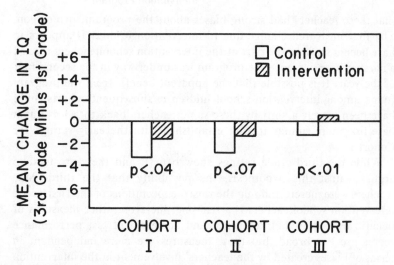

Figure 6. Mean Change in IQ from First to Third Grade (Intervention vs. Control). These populations consisted of children in control or intervention schools from the middle to the end of first grade (early to end for Cohort I) and who had first-grade and third-grade IQ scores, first-grade Metropolitan Readiness scores and third-grade Metropolitan Reading Achievement scores. Change in IQ scores from first grade to third grade were compared for control vs. intervention groups by t-tests.

The p values below the bars indicate level of significance.

Control population, Cohort I: N=318	Intervention population, Cohort I: N=259
Cohort II: N=334	Cohort II: N=310
Cohort III: N=203	Cohort III: N=255

third-grade classrooms of Cohort III. These results were consistent with those of the public school testers. See Appendix G for a description and results of these studies.

The benefit from intervention resulted sometimes from the fact that children in the program actually performed better on the tests than did control schoolchildren; at other times the apparent benefit resulted from *less deterioration* in IQ performance among intervention schoolchildren. In Cohort III, for example, there was a significant tendency for control children to perform less well on their IQ tests, while the intervention schoolchildren actually showed a gain.

Achievement tests. The public schools administered the Metropolitan Readiness Test early in first grade and the Metropolitan Achievement Test in third grade. We collected only the reading scores for use here, but we administered the entire Metropolitan Achievement Test to

Cohort III third-graders, as mentioned above. Again, parochial schools were not included because of the difference in their test schedules. An analysis of covariance on the third-grade reading achievement test scores was performed using first-grade Metropolitan Readiness Test scores as covariate. Cohort I did not show any significant difference between the control and intervention groups (although intervention had a gain of less than one month over control). The results for Cohort II were the opposite; intervention schools were over a month behind. We do not have an explanation for this result, since IQ scores for intervention schools for this cohort had shown some benefit. Cohort III intervention schoolchildren showed a gain of about two months in reading achievement compared to control schoolchildren. We also performed analysis of covariance on the scores of the Metropolitan Achievement Test battery that was administered by outside testers in third grade, again using first-grade readiness scores as covariate. There was only one significant difference, and that was on the language subtest. These results are summarized in table 43. From them, we concluded that if there was any impact of intervention on achievement, the benefit was very small.

Grades. After the public school grades of excellent, good, fair and unsatisfactory were converted to numbers, we calculated the change in grades from middle to end-of-first-grade and from mid-first-grade to mid-third-grade on those subjects which were taught across the span of time. (See table 44.) These values were then compared on the basis of intervention and control for Cohorts I, II, and III. The grades of parochial schoolchildren were excluded because of their lack of comparability with subjects in which public schoolchildren were graded. The results indicate that there was short-term benefit in arithmetic in Cohorts I and II, but not in Cohort III. In all three cohorts, there was long-term impact in either reading or oral language or both—the last being consistent with the achievement test results for Cohort III. These results, while not dramatic, do reveal some impact of the intervention process on grades.

Intervention and Special Subgroups

With the exception of the first year with Cohort I, during which we focused on the moderately and severely maladapting children in each classroom, the intervention process was not specifically designed for impact on any special subgroup of children. Yet one of the questions

TABLE 43. IMPACT OF INTERVENTION ON ACHIEVEMENT TEST SCORES

Cohort	Metropolitan Achievement Test Areas	Benefit in Months	p value	N
I	Reading	0.8	ns	577
II	Reading	-1.4	0.06†	644
III	Reading	1.9	0.02	458
III	Word knowledge	0.4	ns	363
	Word discrimination	0.2	ns	363
	Reading	-0.1	ns	363
	Language total	1.5	0.04	356
	Part A, usage	0.5	ns	363
	Part B, punctuation and capitalization	1.8	0.02	356
	Arithmetic computation	-0.5	ns	363

Note: Populations included children who had both IQ scores and Metropolitan Readiness scores in first grade and who had IQ and readiness scores in third grade. In addition, these children were either in control schools or intervention schools for middle and end-of-first-grade teacher ratings. Only public schools are included, since parochial schools do not give these tests in first grade.

The scores for each of three cohorts presented in the upper portion of the tables were obtained from tests administered by the public schools. The scores for Cohort III presented in the lower portion of the tables were obtained from tests administered by independent testers hired by the Woodlawn Mental Health Center.

Benefit in months is the difference in the grade level of achievement in third grade between intervention and control children after correction for Metropolitan Readiness Test score differences in first grade by analysis of covariance.

ns indicates not significant at the 0.10 level of probability. Where significant differences existed between the scores of intervention children compared to those of control schoolchildren, actual p values are entered. The scores of intervention schoolchildren were better than those of control schoolchildren unless otherwise indicated by a †.

† indicates that control schools did better than intervention schools.

raised by the results of evaluating the intervention program is: Did the intervention process especially benefit any subgroup of children, even though this was not an expressed goal? If it did, then we have valuable information about the kinds of child mental health problems this type of modest first-level intervention may best address. In addition, we gain some sense of how the intervention process may be modified or redesigned to strengthen its impact on other kinds of mental health problems in children.

TABLE 44. IMPACT OF INTERVENTION ON GRADES

Subject	Cohort I		Cohort II		Cohort III	
	Mid minus End	Mid minus Long-Term	Mid minus End	Mid minus Long-Term	Mid minus End	Mid minus Long-Term
Reading	ns	.09	ns	.01	ns	ns
Oral language	ns	ns	ns	.01	ns	.01
Writing	ns	ns	ns	ns	.02†	ns
Arithmetic	.08	ns	.06	ns	ns	ns
Intervention N	628	232	730	363	666	296
Control N	623	321	593	330	576	286
Total N	1251	644	1323	693	1242	582

Note: The p values are based on t tests comparing change in grade means for intervention schoolchildren versus control schoolchildren. Populations had received all four grades at middle and end of first grade and in third grade. These children were in either intervention schools or control schools for middle and end-of-first-grade teacher ratings except for Cohort I, where the requirement was early to end of first grade. Parochial schoolchildren were excluded because they were not graded on the same subjects.
ns indicates not significant at the 0.10 level of probability.
† indicates control schoolchildren did better than intervention schoolchildren.

Favorable/Less Favorable
Characteristics and Impact of
Intervention on TOCA and IQ

On the basis of available data, there were several ways of approaching an examination of the impact of intervention on TOCA and IQ. One was to divide the population according to the favorable/less favorable characteristics discussed earlier to see whether intervention differentially helped children who were boys or girls, who had been to kindergarten or had not, who were repeaters or were not, and so on. We examined change in TOCA ratings from middle to end-of-first-grade and from mid-first-grade to end-of-third grade, and IQ change from first to third grade. We then conducted analyses of variance on these measures, using favorable versus less favorable and control versus intervention as two classifications. Next, significant interactions were examined to see if either the favorable or less favorable group of children benefited more from intervention. Figure 7 summarizes these results.

In terms of short-term impact on TOCA, sex was found to be an important characteristic. Boys received relatively more benefit from intervention than girls on the authority acceptance, maturation, and concentration scales. The reader may recall that earlier, intervention

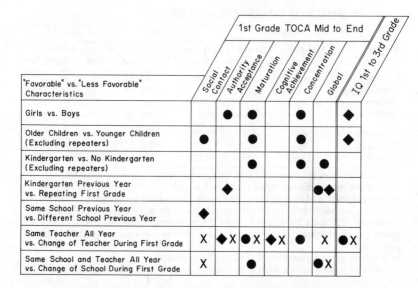

"Favorable" vs. "Less Favorable" Characteristics	Social Contact	Authority Acceptance	Maturation	Cognitive Achievement	Concentration	Global	IQ 1st to 3rd Grade
Girls vs. Boys		●	●	●			◆
Older Children vs. Younger Children (Excluding repeaters)	●		●		●		◆
Kindergarten vs. No Kindergarten (Excluding repeaters)			●		●	●	
Kindergarten Previous Year vs. Repeating First Grade		◆				●◆	
Same School Previous Year vs. Different School Previous Year	◆						
Same Teacher All Year vs. Change of Teacher During First Grade	X	◆X	●X	◆X	●	X	●X
Same School and Teacher All Year vs. Change of School During First Grade	X		●			●X	

Figure 7. Influence of "Favorable" or "Less Favorable" Characteristics on Benefit from Intervention. These interactions between intervention versus control and favorable versus less favorable characteristics were investigated only in those cases where intervention showed significant benefit (see table 40 and figure 6). The TOCA results are based on all four cohorts and the IQ results are based on Cohorts I, II and III.

Three symbols indicate significant interactions in analysis of variance with one or more cohorts:

● Indicates that in one or more cohorts children in intervention schools with less favorable characteristics showed maximum benefit

◆ Indicates that in one or more cohorts children in intervention schools with favorable characteristics showed maximum benefit

X Indicates that in one or more cohorts children in control schools with either favorable or less favorable characteristics showed maximum benefit

boys were shown to have a disadvantage compared to girls on these three TOCA scales as well as two others. Younger children received more benefit from intervention than older children on the social contact, maturation, and concentration scales. Younger children were shown earlier to have a disadvantage compared to older children on the first two of these scales. When we looked at children who had not had kindergarten and those who had, children who had not appeared to benefit more on the maturation, concentration, and TOCA global scales, and the maturation and global scales were among those on which these children had shown disadvantage earlier. Clearly, comparison of the sex, age, and kindergarten characteristics suggests that intervention provided support where it was needed—benefiting the children with disadvantages by moving their SAS toward greater similarity to the SAS of the other children. The remaining characteristics present a different picture. On the social contact scale, intervention benefited children who had been in the same school the previous year more than it did children who had been in a different school prior to first grade. In other words, here intervention helped children who were already advantaged. It did not make new children feel more at home in the new setting; they continued to be more shy than their classmates who had remained in the same school for first grade.

The results for the other characteristics were difficult to interpret. At times one group would benefit more, at other times less. Sometimes control children in one of the groups fared better than intervention children. By third grade all but one of the instances of differential impact of intervention on TOCA had disappeared: intervention children who had had kindergarten continued to benefit more than children who had not had kindergarten. When IQ was examined in relation to the favorable/less favorable variables, a mixed picture resulted. Girls and older children (more favorable) were benefited more; other comparisons showed either no differences in who benefited, or mixed results in one instance.

Severity of TOCA Ratings and
Impact of Intervention on TOCA

Another way of dividing the population for examination of the differential impact of intervention on subgroups is by the severity of the TOCA ratings. In order to determine whether the intervention process helped children whose TOCA ratings were at one level of severity more than children at another level, we compared end-of-year TOCA ratings for control and intervention children on the basis of global ratings at mid-first-grade. These results are contained in table 45 for both short-term and long-term impact for those cohorts and scales where intervention had a favorable impact on TOCA, as reported in tables 39 and 40.

In Cohort I, where intervention had an apparent unfavorable impact, we found no special pattern. In Cohorts II, III, and IV, where intervention had shown a favorable short-term impact, there was relatively more benefit among children rated mildly or moderately maladapting on TOCA. We concluded that this particular kind of intervention offered no greater immunity against later maladaptation to adapting children in the intervention group than to those in the

TABLE 45. IMPACT OF INTERVENTION ON VARIOUS LEVELS OF SEVERITY OF TOCA RATINGS

TOCA SCALES	Cohort	Significance of impact by end of first grade TOCA rating on Global Scale at mid-first grade§				Significance of impact by end of third grade TOCA rating on Global Scale at mid-first grade§			
		0	1	2	3	0	1	2	3
Social contact	I								
	II					.06	.09	ns	ns
	III	ns	.05†	ns	ns				
	IV	ns	ns	ns	ns	ns	ns	ns	ns
Authority acceptance	I								
	II	ns	.01	ns	ns	ns	ns	ns	ns
	III	ns	ns	.01	ns				
	IV	ns	.06	.03	ns				
Maturation	I								
	II	ns	.01	ns	ns	ns	.10	ns	ns
	III	.08	.01	.01	ns				
	IV	ns	ns	ns	ns	ns	ns	ns	ns
Cognitive achievement	I								
	II	ns	.01	ns	ns	ns	ns	ns	ns
	III	ns	.04	ns	ns				
	IV	ns	ns	ns	.06†	ns	ns	ns	ns
Concentration	I								
	II	ns	.01	ns	ns	ns	.01	ns	.09
	III	ns	.02	.01	ns				
	IV								
Global	I								
	II	.07†	.01	ns	ns	ns	.01	.07	ns
	III	.04	.05	.09	.05				
	IV	ns	ns	.02	ns	ns	ns	ns	.04

Note: The numbers above are probability levels representing significant differences between control and intervention children on TOCA ratings. The table is based on only those scales and cohorts where intervention had a favorable impact compared to control.
ns indicates that the results were not significant at the 0.10 level.
† control group children did better than intervention children.
§ there was no middle-of-first-grade rating for Cohort I; so the early TOCA rating was used.

control group. In addition, severely maladapting children were not especially helped by this intervention process. We can conjecture that some of these children would have received more benefit from a second-level intervention, where greater specialization of service would be available for more acute problems.

Favorable long-term impact of intervention on TOCA resulted only in Cohort II and Cohort IV. In Cohort II, when middle-first-grade global ratings were followed up in third grade, we found that intervention helped the mildly maladapting children more than any other group, although this finding was not replicated in Cohort IV.

Intervention and
Psychological Well-Being

Studies of the impact of intervention on psychological well-being revealed important results in two respects: first, in regard to differences in the frequencies of symptoms between intervention and control children; and second, in differences in the relationships between symptoms and SAS in intervention children compared to control children.

The DCO procedure was done with Cohort I early in first grade, at the end of first grade, and in third grade. Cohort III was assessed early and at the end of first grade. No significant differences were found to exist in the frequency of DCO symptoms between intervention and control children at any of these times. The small numbers of children rated symptomatic by the clinical raters precluded studies of changes in the relationship of specific DCO symptoms and SAS intervention children compared to control children. Studies of the global DCO scale, on which more children were rated symptomatic than on the other DCO scales, did not reveal differences in the quantity or kinds of relationships with social adaptational status measures.

Ratings on the Mothers Symptom Imventory were made for Cohort I and Cohort III. Here again, there were no differences between intervention and control children in the frequency of ratings of symptomatic. However, there were marked differences in the relationships of the thirteen MSI symptom categories to the child's SAS in the classroom as measured by TOCA. There were many more associations between these two dimensions of mental health in intervention children than in control children, with the shy-aggressive children showing the biggest differences in numbers of associations. Not only were there a larger number of associations, there were more replications from one study to the next (see note 1). These results become more important when we examine the results of a similar study of HIF, which showed that the shy-aggressive children in the intervention program had stronger relationships between feelings of sadness and social maladaptation than did control children. The HIF data for intervention and control children in table 46 indicate these relationships.

How I Feel was administered to Cohort III and Cohort IV in third

TABLE 46. PERCENTS OF CHILDREN SYMPTOMATIC ON HIF CONTROL
VS. INTERVENTION

| | Percent (2 + 3)† | | Significance |
	Control	Intervention	Level
Nervous			
Cohort III	36.4	28.7	(*)
Cohort IV	39.7	32.4	(*)
Sad			
Cohort III	26.8	26.3	ns
Cohort IV	31.8	30.7	ns

Note: Results are based on chi square tests comparing 0 + 1 vs. 2 + 3 ("not at all"
and "a little" vs. "pretty much" and "a lot") ratings on HIF Nervous and Sad, and
Control vs. Intervention.
Population consists of children in control or intervention schools during the first-
grade intervention period.
  † percent (2 + 3) is the percent of children that rated themselves "pretty much" or
  "a lot" nervous or sad on HIF.
(*) indicates chi square significant at the 0.10 level of probability.
ns indicates chi square not significant at the 0.10 level of probability.
Ns: Cohort III = 470, Cohort IV = 570.

grade; we did not have base line data for either HIF or MSI against
which to assess the frequencies of symptomatic ratings in intervention
children versus control children. With this caution in mind, we
examined frequencies on HIF in the two populations, and found that
the frequency of sadness was not different for intervention and control
children, just as the frequencies of DCO and MSI symptoms were not
different between the two groups. However, there was somewhat less
nervousness among the intervention children as compared to control
children in both Cohort III and Cohort IV. (See table 46 for these
frequencies.)

Having found stronger relationships between social adaptational
status and psychological well-being in intervention children than in
control children, we had to determine whether the intervention program was the cause. There were no base line measures of HIF or the
MSI, both of which were administered after intervention, and the
number of children rated symptomatic on DCO was too small to study
intervention and control separately. Therefore, the examination of
other base line data became very important in the effort to determine
whether the two groups were different beforehand in any way that
could provide an explanation—other than intervention—for the
stronger linkage between symptoms and social adaptational status in

intervention schoolchildren. While we could not find an alternative explanation, as the following data indicate, we cannot definitely rule out the possibility that one exists.

As indicated in table 11, control and intervention schools were matched on a number of criteria. Of course, that does not guarantee that various combinations of criteria would be similar in the two groups. We therefore examined as many other criteria as we had available data to seek out possible a priori differences between intervention and control.

In Cohort I, control and intervention were matched on early TOCA ratings. However, after the first year, intervention teachers moved to a harsher base line. In the remaining cohorts, therfore, control and intervention differed on TOCA. We will return to the implications of this for our results later.

Intervention schools were one to two points behind control schools on IQ. Readiness test scores revealed either no difference or one to two points' difference in each direction, depending on the year.

The family life characteristics of the intervention and control schoolchildren were assessed during the same home interviews in which MSI ratings were done. Control and intervention children were astonishingly similar in all the aspects of family life studied. These aspects included the affectional resources of the child and the family, including who the adults in the family were; income; physical and emotional well-being of the child and other family members; education; occupation; and value orientation about the child in regard to his or her education and in regard to such issues as civil rights and how such rights could be obtained.

In addition to the fact that family life characteristics of the intervention and control populations were almost identical, frequencies of symptoms on DCO and MSI were also strikingly similar. This leaves only two areas of difference: TOCA, which was not different early but became different after intervention; and IQ, on which intervention differed from control by a slight one or two points. The small differences in IQ or even those on TOCA do not seem to be likely explanations for the increased relationship between psychological well-being and social adaptational status found in intervention schoolchildren.

If either IQ or TOCA were the cause, we would expect intervention children to have had greater frequencies of symptoms, because lower IQ or worse adaptational status in this population was associated with a higher risk of symptoms. The difference in risk of symptoms between maladapting and adapting children was greater in the intervention schools, and there does not appear to be a viable explanation other than that intervention caused succeeding or failing at the social tasks set by the teacher to be more important to the intervention child's psychological well-being. Hypothetically, intervention may have caused adapting children to have less risk of symptoms, or maladaptive children to have more risk of symptoms, or a combination of both these effects could have occurred in intervention children. In fact, after examining the data, we concluded that all three possibilities probably occurred (see note 1).

5   An Overview

The Woodlawn program began with several explicit goals on the part of both the board and the staff. The first goal was to help Woodlawn first-graders get off to a good start in school. This was to be accomplished by means of a systems approach to intervention rather than a "child-only" approach. In concert with this goal and the theoretical formulations described at the beginning of this report, we set about developing a community-wide first-level mental health program, based in the schools, that was a product of close collaboration among community leaders, mental health staff, and school staff, and that was sanctioned by the community.

This general goal rested on a firm commitment to the idea that research and service in mental health programming should be closely related. There was thus an opportunity to put this theoretical relationship into operation in order to maximize its benefit to the recipients of service—in this case, young boys and girls beginning their elementary school careers.

We wanted also to increase our understanding of mental health by viewing it as a two-dimensional concept, testing the viability of "social adaptational status" as one dimension of mental health and investigating its link, if any, to the other dimension, that of psychological well-being. Finally, we sought to determine whether social adaptational status and psychological well-being are amenable to change using a systems approach to intervention and whether the system itself (i.e., the child-family-school-community system) is accessible to change.

All of these goals, taken together, form an intricate pattern of interrelationships that makes consideration of each of them in isolation of only limited usefulness. Most have been discussed already, directly or indirectly, earlier, and it is not the purpose of this overview to recount these discussions. We have restated these broad goals here because there are certain aspects of the project, brought to the fore by our pursuit of these goals, that warrant further explication in view of the findings. All of these aspects did not emerge at the same level of abstraction, but all seem important to address in a final overview of the project.

Stress and Social Adaptive Capacity

A major finding of the Woodlawn studies concerned the link between social adaptational status and psychological well-being in children who had experienced the intervention program. Compared to control children, the ratings of these children demonstrated a strong association between maladaption to the social tasks of the classroom and a higher risk of psychiatric symptoms.

The most likely explanation for this increased linkage between SAS and psychological well-being is that the intervention process heightened the importance of school task performance and thus increased the stress of school failure. Intervention schoolchildren who succeeded at the social tasks set for them by the teacher in the classroom showed some tendency toward a lower risk of psychiatric symptoms. It appears, then, that it was not the increased importance of classroom tasks alone that was the source of stress, but the increased importance *plus* the failure to perform these tasks satisfactorily in the eyes of the teacher.

On the basis of these results, we can hypothesize that, as individuals pass through various stages of life and enter new social fields, the risks of developing psychiatric symptoms is not simply the result of being confronted with new social tasks set by the natural rater but is more likely the result of being confronted with new tasks and then failing to perform them adequately. After failing to perform at one stage of life in the view of the natural rater, the child may at subsequent stages of life anticipate further failure and be overly fearful and cautious, thus perpetuating poor social adaptational status. The Woodlawn studies provide some evidence that, when one succeeds at the social tasks in the eyes of the natural rater, one's risk of psychiatric symptoms later on is diminished. It is important to note, however, that the increased relationship between psychological well-being and social adaptational status in intervention schoolchildren did not result in a greater number of symptomatic children in this group.

School task performance was clearly important to control schoolchildren also, or we would not have found relationships between specific symptom ratings and specific measures of SAS in this group. Intervention, however, seems to have intensified this importance, and this raises an issue that is fundamentally important to the development of mental health treatment programs at all levels of care. Is the therapist's goal to improve an individual's psychological well-being compatible with the goal that society holds for the individual (and which the individual may or may not hold for himself) to improve his social adaptational status? What are the consequences of the Woodlawn results for the design of intervention programs?

The Optimal Proximity of
Intervention

Mental health professionals often maintain the position, at least in theory, that their proper function concerns only psychological well-being—that it is up to the individual to choose what is important in his life. While such a separation may be possible on a theoretical level, our own studies have shown that these two aspects of an individual's existence are closely related. It seems improbable—if not impossible—for mental health therapists to avoid completely any concern with the social tasks confronting a client or that client's response to the demands of the social fields in which he is involved.

Psychotherapy usually must involve the client's social adaptational status, and the therapist is frequently called upon to remind the client of "reality." Perhaps reality is another name for the pressures natural raters exert upon individuals in an effort to obtain adequate performance of the social tasks required in a specific social field. One would expect this to be an especially important issue in child psychiatry, where therapists are often faced with the need to involve themselves in the child's "proper" performance in school or in the family.

What should the mental health worker's position be? Should he or she support the social task definition of the natural rater and reinforce the idea that these social tasks are important? The traditional mental health position, at least for adults, is that the choice of important areas of life should, as much as possible, be the individual's. But how much is possible—particularly for children? Should a mental health worker support a child's choice not to consider school tasks important? There are no easy, obvious answers to these questions.

The Woodlawn program did not allow us to escape this issue, as evidenced by the finding that intervention apparently increased the relationship between social adaptational status and psychological well-being. Was this result desirable or undesirable? One may answer that, for those children who succeeded at the school tasks, the intervention process was good; but for those in intervention who continued to maladapt, the process was undesirable because it increased the risk of psychiatric symptoms.

Ultimately, the answer may lie in the value system of a society whose institutions support or inhibit the life processes of all individuals. Clearly, the old medical doctrine that says the treatment should not be worse than the problem is not very helpful here, since the size and complexity of the problem this program addressed were great. For the last decade, community mental health theoreticians have urged the value of bringing intervention programs as close as possible to the individual or situation in need. Our results suggest a need for research into the question of how close intervention should be to be optimally effective and yet not create a different kind of risk—one associated with reinforcing the stressful importance of failing at the social tasks in an individual's social fields.

If there is such a thing as *optimal proximity* of intervention programming, we shall have to look for intervention techniques that do not relate the problem and the stress so intimately. In other words, we shall need to develop interventions which enhance social adaptive capacity but which do not, for some individuals at least, intensify the stress associated with the problem. The longitudinal nature of the relationship between social adaptational status and psychological well-being, which is considered next, supports the necessity for such research.

The Advantages of Longitudinal Study

The advantages that accrued to the Woodlawn first-grade program because it was longitudinal were many. As a result of following the course of social adaptational status and psychological well-being in the same children, we were able to show that the relationship between these two dimensions of mental health was not only concurrent but longitudinal; it persisted over time. Early maladaptation to school was related to later psychiatric symptoms, and early psychiatric symptoms were related to later social maladaptation.

The fact that these relationships were longitudinal as well as concurrent strengthens the hypothesis that social adaptational status and psychological well-being may each contribute to an individual's status in the other dimension. Dohrenwend and Dohrenwend comment on this advantage of longitudinal studies (1969). While a concurrent correlation between symptoms and social adaptation may be accidental, the capacity that longitudinal studies gave us to predict from Time 1 to Time 2 adds strength to a causation hypothesis. The replication of these studies over several different populations tends to add further support. We must caution, however, that the possibility of a cause-effect relation between these two variables does not rule out contributing causes from other biological, psychological, and social sources.

In previous "true prevalence" studies conducted by other investigators, the prevalences of symptoms were drawn from cross-sections of the communities studied, but there were few longitudinal studies of symptoms. Thus there was no way of determining whether symptoms persisted over time or if they were temporary. In the Woodlawn longitudinal studies, we found that clinically observed symptoms were not strongly persistent from one rating period to the next; children who had been rated symptomatic by clinicians previously did not show much of an increased risk of being symptomatic again. Coupled with the finding that early maladaptation was associated with later symptoms and early symptoms were associated with later maladaptation, this result broadened our understanding of the relationship of social adaptation and psychological well-being in a way that would not have been possible with concurrent studies only.

Issues Raised by the
Longitudinal Studies

Given the results of the longitudinal studies, one may ask why such relationships should occur between social adaptational status and psychiatric symptoms. One part of the explanation may be that failing at social tasks is stressful and induces symptoms in the child who considers it important to succeed at the tasks. On the other hand, one may conjecture that children who are symptomatic do not perform well in the view of their teachers and are thus rated maladapting.

In any attempt to explain these relationships, it is important to remember that they were relatively specific relationships; specific symptoms were related to specific social maladaptational modes. We must recall also that depression as rated by clinicians functioned differently than most other symptoms in that it was associated with better performance on many SAS measures, although it was also associated with the shy social maladaptive mode. Self-ratings of mild nervousness by the children in third grade were also associated with better performance. When one examines the longitudinal character of these results, they suggest that certain symptoms appear to be part of the cause of certain kinds of social maladaptation, while certain kinds of maladaptation appear to be part of the cause of certain kinds of symptoms; further, other kinds of symptoms seem to be associated with better adaptation. Thus there may be a possibility that the causes, as well as the long-term effects, of maladaptation and of symptoms may vary with each social maladaptive mode and with each kind of symptom.

These relationships have theoretical importance for the issue of the kinds of stress that social tasks engender in children and for a child's capacity for social adaptation over the early school years, and perhaps into adolescence and later life. We have cited results that showed that a change of school between kindergarten and first grade was associated with maladaptation, while the same children, when faced with the teacher change during first grade, exhibited an improved capacity to cope compared to children who had not experienced the prior stress of changing schools. Yet repeating first grade because of prior failure was associated with a decreased capacity for adaptation when the first-grade teacher left. In other words, the child's capacity for adaptation increased or decreased depending on the *kind* of prior stress he had experienced. Apparently, it made a difference whether the prior stress was damaging to the child's self-esteem or whether it was a "fateful event," that is, outside the control of the child.

The longitudinal studies of ratings made from first to third grade reveal that, for some children, maladapting was associated with psychiatric symptoms. How important are these relationships and what do they portend for the child's future? This question can be answered absolutely only by conducting additional follow-up studies at later stages of the children's lives. Meanwhile, if we infer that part of the cause of symptoms was the failure to perform adequately in the eyes of the teacher, we may also infer that such failure does not represent the same degree of stress for some children that it does for others. The symptoms may represent, in a sense, the degree of involvement the child has with the social tasks confronting him. From this point of view, early maladapting with symptoms may be good or bad—depending on whether the child also experiences damage to his self-esteem, thereby decreasing his capacity to adapt later on, or whether the child considers it to be a reality experience and an early warning, causing him to exert a more intense effort to perform adequately in the view of the natural rater.

Our first reaction to this question was that early failure at the social tasks had to be damaging to self-esteem for those children who showed symptoms; it is conceivable, however, that early maladapting may stimulate greater effort in some children and thus better social adaptational status later on. These alternative hypotheses can be tested by reassessing the children later in their school careers. If children who were maladapting and symptomatic early in elementary school are found to have better SAS and psychological well-being in high school, for example, than children who were maladapting early without symptoms, it will support the hypothesis that early failure can act as a forewarning for some children and strengthen their later social adaptive capacity. Should later assessment reveal children who were maladapting and symptomatic early to be worse off in terms of SAS and psychological well-being, this would support the hypothesis that early maladaptation is damaging to self-esteem in children rated symptomatic early in their school careers, thus decreasing their capacity for adaptation later on.

The different social maladaptive modes all entailed learning problems, but differed in regard to shyness and aggression. Each of them—shy, shy-aggressive, aggressive, and neither shy nor aggressive—were related to specific symptoms, and the long-term function of these relations may well differ. At the start of high school, for example, we may find that, for children in the shy maladaptive mode, the symptoms are debilitating, injuring self-esteem and resulting in poor SAS as well as a continuing risk of symptoms. On the other hand, we may find that the aggressive mode does not relate to symptoms in this way over time.

For the time being, we can only conjecture about the possible functions of the relationships between social maladaptive modes and specific symptoms, as we have done here. It is clearly important to test these alternative hypotheses, and this is possible only by longitudinal examination of symptoms and adaptation early in a child's life course and periodically thereafter. It is important to be able to predict, from a foundation of empirical evidence, the course of social adaptational status and psychological well-being in a child from a point early in his school career. The implications for treatment at all levels of care are compelling and again emphasize the benefit to be derived from longitudinal studies of this kind.

The Relationship between
Research and Service

Almost all of the discussion thus far in this chapter points up the reason for our commitment to relate research and service closely—not only in mental health but in all fields of human service. In the case of the Woodlawn studies, the intervention process was useful to the research because it helped to clarify the relationships that existed between the main concepts under study—social adaptational status and psychological well-being. On the other hand, the results of assessment and evaluation of impact indicated the directions in which the design of intervention should go and allowed us to modify intervention design on the basis of evaluation.

The relationship between assessment, evaluation, and intervention was an important part of this project from the beginning. The facts that there was a high prevalence of social maladaptation among first-grade students as rated by their teachers, and that social maladaptation was associated with symptoms, suggested that the classroom, including children, teachers, and, finally, parents, could be an appropriate setting for intervention. If there had been no relationship between social adaptation and psychological well-being, the intervention would have been less closely linked to the classroom. In the long run, the evaluation measures continued to influence our thinking in regard to the value of this specific intervention and the characteristics of alternative interventions.

Beyond the goal of evaluating whether the intervention program had been successful in reducing maladaptation or the risk of psychiatric symptoms, the research also revealed some unanticipated results of intervention. First, ratings by intervention teachers became harsher, indicating that these teachers had raised their expectations with regard to the children's performance of the classroom tasks. The research provided an opportunity to make this observation. Another important result of the close link between research and service in the Woodlawn program was the discovery of the increased relationship between social maladaptation and psychiatric symptoms in intervention school-children.

The tremendous advantages that the hand-in-hand development of research and service provide the researcher and mental health worker, and those who receive the services, are clear. What is perhaps not so clear is that the only way to derive maximum benefit from the relationship between research and service is to view them both as necessary components of an integrated system of care such as that described earlier.

The Woodlawn studies, particularly the results of evaluation of intervention and data which are not presented here concerning the family life of the children, led us to conclude that efforts to improve social adaptational status and psychological well-being will be most effective when they are part of a total human service system in which mental health interventions are but one component. First-level programming for populations such as elementary schoolchildren will need to draw upon a variety of professional disciplines and develop supports, such as financial assistance to families, remedial education for specific social maladaptive modes, and short- and long-term individual and group psychotherapeutic processes—that last involving both the more traditional interpersonal type and the newer behavioral modification. There is also a growing awareness that certain kinds of drugs may be beneficial to some children, and current research is seeking to identify such children more specifically. There are still many important questions to be answered in all of these areas of research, and, ideally, such research should be closely related to the services it is intended to improve.

Before we leave the subject of research and service, it may be of interest to discuss briefly how child mental health services in Woodlawn have changed since the program reported here. The child mental health program is now removed from the classroom to some extent. Services are based in nearby church recreation centers made available through arrangements negotiated by the Woodlawn Mental Health Center Board. While these church centers are near the schools and classrooms, they are not within the schools themselves.

Services for children now increasingly involve multi-disciplined interventions which focus on a variety of social maladaptive and/or psychological problems defined during the Woodlawn studies. There are a variety of group, crisis, and individual therapies, pharmacotherapies, home visits, and other activities, including a continuing effort to maintain close collaboration among family, teacher, and child around the social field of the classroom. Many of the changes reflected in this modification of programming were based directly on the results of the research.

**Epidemiology
and Community Studies**

The actualization of multi-disciplined approaches to services is dependent not only on the development of an integrated system of care but on a more adequate epidemiology as well. The Woodlawn studies attempted to incorporate the beginnings of such an epidemiology within the context of a framework that included social contextual variables in the counting and characterizing of the problems under study. By collecting data that would allow for social maladaptive modes to be designated and studying the risk of psychiatric symptoms attendant on each mode, we could compare a variety of kinds of treatments for relative effectiveness with specific categories of problems.

The kinds of diagnostic categories as well as the kinds of treatments tested depend to a great extent on whether the epidemiology is done at the first level in the community, at the second level with populations of patients who come to clinics and private practitioners, or at the third level with the population of patients who are in the hospital. The social maladaptive modes with their attendant symptoms are derived from first-level community-wide assessment of all first-grade children in Woodlawn. The categories of problems derived would have been different had these studies been done at the clinic or the hospital.

The diagnostic categories in child psychiatry, then, will be different for each of the levels of care, since each level involves a different base population. One can easily predict that the first level will yield categories of social maladaptive modes. At the second level, categories of problems in psychological well-being, and at the third level categories of psychoses or severe emotional disturbance, will be more prominent. All of this assumes a rational mental health system in which the problem is assessed at the first level and the individual referred to second or third levels from the first level only when the basic aspect of treatment has been determined to be the individual and that aspect to require highly specialized professional care.

Many such studies of both assessment of need as well as methods of intervention can be done in the context of first-level care in strategic social fields in a single community. Such studies would take into account the psychological, social, political, and even biological differences across various groupings of individuals within the community while holding constant important differences between the study community and other communities.

What one gives up in conducting such community studies is immediate generalizability of the results to other populations. A community study, by its nature, does not sample all of a broad population, such as lower-class blacks or Jews. Thus the results of a community study can be generalized only to similar communities, and the criteria for defining comparability are themselves a subject of study. Rutter and his colleagues (1970) discussed the relative advantages and disadvantages of local and national surveys with regard to generalizability.

They state:

Local studies ... have sometimes been criticized because they are not representative of the whole country. This is true but it is not always appreciated that the converse is also true. A national survey no more represents the Isle of Wight, London, or the Lake District than surveys in these areas represent the national scene. Planning for the country as a whole cannot be based on national figures for the very same reason—that is, that the different areas have different problems and different needs. [p. 360]

By doing studies in communities which are selected in systematically definable ways, we can determine which characteristics of the community, if any, influence the results of the studies. An example of the importance of such studies is the question of whether differences in socioeconomic or ethnic characteristics require different treatments. It is a reasonably well established fact that different treatments are offered different groups with the same diagnosis (Hollingshead and Redlich, 1958). Lerner (1972) has recently cast doubt on whether different treatments are required for different class and racial groups. We can tell whether there are other critical characteristics which transcend community characteristics, for example, social class, or whether the prevalences, relationships, and results of evaluation of effectiveness are dependent on (or interactive with) local community characteristics.

Given the importance of the social system view, characteristics of children, such as their membership in specific communities in specific classrooms, the school they attend, or the part of the neighborhood from which they come, permit consideration of the social system together with the child as available for assessment and intervention. A community-wide strategy seems indicated, at least for first-level prevention and early intervention.

If we accept the concept of first-level community-wide assessment and programming, we are immediately confronted with the question of the portion of the social system we should consider. It appeared to us that all the first-grade classrooms in a school should be involved in intervention. Classrooms are very closely related to each other in the structure of an elementary school. It would have been hard to establish adequate research control if some of the classes in a given school were control groups and others were intervention groups. Informal communication processes, modeling processes, and the competitions which inevitably arise across social units may well have confounded the two groups. In addition, it seemed to us that the school as a whole had an integrity important to consider. For these reasons we concluded that the school was the appropriate unit for intervention—even though the primary focus was to be the activities of the classroom.

Including all twelve of Woodlawn's elementary schools in our studies provided an opportunity to examine various aspects of the social system of Woodlawn first-grade families and schools. It was quite clear, for example, that no two schools could be considered representative of schools in Woodlawn generally. Not only were there socioeconomic differences; there were a variety of values and characteristics in different schools. Including all twelve schools was highly useful in providing the range of information which characterized Woodlawn as a whole.

The study of Woodlawn first-graders needs to be distinguished from two other types of studies commonly referred to as "community" studies. First, there are frequent references in the sociological literature (see Vidich, Bensman, and Stein 1964) to community studies which are concerned with the power structure, institutions, values, social hierarchy, and way of life within a particular community. While in our studies we attempted to be aware of and to take into account these aspects, we did not set out to describe or analyze the Woodlawn community in those terms. Our main interest centered on the definition, characteristics, and prevalence of social adaptation and psychological well-being, the relationship between social adaptation and psychological well-being in first-grade children, and the evaluation of the Woodlawn first-grade intervention program. Second, in psychiatric epidemiology, "community" studies often mean studies of the prevalence of mental disorder in which counts of untreated as well as treated cases are made. These have also been called "true prevalence" studies (Dohrenwend and Dohrenwend 1969). Typically, in such studies, the population in a specified geographic area is the subject of study and this is the population on which prevalence rates are obtained.

It is true that the Woodlawn study was concerned with certain aspects of the community and that it obtained prevalence rates of untreated psychiatric symptoms. It differs, however, from both types of studies described above. This study focused on the interaction between the community and the child—that is, the social adaptational process in the context of the elementary school classroom. The longitudinal character of this study and the fact that it was intimately related to an intervention program also distinguish it from the other two kinds of community studies.

The fact that this is a report of a community study raises particular questions about generalizability. The conceptual framework concerning the two dimensions of mental health, the concepts of social adaptational status and the natural rater, and the method of assessing SAS would seem to be capable of being generalized universally. We must be cautious, however, about generalizing the inferences drawn from the measurements themselves—including the prevalences of social maladaptation to the classroom and of symptoms among first-graders, the relationships between these two dimensions of mental health, and the evaluation of impact of intervention.

It is essential to note that the main purpose of this community study was not to provide results generalizable to a broad population, but rather to study the mental health of children in a particular community. In so doing we have learned not only about the children's mental health but also about various aspects of the children's social system. Very early in this report we described some of the social, economic, and political characteristics of the Woodlawn community over the last decade, with particular emphasis on the period of time during which this project was carried out (the mid-1960s). It is possible that the particular social, political, and economic forces that exist within Woodlawn and between Woodlawn and the larger city affected the results of this study.

Once there are similar studies of other communities, we can compare prevalences of maladaptation, symptoms, and their specific inter-relationships. We may then learn which community characteristics are related to these aspects of mental health. Some aspects may be uniform across communities; others may be highly specific to particular kinds of communities. This suggests that future community studies should include clear specification of the population and the community under study. The effort to classify communities should be part of research design along with the classification of independent and dependent variables relating more intimately to the subject individuals. Greater specification of the social and political processes within the community is also a potentially important part of community study.

In considering community studies in overview, we must point out again that community research and service should be closely integrated into the community. A number of approaches have been utilized in attempts to develop viable working relationships between human service agencies and the communities they serve. In Woodlawn, the ongoing involvement of the Woodlawn Mental Health Center staff with a community board made up of citizen leaders representing a variety of neighborhood groups and interests has been critical. Both the research and service functions at this first level of care have depended to a large extent on an ongoing collaboration with the community in decision-making processes involving the setting of priorities and the design and implementation of programs.

It is important that, prior to the establishment of the Woodlawn Mental Health Center, the community—through its citizen leaders—had requested a mental health facility. Thus, in a very real sense, the community has been fully participatory in establishing and maintaining its mental health services and has been in a position to see that the community's point of view, and especially its values, have been taken into account.

Appendixes

Appendixes

Appendixes

Appendixes

Appendix A

Original Pupil Code

S	S	C	X	P	P

New Pupil Code:

S	S	C	X	P	P

TEACHER OBSERVATION OF CLASSROOM ADAPTATION

Pupil's Name: _____

Teacher Code:

S	S	T	T

School: _____

Date:

M	M	D	D	Y	Y

Room No.: _____

Teacher: _____

Number of Weeks Teaching This Child

Rating Scale (0 – 3)

0 = Within minimal limits of acceptable behavior
1 = Mildly excessive
2 = Moderately excessive
3 = Severely excessive

Please rate each pupil from 0 to 3 for each of the following kinds of maladaptive behavior observed in the classroom, using the above rating scale. The examples given for each category of maladaptive behavior are merely illustrative suggestions, and should not be thought of as an exhaustive list.

1. **EXCESSIVELY LACKING IN INVOLVEMENT WITH CLASSMATES** – e.g. shy, timid, alone too much, day-dreamer, friendless, aloof . . . .

2. **EXCESSIVELY AGGRESSIVE BEHAVIOR** – e.g. fights too much, steals, lies, resists authority, is destructive to others or property, obstinate, disobedient, uncooperative . . . .

3. **EXCESSIVELY IMMATURE BEHAVIOR** – e.g. acts too young physically and/or emotionally, cries too much, has tantrums, sucks thumb, is physically poorly coordinated, masturbates, urinates in class, seeks too much attention . . . .

4. **EXCESSIVELY NOT WORKING UP TO HIS ABILITY** – e.g. does not learn as well as your assessment of his ability indicates he is able to . . . .

5. **EXCESSIVELY RESTLESS** – e.g. fidgets, is unable to sit still in classroom . . . .

- -

6. **GLOBAL RATING OF CLASSROOM ADAPTATION** – This is not a summary of the other behavior ratings but a general overall rating of the child's state of classroom behavior adaptation. However, if a child has been rated as maladapted in one of the classroom behavior categories, he should have a maladapted rating in the global category. If he has received a '0' in each of the boxes above he should have a '0' in this box . . . .

Appendix B

Schedule of Assessment and Intervention (First and Third Grade)

	COHORT I 1964-65				COHORT II 1965-66				COHORT III 1966-67				COHORT IV 1967-68			
	Early 1st	Mid 1st	End 1st	End 3rd	Early 1st	Mid 1st	End 1st	End 3rd	Early 1st	Mid 1st	End 1st	End 3rd	Early 1st	Mid 1st	End 1st	End 3rd
TOCA	●		●	●	●	●	●	●	●	●	●	●	●	●	●	●
DCO	●		●	●					●		●					
MSI			●								●					
HIF												●				●
MRT	●				●				●							
MAT				●				●				●				
IQ	●			●	●			●	●			●				
GRADES		●	●	●		●	●	●		●	●	●				
VMI, MAT, IQ (WMHC)												●				
INTER- VENTION		●——●				●——●				●——●				●——●		

Appendix C

APPENDIX C

WOODLAWN MENTAL HEALTH CENTER

DIRECT CLINICAL OBSERVATION

**PSYCHOPATHOLOGY RATING SCALES
AND
SOCIAL CONTACT MEASUREMENTS**

DEFINITION OF SOCIAL CONTACT

Social contact is defined as two or more children sitting or standing close to each other with any evidence of interchange between them, such as touching, talking, mutual play on a single project or object, hitting, etc.

HOW TO USE THE SYMPTOM SCALES

Each of the symptom scales is described inside with a series of descriptive phrases at the top and each level described with variations of the phrases below. These phrases are not to be used as scale items, without which a child cannot be rated as sick, but rather as descriptions of a level of behavior against which to judge the severity of symptoms in a given child. Some children's symptoms may not be included in the list of phrases in a given scale. The child may be rated anyway if his or her behavior is seen as of the same kind and level of sickness as the descriptive phrases of that scale and level.

FLATNESS – bland fixed expression; "zombie-like" behavior; emotional unresponsiveness; autistic; distant; "walled-off."

0 – **within minimal limits:** outer limits of this rating would be a state of slight blandness and tangential relatedness to others, or a mild "stranger-in-town" quality.

1 – **mild:** bland mostly fixed expression, some relatedness but not prolonged or intense, mostly distant.

2 – **moderate:** bland, fixed expression plus no relatedness to other children; a "zombie-like" or mechanical responsiveness to overtures from others with no initiation of socializing.

3 – **marked:** any or all of the above with facial immobility and increased "zombie-like" behavior, markedly slow movements.

4 – **severe:** any or all of the above with severely slowed movement.

5 – **extreme:** totally affectless expression, total unresponsiveness; immobile, seeming total unawareness.

DEPRESSION – sad faces; motor retardation; slumped posture; crying without external reason.

0 – **within minimal limits:** not excessively depressed, though may be somewhat sad looking, or may be generally cheerful but have a sudden transitory outburst of crying.

1 – **mild:** sad faces; some slowing; tearfulness; sad posture; some lack of interest in surroundings and other children to a degree interfering with play and relatedness to others.

2 – **moderate:** most of the above with increasing and deepening of sadness; tearfulness; increasing and deepening disinterest in play and other children.

3 – **marked:** most of the above plus marked sadness and almost total loss of interest in play or other children. Some evidence of self-mutilating behavior, such as deep scratching, digging to the point of bleeding, etc.; marked motor retardation or agitation.

4 – **severe:** most of the above plus increased intensity of sadness to a severe degree; total lack of interest in environment with severe suicidal or self-mutilating tendencies; severe motor retardation or agitation.

5 – **extreme:** extremely sad faces; continual tearfulness, weeping; extreme motor retardation or agitated behavior with extreme self-destructiveness.

ANXIETY – fearful faces; excessive startle reaction; tremulousness; tics; rocking; anxiety posture, etc.

0 – **within minimal limits:** not excessively anxious.

1 – **mild excessive anxiety:** mild evidence of any or all of the above **over the predominant part** of the session plus difficulty with more complex play or interpersonal transaction.

2 – **moderate excessive anxiety:** moderate evidence of any or all of the above plus difficulty with even less complex play and rudimentary interpersonal transactions.

3 – **marked excessive anxiety:** any or all of the above plus difficulty with almost all play and interpersonal transactions.

4 – **severe excessive anxiety:** any or all of the above plus difficulty in taking part with all play and interpersonal transaction.

5 – **extreme excessive anxiety:** any or all of the above to a degree that it characterizes and dominates all behavior; total inability to carry out purposive behavior, including all interpersonal transactions.

HYPERKINESIS — excessive motion implying difficulty in self-control of movement.

0 — **within minimal limits:** may be an active child but has, to a great extent, control over movement.

1 — **mild:** excessively in motion; difficult to contain child; running and moving predominant behavior; very limited degree of involvement in sedentary play.

2 — **moderate:** more excessive motion; greater difficulty in containing child; difficulty in sitting even for brief moments.

3 — **marked:** markedly excessive motion; impossible to contain without some physical restraint; otherwise constantly in motion.

4 — **severe:** severely excessive motion; cannot stop without great physical restraint.

5 — **extreme:** continual driven motion, without pause, permitting no purposive behavior or sustained relationship; stopped only by exhaustion and collapse or constant great physical restraint.

BIZARRE BEHAVIOR — grimacing, posturing; unusual and weird body movements, behavior and speech.

0 — **within minimal limits:** not clearly bizarre.

1 — **mildly bizarre:** intermittent weird movements, behavior or speech; may include grimacing, posturing, bizarre ideation more than transient but only to a mild degree; a subtle sense of unrelatedness.

2 — **moderately bizarre:** any or all of the above to a moderate degree with an increase in the obviousness of the unrelatedness; a moderate amount of the totality of behavior being seen as bizarre.

3 — **markedly bizarre:** any or all of the above to a marked degree, most of the behavior been seen as bizarre; obvious unrelatedness with possible evidence of hallucination and delusion.

4 — **severely bizarre:** obviously unrelated with any or all of the above items of bizarreness with only islands of behavior seeming appropriate.

5 — **extremely bizarre:** totally inappropriate speech and behavior; totally unrelated to others; any or all variety of bizarre behavior may be present.

GLOBAL — This is a rating of how sick the child is. A global rating other than zero has to have been preceded by a rating other than zero on one or more of the symptom scales. The level of the global rating can be higher or lower than the rating on the symptom scale. If the rating in one or more of the symptom scales is more than 0, the rating on the global scale must be more than 0.

0 — **within minimal limits** — not clearly sick.

1 — **mildly sick**

2 — **moderately sick**

3 — **markedly sick**

4 — **severely sick**

5 — **extremely sick**

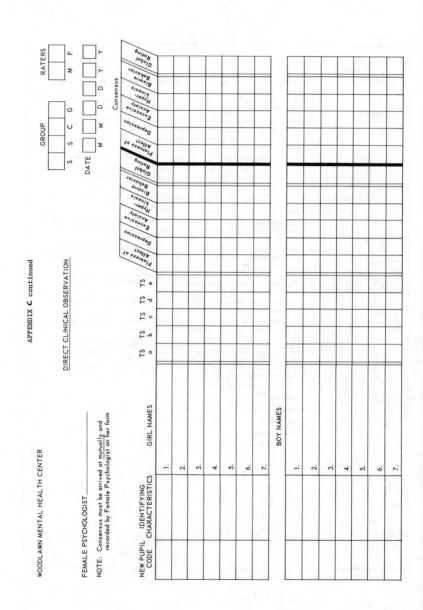

APPENDIX C continued

WOODLAWN MENTAL HEALTH CENTER

DIRECT CLINICAL OBSERVATION

FEMALE PSYCHOLOGIST

NOTE: Consensus must be arrived at mutually and
recorded by Female Psychologist on her form

Appendix D

SURVEY RESEARCH SERVICE

SRS-730

Deck 06

National Opinion Research Center
University of Chicago
Chicago 37, Illinois

Case Number   (1-4)

Child's Name

MOTHER'S QUESTIONNAIRE

CIRCLE THE CODE NUMBER IN THE PROPER BOX ON EACH LINE
TO INDICATE HOW TRUE THE PROBLEM IS OF YOUR CHILD. IF
YOU NEED HELP, THE INTERVIEWER WILL EXPLAIN.

	How true is this of your child?				
	Not at all	Just a little	Pretty much	Very much	
1. Picky and finicky about food	0	1	2	3	7/y
2. Underweight	0	1	2	3	8/y
3. Overweight	0	1	2	3	9/y
4. Restless or awakens at night	0	1	2	3	10/y
5. Has nightmares	0	1	2	3	11/y
6. Afraid of new situations	0	1	2	3	12/y
7. Afraid of people	0	1	2	3	13/y
8. Afraid of being alone	0	1	2	3	14/y
9. Worries about illness and death	0	1	2	3	15/y
10. Afraid to go to school	0	1	2	3	16/y
11. Looks sad	0	1	2	3	17/y
12. Cries and sobs for unexplained reasons	0	1	2	3	18/y
13. Muscles get stiff and rigid	0	1	2	3	19/y
14. Twitches and jerks, etc.	0	1	2	3	20/y
15. Body shakes	0	1	2	3	21/y
16. Stutters	0	1	2	3	22/y
17. Doesn't speak clearly, other than stuttering	0	1	2	3	23/y
18. Keeps anger to himself	0	1	2	3	24/y
19. Lets himself get pushed around by other children	0	1	2	3	25/y

COMPLAINS OF THE FOLLOWING EVEN WHEN DOCTOR FINDS NOTHING WRONG:	How true is this of your child?				
	Not at all	Just a little	Pretty much	Very much	
20. Headaches	0	1	2	3	26/y
21. Stomach-aches	0	1	2	3	27/y
22. Vomiting	0	1	2	3	28/y
23. Aches and pains	0	1	2	3	29/y
24. Loose bowels	0	1	2	3	30/y
25. Sucks thumb	0	1	2	3	31/y
26. Bites or picks nails	0	1	2	3	32/y
27. Chews on clothes, etc.	0	1	2	3	33/y
28. Picks at things, such as hair, clothing, etc.	0	1	2	3	34/y
29. Clings to parents or other adults	0	1	2	3	35/y
30. Plays with own sex organs	0	1	2	3	36/y
31. Involved in sex play with other children	0	1	2	3	37/y
32. Looks stony-faced	0	1	2	3	38/y
33. Has weird, odd, strange movements or looks	0	1	2	3	39/y
34. Says weird, odd, or strange things	0	1	2	3	40/y
35. Runs to bathroom constantly	0	1	2	3	41/y

	Once a month or less	About every 3 weeks	About every 2 weeks	Once a week or more	
36. Wets bed	0	1	2	3	42/y
37. Wets self during day	0	1	2	3	43/y

	None	Once	Twice	3 times or more	
38. Has had accidents with bowel movements in the last year	0	1	2	3	44/y

Appendix E

HOW I FEEL

My Name _____

My Teacher _____

My School _____

PRACTICE QUESTION.

I feel like skating.

☐ almost not at all

☐ a little

☐ pretty much

☐ a lot

1. I feel sad.

    ☐ almost not at all

    ☐ a little

    ☐ pretty much

    ☐ a lot

2. I feel nervous.

    ☐ almost not at all

    ☐ a little

    ☐ pretty much

    ☐ a lot

3. I feel shy and lonely.

    ☐ almost not at all

    ☐ a little

    ☐ pretty much

    ☐ a lot

4. I break rules in the school classroom.

    ☐ almost not at all

    ☐ a little

    ☐ pretty much

    ☐ a lot

5. I act too young for my age.

    ☐ almost not at all

    ☐ a little

    ☐ pretty much

    ☐ a lot

6. I could do my work better in school.

    ☐ almost not at all

    ☐ a little

    ☐ pretty much

    ☐ a lot

7. I get restless in school and don't pay attention.

    ☐ almost not at all

    ☐ a little

    ☐ pretty much

    ☐ a lot

8. All in all how do I feel I am doing in school?

    ☐ I feel I'm doing pretty well

    ☐ I feel I'm having a little trouble

    ☐ I feel I'm having pretty much trouble

    ☐ I feel I'm having a lot of trouble

Appendix F

**Various Methods of Analysis for
Evaluating Impact of Intervention
(Cohort III)**

The results we obtained using certain statistical methods raises the question of whether the results would be different with other methods. For example, would an analysis of covariance reveal impact similar to that found when end-of-year minus midyear TOCA ratings of intervention children were compared to those of control children?

This appendix presents results from three kinds of analysis done to validate the results reported in the text. These studies were done with Cohort III first-grade ratings at midyear and at end of first grade. Analysis of covariance was done with the six TOCA scales using end-of-year ratings as the dependent variable and midyear ratings as covariate in the following ways:

1. midyear ratings on all five scales as covariate;
2. only midyear ratings on the global scale as covariate;
3. midyear ratings on individual scales as covariate for each of the same scales at end of year.

In addition, we separated the pupils rated 0, 1, 2, and 3 on the basis of midyear global TOCA ratings, comparing end ratings of control children to those of intervention children. This method controlled for differences at midyear and yielded separate results for each group. The table in this appendix shows the p values for these several comparisons also.

Analysis of covariance revealed impact similar to that achieved with the method reported in the text (t tests on middle minus end ratings which are presented in the first column of the table) regardless of the way midyear scales were used as covariate. Analysis of variance on each of the TOCA adaptational levels by midyear global ratings indicated that benefit accrued more to moderately and mildly maladapting children, and this appears to suggest a way of finding out more about the effects of intervention.

TOCA Scales	t tests Mid minus End	ANACOVA,‡ mid as covariate			ANOVA, § each level of TOCA Global at mid			
		All 5 Scales	Global	Each Scale	0	1	2	3
Social contact	0.01	ns	ns	ns	ns	0.05†	ns	ns
Authority acceptance	0.04	ns	0.05	ns	ns	ns	0.01	ns
Maturation	0.01	0.01	0.01	0.01	0.08	0.01	0.01	ns
Cognitive achievement	0.08	ns	ns	ns	ns	0.04	ns	ns
Concentration	0.01	0.01	0.01	0.01	ns	0.02	0.01	ns
Global	0.01	0.01	0.01	0.01	0.04	0.05	0.09	0.05

Note: Population consisted of children who had TOCA ratings at early, middle, and end of year and who were either in control or intervention schools at midyear and the end of first grade. Although all tests were two-tailed, intervention had a favorable impact except in that case noted by the symbol †. ns indicates not significant at the 0.10 level of probability. N = 1485.
‡ Analysis of covariance.
§ Analysis of variance.

Appendix G

The Woodlawn Mental Health Center employed outside testers and proctors in order to study independently various aspects of achievement and intelligence performance—particularly with regard to the kinds of factors which influence test scores. The following procedures were used to sample and test the mean improvement in IQ from first to third grade among Cohort III children:

1. Twenty children from each third-grade class were randomly selected to be tested.
2. The *B* form of the Kuhlmann-Anderson test was administered to a randomly selected 50 percent of the classes in control schools and 50 percent of the classes in intervention schools. The other 50 percent of the classes were given the *CD* form.

MEAN IMPROVEMENT IN IQ FROM FIRST TO THIRD GRADE
(results obtained by independent testers)

Kuhlmann-Anderson Test Form B			Kuhlmann-Anderson Test Form CD		
Mean IQ Change (3d–1st Grade)			Mean IQ Change (3d–1st Grade)		
Intervention	Control	t† (Intervention-	Intervention	Control	t (Intervention-
N = 103	N = 74	Control)	N = 85	N = 87	Control)
2.93	0.16	1.67(*)	–3.04	–5.87	2.03*

Note: The populations consisted of Cohort III children who were in control or intervention schools for TOCA at middle and end of first grade and who had readiness and IQ scores in first grade and IQ scores in third grade from independent testing. Significance results are based on t tests comparing change in IQ from first to third grade between control and intervention schoolchildren.

† A positive *t* value indicates intervention did better than control in terms of improvement.

* indicates significant at the 0.05 level of probability.

(*) indicates significant at the 0.10 level of probability.

We were interested in comparing the scores obtained on each of the test forms for both intervention and control schools. Intervention schoolchildren showed significant gain in IQ scores from first to third grade when the *B* form was used, whereas control remained unchanged. The *CD* form showed a loss in IQ scores over the same period of time for both control and intervention, but there was less decline in the scores of the intervention schoolchildren than in those of control schoolchildren. The results of t tests comparing control and intervention on IQ scores from *B* and *CD* forms are presented in the table in this appendix.

Notes

1. In order to avoid burdening the reader with even more numbers, we have not included data which would be of interest to some. Additional data may be obtained from Dr. Kellam.

2. For the first four years of these studies, Jeanette Branch, formerly chief of the center's Children's Mental Health Services and currently the center's director, conducted teacher interviews. In the fifth year, Jane Ryder and Norma Smith joined the center staff and assisted Mrs. Branch.

3. Chicago Board of Education 1973: personal communication.

4. For the most part, "non-antisocial reasons" included items we would have categorized as symptoms, with one important exception—school failure.

5. With the exception of the first DCO assessments, the rating teams were supervised by Barbara Lerner, Ph. D.

6. The National Opinion Research Center gave technical consultation in devising the interview schedule and was responsible, under Dr. Kellam's supervision, for conducting the mother interviews. Paul Sheatsley and the senior staff of NORC contributed greatly to these studies.

7. C. K. Conners, Massachusetts General Hospital, 1964-65: personal communication.

8. Conners altered the list used in a study by Cytryn (Cytryn, Gilbert, and Eisenberg 1960). The Cytryn list was reported to have been developed from a list used in Glidewell's St. Louis studies (Glidewell, Gildea, Domke, and Kantor 1959). The St. Louis group reported their list was based on symptom descriptions in Leo Kanner's child psychiatry text (1957).

9. Cohort III ratings of nervous were compared to those in Cohort IV ($t=3.3$, $p<0.01$) and Cohort III ratings of sad were compared to those in Cohort IV ($t=3.7$, $p<0.01$).

10. DCO was the only instrument used to assess symptoms periodically. It was not used with Cohort III in third grade.

11. Dr. Sheldon K. Schiff directed the intervention program during all of these years, although the general design of the program was a collaborative effort. Dr. Schiff was responsible for training the school and mental health staff connected with the program. He was assisted by Mr. Douglass Turner, who coordinated the program. Organizing parent involvement, monitoring the intervention process in all intervention schools

through the use of audio and video tape, and linking the intervention program with back-up crisis response resources were all part of the role played by the school mental health intervention staff under Dr. Schiff's direction.

12. Dr. Sheldon K. Schiff and Dr. Kellam each worked in two of the six intervention schools for all four years of the program reported here. The remaining two schools were covered by different people at different years, as follows: 1964-65, Dr. Edward H. Futterman; 1965-66, Norman A. Buktenica, Ph.D.; and 1966-68, Dr. Donald H. Williams.

13. Parochial schoolchildren were not included in these studies, since the schedule of testing in parochial schools was not comparable to that in public schools.

Bibliography

Aberle, D. F. 1950. Introducing preventive psychiatry into a community. *Human organization* 9:5-9.

Achenbach, T. M. 1966. The classification of children's psychiatric symptoms: a factor analytic study. *Psychological monographs: general and applied* 80:1-37.

Albee, G. W. 1967. The relation of conceptual models to manpower needs. In *Emergent approaches to mental health problems*, ed. E. L. Cowen, E. A. Gardner, and M. Zax. New York: Appleton-Century-Crofts.

American Psychological Association. 1966. *Standards for educational and psychological tests and manuals.* Washington, D.C.

Andrew, G., and Lockwood, H. 1954. Teachers' evaluations of the mental health status of their pupils. *Journal of educational research* 47:631-35.

Anthony, E. 1970. The behavior disorders of childhood. In *Carmichael's handbook of child psychology.* 3d ed., ed. P. H. Mussen. New York: Wiley.

Battle, E. S., and Lacey, B. 1972. A context for hyperactivity in children, over time. *Child development* 43:757-73.

Beller, E. K., and Neubauer, P. B. 1963. Sex differences and symptom patterns in early childhood. *Journal of the American Academy of Child Psychiatry* 2:417-33.

Bentzen, F. 1963. Sex ratios in learning and behavior disorders. *American journal of orthopsychiatry* 33:92-98.

Blalock, H. M. 1960. *Social statistics.* New York: McGraw-Hill.

Bloom, B. S. 1964. *Stability and change in human characteristics.* New York: Wiley.

Blum, R. H. 1962. Case identification in psychiatric epidemiology: methods and problems. *Milbank Memorial Fund Quarterly* 40:253-88.

Bower, E. M. 1960. *Early identification of emotionally handicapped children in school.* Springfield, Ill.: Charles C. Thomas.

Brazier, A. M. 1969. *Black self-determination.* Grand Rapids, Mich.: Eerdmans.

Clausen, J. A., and Kohn, M. L. 1959. Relation of schizophrenia to the social structure of a small city. In *Epidemiology of mental disorder*, ed. B. Pasamanick. Washington, D.C.: American Association for the Advancement of Science.

Conners, C. 1967. The syndrome of minimal brain dysfunction: psychological aspects *Pediatric clinics of North America* 14:749–66.

Conners, C. K. 1970. Symptom patterns in hyperkinetic, neurotic and normal children. *Child development* 41:667- 82.

Cowen, E. L.; Izzo, H. M.; Telschow, E. F.; Trost, M. A.; and Zax, M. 1963. A preventive mental health program in the school setting: description and evaluation. *Journal of psychology* 56:307–56.

Cytryn, L.; Gilbert, A.; and Eisenberg, L. 1960. The effectiveness of tranquilizing drugs plus supportive psychotherapy in treating behavior disorders of children: a double-blind study of eight outpatients. *American journal of orthopsychiatry* 30:113–29.

De Vise, P. 1967. *Chicago's widening color gap.* Interuniversity Social Research Committee, Report No. 2. Chicago Regional Hospital Study.

Dohrenwend, B. P., and Dohrenwend, B. S. 1969. *Social status and psychological disorder: a causal inquiry.* New York: Wiley.

Erikson, E. H. 1959. Identity and the life cycle, selected papers. In *Psychological issues*, ed. G. S. Klein. New York: International Universities Press.

Erikson, E. H. 1963. *Childhood and society.* Rev. ed. New York: Norton.

Faris, R. E., and Dunham, H. W. 1939. *Mental disorders in urban areas.* Chicago: University of Chicago Press.

Fein, L. G. 1963. Evidence of a curvilinear relationship between IPAT anxiety and achievement at nursing school. *Journal of clinical psychology* 19:374–76.

Fish, J. H. 1973. *Black power/white control: the struggle of The Woodlawn Organization in Chicago.* Princeton, N. J.: Princeton University Press.

Fisher, M. L. 1934. Measured differences between problem and non-problem children in a public school system. *Journal of educational sociology* 7:353–64.

Fisher, R. A. 1963. *Statistical methods for research workers.* 13th ed. New York: Hafner.

Fuller, E. M. 1960. Early childhood education. In *Encyclopedia of educational research*. 3d ed., ed. C. W. Harris. New York: Macmillan.

Glidewell, J. C.; Gildea, M. C.-L.; Domke, H. R.; and Kantor, M. B. 1959. Behavior symptoms in children and adjustment in public school. *Human organization* 18:123–30.

Goldfarb, A. 1963. Teacher ratings in psychiatric case-finding. I. Methodological considerations. *American journal of public health* 53:1919–27.

Goodlad, J. I. 1954. Some effects of promotion and non-promotion upon the social and personal adjustment of children. *Journal of experimental education* 22:301–28.

Goodman, L. A., and Kruskal, W. H. 1954. Measures of association for cross classifications. *Journal of the American Statistical Association* 49:732–64.

Haggerty, M. E. 1925. The incidence of undesirable behavior in public school children. *Journal of educational research* 12:102-22.

Hamalainen, A. E. 1952. Kindergarten-primary entrance age in relation to later school adjustment. *Elementary school journal* 52:406–11.

Harman, H. H. 1967. *Modern factor analysis.* 2d ed. Chicago: University of Chicago Press.

Hartmann, H. 1964. Psychoanalysis and the concept of health. In *Essays on ego psychology.* New York: International Universities Press.

Havighurst, R. 1952. *Developmental tasks and education.* 2d ed. New York: Longmans Green.

Hefferman, H. 1971. Early childhood education: overview. In *Encyclopedia of education.* Vol. 3, ed. L. C. Deighton. New York: Macmillan.

Hildreth, G. 1928. A survey of problem pupils. *Journal of educational research* 18:1–14.

Hollingshead, A. B., and Redlich, F. C. 1958. *Social class and mental illness.* New York: Wiley.

Hughes, C. C.; Tremblay, M. A.; Rapoport, R. N.; and Leighton, A. H. 1960. *People of cove and woodlot. The Stirling County study of psychiatric disorder and sociocultural environment.* Vol. 2. New York: Basic Books.

Jahoda, M. 1958. *Current concepts of positive mental health.* New York: Basic Books.

Janowitz, M. 1967. *The community press in an urban setting: the social elements of urbanism.* 2d ed. Chicago: University of Chicago Press.

Kaiser, H. F. 1958. The varimax criterion for analytic rotation in factor analysis. *Psychometrika* 23:187–200.

Kanner, L. 1957. *Child psychiatry.* 3d ed. Springfield, Ill.: Charles C. Thomas.

Kellam, S. G., and Schiff, S. K. 1966. The Woodlawn Mental Health Center: A community mental health center model. *Social service review* 40:255–63.

Kellam, S. G., and Schiff, S. K. 1968. An urban community mental health center. In *Mental health and urban social policy,* ed. L. J. Duhl and R. L. Leopold. San Francisco: Jossey-Bass.

Kellam, S. G., and Branch, J. D. 1971. An approach to community mental health: analysis of basic problems. *Seminars in psychiatry* 3:207–25.

Kellam, S. G.; Branch, J. D.; Agrawal, K. A.; and Grabill, M. E. 1972. Woodlawn Mental Health Center: an evolving strategy for planning in community mental health. In *Handbook of community mental health,* ed. S. G. Golann and C. Eisdorfer. New York: Appleton-Century-Crofts.

Kitagawa, E. M., and Taeuber, K. E., eds. 1963. *Local community fact book, Chicago metropolitan area 1960.* Chicago: Chicago Community Inventory.

Langner, T. S., and Michael, S. T. 1963. *Life stress and mental health: the Midtown Manhattan study.* Vol. 2. New York: Free Press of Glencoe.

Lapouse, R., and Monk, M. 1958. An epidemiologic study of behavior characteristics in children. *American journal of public health* 48:1134–44.

Leighton, A. H. 1959. *My name is legion. The Stirling County study of psychiatric disorder and sociolcultural environment.* Vol. 1. New York: Basic Books.

Leighton, D. C.; Harding, J. S.; Macklin, D. B.; Macmillan, A. M.; and Leighton, A. H. 1963. *The character of danger. The Stirling County study of psychiatric disorder and sociocultural environment.* Vol. 3. New York: Basic Books.

Lerner, B. 1972. *Therapy in the ghetto.* Baltimore: Johns Hopkins University Press.

Levine, M.; Wesolowski, J. C.; and Corbett, F. J. 1966. Pupil turnover and academic performance in an inner city elementary school. *Psychology in the schools* 3:153–58.

Lewis, W. D. 1947. Some characteristics of children designated as mentally retarded, as problems, and geniuses by teachers. *Journal of genetic psychology* 70:29–51.

Lippitt, R. 1968. Improving the socialization process. In *Socialization and society,* ed. J. A. Clausen. Boston: Little,Brown.

MacClenathan, R. H. 1934. Teachers and parents study children's behaviors. *Journal of educational sociology* 7:325–33.

McClure, W. E. 1929. Characteristics of problem children based on judgments of teachers. *Journal of juvenile research* 13:124–40.

Macfarlane, J. W.; Allen, L; and Honzik, M. 1954. *A developmental study of the behavior problems of normal children between twenty-one months and fourteen years.* Berkeley: University of California Press.

McNemar, Q. 1963. *Psychological statistics.* New York: Wiley.

Martens, E. H. 1932. *Adjustment of behavior problems of school children—a description and evaluation of the clinical program in Berkeley, California.* U. S. Bureau of Education, Bulletin 18. Washington, D. C.: U. S. Government Printing Office.

Menkes, M. M.; Rowe, J. S.; and Menkes, J. H. 1967. A twenty-five year follow-up study on the hyperkinetic child with minimal brain dysfunction. *Pediatrics* 39:393-99.

Mensh, I. N.; Kantor, M. B.; Domke, H. R.; Gildea, M. C.-L.; and Glidewell, J. C. 1959. Children's behavior symptoms and their relationships to school adjustment, sex, and social class. *Journal of social issues* 15:8-15.

Merton, R. K. 1968. *Social theory and social structure.* Rev. ed. New York: Free Press of Glencoe.

Meyer, A. 1948. *The commonsense psychiatry of Dr. Adolf Meyer,* ed. A. Lief. New York: McGraw-Hill.

Michael, C. M; Morris, D. P.; and Soroker, E. 1957. Follow-up studies of shy withdrawn children. II. Relative incidence of schizophrenia. *American journal of orthopsychiatry* 27:331-37.

Mindness, M., and Keliher, A. V. 1967. Review of research related to the advantages of kindergarten. *Childhood education* 43:505-12.

Mitchell, S., and Shepherd, M. 1966. A comparative study of children's behavior at home and at school. *British journal of education psychology* 36:248-254.

Morris, D. P.; Soroker, E.; and Burruss, G. 1954. Follow-up studies of shy withdrawn children. I. Evaluation of later adjustment. *American journal of orthopsychiatry* 24:743-54.

Morrison, J. R., and Stewart, M. A. 1973. The psychiatric status of the legal families of adopted hyperactive children. *Archives of general psychiatry* 28:888-91.

Neugarten, B. L. 1968. The awareness of middle age. In *Middle age and aging: a reader in social psychology,* ed. B. L. Neugarten. Chicago: University of Chicago Press.

Parsons, T. 1964. *Social structure and personality.* New York: Free Press of Glencoe.

Peterson, D. R. 1961. Behavior problems of middle childhood. *Journal of consulting psychology* 25:205-9.

Robins, L. N. 1966. *Deviant children grown up: A sociological and psychiatric study of sociopathic personality.* Baltimore: Williams & Wilkins.

Rogers, C. R. 1942. Mental-health findings in three elementary schools. *Educational research bulletin* 21:69–79, 86.

Roman, M. 1969. Community control and the community mental health center: a view from the Lincoln Bridge. Paper presented at NIMH staff meeting on metropolitan topics, Washington, D.C.

Rosenthal, R., and Jacobson, L. 1966. Teachers' expectancies: determinants of pupils' IQ gains. *Psychological reports* 19:115–18.

Rosenthal, R., and Jacobson, L. F. 1968. Teacher expectations for the disadvantaged. *Scientific American* 218:19–23.

Rutter, M., and Graham, P. 1966. Psychiatric disorder in 10- and 11-year-old children. *Proceedings of the Royal Society of Medicine* 59:382–87.

Rutter, M.; Tizard, J.; and Whitmore, K., eds. 1970. *Education, health and behavior*. New York: Wiley.

Ryle, A.; Pond, D. A.; and Hamilton, M. 1965. The prevalence and patterns of psychological disturbance in children of primary age. *Journal of child psychology and psychiatry* 6:101–13.

Scheff, T. J. 1966. *Being mentally ill*. Chicago: Aldine-Atherton.

Schiff, S. K., and Kellam, S. G. 1967. A community-wide mental health program of prevention and early treatment in first grade. In *Poverty and mental health*. Psychiatric Research Report No. 21, ed. M. Greenblatt, P. E. Emery, and B. C. Glueck, Jr. Washington, D.C.: American Psychiatric Association.

Scott, W. A. 1958. Research definitions of mental health and mental illness. *Psychological bulletin* 55:29–45.

Shepherd, M.; Oppenheim, A. N.; and Mitchell, S. 1966. Childhood behavior disorders and the child-guidance clinic: an epidemiological study. *Journal of child psychology and psychiatry* 7:39–52.

Silberman, C. E. 1964. *Crisis in black and white*. New York: Random House.

Snyder, L. M. 1934. The problem child in the Jersey City elementary schools. *Journal of educational sociology* 7:343–52.

Spitzer, S. P., and Denzin, N. K. 1968. *The mental patient: studies in the sociology of deviance*. New York: McGraw-Hill.

Spivak, G., and Spotts, J. 1965. The Devereux child behavior scale of symptom behaviors in latency age children. *American journal of mental deficiency* 69:839–53.

Srole, L.; Langner, T. S.; Michael, S. T.; Opler, M.; and Rennie, T. A. C. 1961. *Mental health in the metropolis: the Midtown Manhattan study*. Vol. 1. New York: McGraw-Hill.

Suttles. G. D. 1972. *The social construction of communities*. Chicago: University of Chicago Press.

Szasz, T. S. 1960. The myth of mental illness. *American psychologist* 15:113–18.

Thompson, L. J. 1973. Learning disabilities: an overview. *American journal of psychiatry* 130:393–99.

Tuddenham, R. D. 1962. The nature and measurement of intelligence. In *Psychology in the making*, ed. L. Postman. New York: Knopf.

Ullmann, C. A. 1952. *Identification of maladjusted school children*. Public Health Monograph No. 7. Public Health Service Publication No. 211. Washington, D.C.: U.S. Government Printing Office.

Vidich, A. J.; Bensman, J.; and Stein, M. R. 1964. *Reflections on community studies*. New York: Wiley.

Warren, R. L. 1963. *The community in America*. Chicago: Rand McNally.

Wender, P. H. 1971. *Minimal brain dysfunction in children*. New York: Wiley-Interscience.

Wickman. E. K. 1928. *Children's behavior and teachers' attitudes*. New York: Commonwealth Fund.

Wolff, S. 1967. Behavioural characteristics of primary school children referred to a psychiatry department. *British journal of psychiatry* 113:885–93.

World Health Organization. 1960. *Epidemiology of mental disorder: eight reports of expert committee on mental health*. Geneva: World Health Organization Technical Report Series No. 185.

Young-Masten, I. 1938. Behavior problems of elementary school children: a descriptive and comparative study. *Genetic psychology monographs* 20:123–81.

Index

205

shy, as important group, 135; under-
achieving, 137; young, major social
fields of, 23, 26
Children, age of: factor in intervention,
160, 161; relation to adaptation, 44
Children, aggressive: hyperkinesis in, 117
Children, anxious: relation to TOCA
aggressive cluster, 105
Children, bizarre: relation to MSI,
102, 104
Children, change of school by, 46-49
Children, change of teacher by, 47-48
Children, characteristics of, in study of
construct validity, 40-41
Children, flatness in: relation to grades,
119, 122; to IQ, 119, 122; to MSI, 101,
104; to TOCA shy cluster, 105
Children, hyperkinesis in, 104, 105
Children, kindergarten experience of,
44-45
Children, maturation of, 102
Children, sex of: factor in intervention,
159-161; relation to adaptation, 43-44;
to DCO prevalences, 80; to MSI
frequencies, 84
Children, sex problems of, 102
Childrens' services, 175
Church centers, use of in child
program, 175
Circumscribing the community, 12-13
Classroom: assessment in, 23; intervention
in, 24, 142, 174, 178; as major social
field, 23, 26; social adaptational tasks
in, 26
Classroom meetings, 143-48
Classrooms, first-grade, number in
Woodlawn, 27
Classrooms, in school structure, 177
Clausen, J. A., 9
Clinical judgments: as basis of program
modification, 143; as measure of
symptoms, 73
Clinical raters, use and selection of, 75-76
Clinical ratings. See Direct clinical
observation (DCO)
Cognitive achievement category, 28
Cognitive achievement scale, 34, 36
Cohort I, defined, 30
Community: as aspect of social system, 31;
circumscribing of, 12, 14; defined, 10;
formalizing relation to, 13, 15, 20; and
hospitalization, 9; as local entity, 13, 16;
and mental health system, 9-11, 15;
models for relating to, 4, 20; role of, in

policy making, 4, 14, 15; as site of social
process, 6. See also Woodlawn
Community boards, 20; in Woodlawn, 5,
19, 20
Community boundaries, 10, 13, 14, 119
Community involvement, early, 15, 19
Community leaders: as board members,
19; collaboration of, 167; concerns of,
20; sanction from, 21; support of, for
information system, 15
Community mental health: as broadened
purview, 5, 134; as broadening services,
3; influence of on concepts of mental
health, 7; conceptualization of, 5; in
integrated mental health system, 9;
examination of aspects of, 4; research
and service in, 9
Community mental health center, in
Woodlawn, 9, 19, 180
Community organizations, in Woodlawn,
16
Community residents: on boards and
councils, 19-20; concerns of, 19; ideas
of boundaries of, 13; involvement of in
policy-setting, 4; support of, 15; as
workers, 11
Community sanction in Woodlawn, 4, 15,
19, 21, 167
Community studies, 176-79
Community-wide assessment, 14, 30, 141;
need for records in, 24; of symptoms, 73
Community-wide studies, 11. See also
Woodlawn program
Concentration category, 28
Concentration scale, 53
Conners, C. K., 55, 84, 85, 136, 198nn
Construct validity: of symptom measure,
72, 73; of TOCA, 40-49
Content validity: defined, 33; in measure-
ment of symptoms, 71; of TOCA, 33-34
Control school children, 165
Cooley, C. H., 8
Corbett, F. J., 48
Cowen, E. L., 153
Criterion-related validity: in measurement
of symptoms, 72; of TOCA, 34-40
Cytryn, L., 197n

DCO. See Direct clinical observation
Denzin, N. K., 68
Depression, 171
de Vise, P., 18
Diagnosis, of symptoms, 71-72
Direct clinical observation (DCO), 75-83;